A Special Issue of the
International Journal of Behavioral Development

The Development of Working Memory

Edited by

Anik de Ribaupierre

University of Geneva, Switzerland

Graham J. Hitch

Lancaster University, UK

Routledge
Taylor & Francis Group

LONDON AND NEW YORK

First published 1994 by Lawrence Erlbaum Associates

Published 2018 by Routledge
2 Park Square, Milton Park, Abingdon, Oxon OX14 4RN
52 Vanderbilt Avenue, New York, NY 10017

First issued in paperback 2018

Routledge is an imprint of the Taylor & Francis Group, an informa business

British Library Cataloguing in Publication Data

A catalogue record for this book is available from the British Library

Cover design by Joyce Chester
Index by Sue Ramsey
Typeset by Acorn Bookwork, Salisbury, UK

ISBN 13: 978-1-138-87731-3 (pbk)
ISBN 13: 978-0-86377-927-5 (hbk)

Contents

INTERNATIONAL JOURNAL OF BEHAVIORAL DEVELOPMENT, 1994, *17* (1), 1–3

Preface

Working memory refers to the temporary storage of information that is being processed in a wide range of cognitive tasks. In this Special Issue we bring together research on the development of working memory that arises within two quite different approaches. The first is the neo-Piagetian perspective, which attempts to capitalise on the insights of Piaget's work by proposing information-processing accounts of cognitive development. A dominant theme in this approach is the claim that working memory limitations play an important role in the development of cognitive abilities (Case, 1985; Halford & Wilson, 1980; Pascual-Leone, 1970, 1987). The second approach stems from the study of working memory and information-processing in mainstream cognitive psychology. It uses such knowledge to guide and inform investigation of the development of working memory in children (Baddeley, 1986; Hitch & Halliday, 1983; Hulme, Thompson, Muir, & Lawrence, 1984).

Despite their obvious similarities, the two approaches have tended to remain rather separate. This first became apparent to us when we met at a symposium on the Development of Working Memory at the International Conference on Memory at Lancaster in 1991. The idea for a special issue of *International Journal of Behavioral Development* arose in the aftermath of a subsequent poster workshop on Developmental Aspects of Working Memory at the Fifth European Conference on Developmental Psychology at Seville in 1992. The aim of the workshop was to bring together researchers using the two approaches in order to promote the exchange of ideas, methods, and data, and to explore conflicts and agreements. This Special Issue is intended to serve a similar purpose in the context of a much wider audience.

Neo-Piagetian researchers have tended to conceptualise working memory as a set of central limited capacity resources which exert a general constraint on cognitive processes. Accordingly, a major goal of neo-Piagetian research has been to develop techniques for measuring the capacity of working memory and to chart its development. The papers by Alp; de Ribaupierre and Bailleux; Morra; Pascual-Leone and Baillargeon, illustrate different facets of this approach. In contrast, research on adult working memory has emphasised the fractionation of its resources, with evidence suggesting in particular the need to distinguish relatively peripheral phonological and visuo-spatial subsystems from central resources (Baddeley, 1986). Because these subsystems are currently better understood than the central component of adult working memory, they have tended to be the focus of related developmental studies. This tendency is illustrated here in the papers on visuo-spatial working memory (Longoni & Scalisi; Walker, Hitch, Doyle, & Porter) and phonological working memory (Henry). Seen this way, the complementarity of the two approaches is fairly obvious: One has tended to emphasise central aspects of working memory, the other more peripheral aspects. Clearly, however, both are likely to be relevant. This is illustrated here in the paper by de Ribaupierre and Bailleux, which suggests the importance of taking peripheral resources into account in the assessment of central working memory capacity. A further significant strand of research in both approaches, is to investigate links between the development of working memory and various aspects of cognitive development. If knowledge about the development of working memory has any utility, it should inform our understanding of developmental changes in a broad range of cognitive activities. This type of work is illustrated here in the case of the specific cognitive abilities of language acquisition (Blake, Austin, Cannon, Lisus, & Vaughan) and reading (Siegel).

We must emphasise, especially to readers unfamiliar with the field, that we have not attempted to collect a set of papers which gives a representative overview of all the many current approaches to the development of working memory. A call for papers was sent out in the fall of 1992. Among the criteria for inclusion in the issue were that individual papers should address developmental aspects of working memory and that the collection should represent a balanced coverage of topics, ages, and methods. The result is an impressive set of nine papers. We regret, however, not to have more papers on life-span issues, considering the editorial objectives of the *International Journal of Behavioral Development*, and, more importantly, the striking similarities in concepts between work conducted on childhood and on older adults. This is simply a consequence of not having actively solicited papers, but having used a "bottom-up" approach. Nor have we deliberately sought papers that integrate or contrast competing approaches. There are, for example, major questions being raised about the assumption that working memory is important in cognitive development (Brainerd & Reyna, 1993; Halford, 1993). However, we hope that by placing side-by-side a selection of papers approaching the topic from the neo-Piagetian and experimentalist perspectives, we can illustrate the vigour of current research on the development of working memory, the kind of progress that is being made, and the broad range of problems presently being tackled.

We wish to express our thanks to Linda Siegel, Editor of the *International Journal of Behavioral Development*, for giving us the opportunity to edit this issue. We also thank the reviewers, whose names will appear in a later issue. They provided prompt and very helpful expert reviews not only on first versions, but often on revisions.

Perhaps it is fitting to conclude on a more personal note. Coming from different trends of studies on working memory, acting as co-editors considerably fostered our understanding of the other's perspective. We hope that after having read the different papers, the reader will share our view that these two trends are indeed complementary rather than, as some would argue, incompatible.

September 1993
Graham J. Hitch
Lancaster University, UK
Anik de Ribaupierre
University of Geneva, Switzerland

REFERENCES

Baddeley, A.D. (1986). *Working memory*. Oxford: Clarendon Press.

Brainerd, C.J., & Reyna, V.F. (1993). Memory independence and memory interference in cognitive development. *Psychological Review, 100*, 42–67.

Case, R. (1985). *Intellectual development: Birth to adulthood*. New York: Academic Press.

Halford, G.S., & Wilson, W.H. (1980). A category theory approach to cognitive development. *Cognitive Psychology, 12*, 356–411.

Halford, G. (1993). *Children's understanding: The development of mental models*. Hillsdale, NJ: Lawrence Erlbaum Associates Inc.

Hitch, G.J., & Halliday, M.S. (1983). Working memory in children. *Philosophical Transactions of the Royal Society, B302*, 324–340.

Hulme, C., Thompson, N., Muir, C., & Lawrence, A. (1984). Speech rate and the development of short-term memory span. *Journal of Experimental Child Psychology, 39*, 241–253.

Pascual-Leone, J. (1970). A mathematical model for the transition rule in Piaget's developmental stages. *Acta Psychologica, 32*, 301–345.

Pascual-Leone, J. (1987). Organismic processes for neo-Piagetian theories: A dialectical causal account of cognitive development. *International Journal of Psychology, 22*, 531–570.

INTERNATIONAL JOURNAL OF BEHAVIORAL DEVELOPMENT, 1994, *17* (1), 5–35

Developmental Change in a Spatial Task of Attentional Capacity: An Essay Toward an Integration of Two Working Memory Models

Anik de Ribaupierre and Christine Bailleux

Faculté de Psychologie et des Sciences de l'Education, University of Geneva, Switzerland

The objective of this paper is to illustrate the complementarity of two lines of studies on Working Memory, the neo-Piagetian models of Pascual-Leone and Case on the one hand, and Baddeley's model, on the other. After a brief summary of each model, their similarities and differences are reviewed. An empirical longitudinal study is then presented as an illustration. Four cohorts of children, aged 5, 6, 8, and 10 years on the first assessment, were examined once a year over five years, with a short-term memory task (Mr Peanut), asking for the recall of the location of coloured spots in a clown figure. Two versions were used: a unicoloured task (Peanut-P) and a multicoloured task (Peanut-C), in which subjects had to recall both positions and colours. Three aspects of the results are emphasised. First, it was found that performances in Peanut-C increased with item complexity up to a certain level, beyond which they tended to remain stable; this stability was interpreted as reflecting the limits in processing resources which are postulated by neo-Piagetian models. Secondly, a drastic diminution in the performances was observed on the fourth year, corresponding to a change in the way of responding: The task was computerised, and subjects had to answer, using a computer mouse. It is argued that the monitoring of the mouse disrupts performances because it draws on the

Requests for reprints should be sent to Anik de Ribaupierre, Faculté de Psychologie et des Sciences de l'Education, Université de Genève, 9 rte de Drize, CH-1227 Carouge, Switzerland. E-mail: DERIB@UNI2A.UNIGE.CH.

This research was supported by grants from the Fonds National Suisse de la Recherche Scientifique (grants nos 1.437-0.86 and 11.27671.89). We are grateful to Sylvain Dionnet, Ineke Keizer, Thierry Lecerf, Santino Livoti, Caroline Moutia, Francisco Pons, Ana Sancho, Anne Spira, and Laurence Thomas who were actively involved in the collection and analysis of the data. We thank Graham Hitch, Juan Pascual-Leone, and Laurence Rieben, as well as two anonymous reviewers, for their very helpful comments. Finally, we also want to thank the children who willingly participated in the study, despite its length and its, at times, repetitive aspects.

same limited resources as the memory task. Finally, results showed that the monitoring of the mouse interferes more with the recall of positions than with the recall of colours, as could be expected if monitoring a computer mouse represents a spatial interference task. Methodological drawbacks of the studies are also discussed, and suggestions for further research indicated.

INTRODUCTION

There are clearly at least two different, independent streams of research on the development of Working Memory (WM), which define it as a system with limited capacity for storing and actively manipulating mental information, for use in cognitive situations. One direction developed from the Baddeley and Hitch (1974) model, according to which short-term memory is not a unitary phenomenon. It was first proposed to account for short-term memory phenomena in adults and was more recently generalised to children. The second perspective is represented by neo-Piagetians who consider the development of WM as a causal factor of cognitive development (e.g. Case, 1974, 1985; Chapman, 1987; Halford, 1982, 1993; Pascual-Leone, 1970, 1987); although different neo-Piagetian formulations of WM have also been proposed, we focus here on Pascual-Leone's and Case's models only. It is striking that there have been so few cross-references from one trend of studies to the other, or external analyses of their similarities and differences.[1]

The objective of this paper is therefore to argue that the theoretical constructs proposed by Baddeley and Pascual-Leone are in fact much closer than it first appears. We came to this conclusion because of the results obtained in the study which is described below. This is a longitudinal study which was designed to test some of Pascual-Leone's and Case's postulates regarding the existence of stages in the development of attentional capacity. Over the course of the study, modifications were introduced in one of the working memory tasks used, and we realised that the unexpectedly large effect on the subjects performances which ensued could be interpreted in the light of Baddeley's model as well as within Pascual-Leone's framework. This paper is an attempt toward this theoretical rapprochement. First, we give a brief summary of both types of models. Secondly, their similarities and differences are discussed. Thirdly, in order to illustrate our arguments, we present the results of our longitudinal study which led us to consider that the two models are compatible.

---

[1]We thank one of the anonymous reviewers of this paper to have called our attention to Halford's recent book (1993), in which a whole chapter is devoted to a review of different capacity concepts in adult and child cognition.

Brief Summary of Two WM Types of Models

As well documented throughout this issue, *Baddeley and Hitch's* model (1974) suggests a tripartite system, composed of the Central Executive, which is a control mechanism helped by two slave systems: the Articulatory Loop (AL) and the Visuo-Spatial-Sketchpad (VSSP). The two slave systems function independently from each other, as demonstrated by the use of dual task paradigms.

The Articulatory Loop is the most studied part of the system; its role is to hold and manipulate verbal material. It consists of two components: a phonological store, which is relatively passive and to which verbal material presented auditorily has obligatory access; and a rehearsal mechanism which helps to maintain stored items as well as recoding verbal material presented visually. The AL is temporally limited: It contains as many items as can be rehearsed in approximatley 1.5 to 2 seconds. It is therefore closely linked to articulation rate. The functioning of this subsystem accounts for phenomena repeatedly observed in verbal short-term memory studies, such as word length, articulatory suppression, and phonological similarity effects.

The VSSP is responsible for the holding and manipulation of visual and/ or spatial information. Experimental studies are less numerous, although their number has greatly increased in the last five years, and results are sometimes difficult to interpret. In particular, the rehearsal mechanism and the limits of the system remain largely unknown. Recent work (Baddeley, 1988; Logie & Baddeley, 1990; Logie & Marchetti, 1991) tends to show that it consists of two distinct components, a visual and a spatial one.

The Central Executive (CE) is an attentional system, with a limited capacity, which can use either slave system in order to free up some of its own resources. It has been relatively little studied, and remains some kind of a "conceptual black box" (e.g. Van der Linden, 1989). Recently, however, experimental studies have directly addressed the CE. For instance, Baddeley (1992) considers that the greater difficulty Alzheimer's patients have in co-ordinating two simple tasks, one calling for the AL system and the other one for the VSSP system, is due to a deficit of the CE. A task of generating random numbers is considered to directly tap the CE; it probably requires the active rehearsal of instructions and the inhibition of automatic routines. Thus, the CE is mainly viewed as a mechanism for monitoring and co-ordinating the processing of information.

Baddeley's model has generated numerous studies. From a developmental perspective, most studies up to now have attempted to determine whether similar effects are found in children. For instance, Hitch et al. (Hitch, Halliday, Schaafstal, & Schraagen, 1988; Hitch, Halliday, Dodd, & Littler, 1989a; Hitch, Halliday, & Littler, 1989b; Hitch, Woodin,

& Baker, 1989c) have shown that the phonological system grows in importance with age, although the ages at which rehearsal has been observed vary with situations. With auditory presentation of verbal stimuli, word length effects are found as early as 4 years of age (see also Hulme, Thomson, Muir, & Lawrence, 1984; Hulme & Tordoff, 1989). By contrast, with visual presentation (drawings of objects), word length effects do not appear before 7 or 8 years of age. Older children (at least from 8 years onwards) spontaneously use articulatory rehearsal, whether presentation is auditory or visual. Incidentally, it is interesting to note that such results converge with Flavell's (e.g. Flavell & Wellman, 1977) and other researchers' work on spontaneous rehearsal in memory tasks. In their recent work, Hitch et al. also suggest that verbal coding does not merely replace visual coding, but that development consists in a multiplication of the number of possible coding systems.

Developmental increase in tasks tapping the AL system has been well documented over the years, in particular through the use of verbal memory span tasks. For Baddeley (1986; see also Case, 1985; Case, Kurland, & Goldberg, 1982; Nicolson, 1981) this increase is accounted for by the development of articulatory speed, rather than by a development of the Central Executive: The faster words or digits can be pronounced, the more can be recalled. It is our position, however, that the increase in articulatory rate does not play a causal role, but depends on a more general developmental mechanism, which influences both rate and span (see also Henry, 1991). Developmental change in VSSP tasks has been less studied, even with respect to the development of spatial span. For instance, Wilson, Scott, and Power (1987) showed that pattern span increases rapidly between the ages of 5 and 11, by which time it is at the adult level; they also found that the memory decay is rapid. Schumann-Hengsteler (e.g. 1989; Schumann-Hengsteler, Demmel, & Seitz, 1992) showed that there is very little qualitative change from 5 to 10 years of age in the ability to perform visuo-spatial memory tasks which do not vary in terms of complexity.

The *neo-Piagetian models* (e.g. Case, 1985; Chapman, 1987; Fischer, 1980; Fischer & Lamborn, 1989; Halford, 1982; Pascual-Leone, 1987) view working memory from a very different perspective. Derived from the Piagetian model, they have in common that they have looked for constructs other than the Piagetian logical structures in order to account for cognitive development in general, and for the existence of general developmental stages. Most theorists assume that general stages should be defined in terms of constraints or upper limits, under which there can be considerable variation across situations and subjects, rather than in terms of the form that behaviour takes across domains. These upper constraints are set by limits in working memory; development of WM is viewed as a causal factor, although not the only one, of cognitive development. Neo-Piagetian models are not all alike, nor do they all explicitly address working memory (e.g. Case, 1987, 1992; Dasen & de Ribaupierre, 1987). Furthermore, different constructs have been used, such as working memory, attentional capacity, M-space, M-power, mental attention, processing space. We will consider here that these constructs are broadly equivalent, in the sense that they all refer to a limited capacity for storage and manipulation of mental information, for use in cognitive tasks. Thus, the role assigned to WM is the same in these models as in Baddeley's approach. However, the main purpose has not been to determine how working memory functions or whether it is unitary or not, but rather to study whether the developmental increase observed in WM tasks accounts for the developmental differences obtained in cognitive tasks in general. As already mentioned, the focus here is on Pascual-Leone's and Case's models.

Let us first mention that *Pascual-Leone's* model has often been mis-understood as assuming a unitary system to account for the development of working memory. On the contrary, the model is basically multidimensional, whether with respect to working memory or to cognitive development in general. This is in accord with current views of WM (see also Halford, 1993). The multidimensional aspect concerns not only the representational format of items of information but also underlying mechanisms or processes which activate information. Pascual-Leone offers a dynamic view of processing (e.g. Pascual-Leone, 1970, 1984; Pascual-Leone & Ijaz, 1989). Three nested levels of activation are described. First, when an input arrives, a number of schemes (defined as information-carrying functional units or structures) are activated in the repertoire, via their own propensity to be activated and via affective operators; this is referred to as the general *field of activation*, denoted H*. Secondly, affective goals are created which activate relevant executive schemes while a number of silent operators, whose role is to activate schemes, may also be mobilised by patterns of schemes co-activation. This generates a subset of more highly activated schemes, which at times Pascual-Leone himself labels working memory (e.g. Pascual-Leone & Ijaz, 1989).[2] Thirdly, and depending on the type of situations, whether misleading[3] or facilitating, some activated schemes

---

[2]Note that other authors also define WM as the amount of information for which the activation strength is above a certain threshold (e.g. Engle, Cantor, & Carullo, 1992; Salthouse & Babcock, 1991). For instance, Moscovitch and Umilta (1990, p. 31) consider that there is neither a single working memory system nor multiple systems, but that working memory "reflects or represents whatever processes are currently active and whose outcomes or operations are consciously apprehended".

[3]Misleading situations are those in which different silent operators activate incompatible sets of schemes, one of which is often more highly activated while leading to an incorrect solution; in contrast, in facilitating situations, different sets of schemes are activated which all concur to a correct solution.

must then be actively inhibited, whereas others require supplementary activation. The content of this last subset, that is, the nature and number of the hyperactivated schemes which define the "field of *Mental Attention*" or attentional capacity, depends on at least three mechanisms: (a) mental capacity or M-power, applied to relevant schemes to boost their level of activation; (b) an inhibition mechanism, the I-operator, responsible for actively inhibiting less relevant or irrelevant schemes;[4] and (c) executive schemes, that is, plans of actions and regulatory controls.

It is only with respect to the growth in M-power that precise developmental predictions were made. M-power or M-capacity is considered to be strictly limited, and to increase maturationally with age. It is defined as the maximum number of independent schemes (other than executive schemes and schemes activated directly by the input or other operators) which can be simultaneously activated by M in a single mental operation; it grows from 1 at age 3 to 7 at age 15. M-stages (i.e. the period of time during which the same maximum number of schemes can be activated across different situations) have been empirically determined to last two years. These theoretical assumptions have been validated in a number of empirical studies, using different age samples and different tasks. M-power has also proved to be a good predictor of performance in other cognitive tasks (for details, see Pascual-Leone, 1987; Pascual-Leone & Goodman, 1979; de Ribaupierre, 1983). To our knowledge, Pascual-Leone did not specify the developmental characteristics of the other operators, except for stipulating that the influence of the inhibition and learning operators are stronger in the second than in the first year of an *M* stage. Likewise, he did not indicate whether there are limits to the number of schemes that can be activated in the first two fields of activation.

Case (e.g. 1985) uses the term executive processing space to refer to a construct similar to Pascual-Leone's M-capacity; it is defined as the maximum number of independent schemes that a child can activate at any one time. Case has introduced the distinction between the activity of executing an ongoing operation and the activity of storing and/or retrieving the products of such an operation: Operating space refers to the portion of the executive space devoted to the activation of new schemes (the ongoing operation); short-term storage space (STSS) is devoted to the maintenance and/or retrieval of recently activated schemes. A number of STSS tasks was developed for the different qualitative stages that are distinguished in his general developmental model. Several studies were aimed at demonstrating that the same average values (see later) can be obtained at the

---

[4]For the importance of inhibitory processes in development, see also Bjorklund and Harnishfeger (1990); Dempster (1992).

same age in different tasks, thus pointing to the existence of stages (lasting approximately two years, as in Pascual-Leone's model) in the development of processing space.

It is difficult to always empirically distinguish between Case's and Pascual-Leone's models. With respect to the growth of working memory, both models predict the same pattern of results, at least within Case's dimensional stage:[5] from 1 to 4 schemes between 3–4 and 10–11 years of age. The two models present, however, a number of important, theoretical divergences. The role assigned to maturation is different. In Pascual-Leone's model, M-power grows with maturation throughout childhood. For Case, although development in general also undergoes maturational influence, the growth of STSS within a general stage is mainly due to a trade-off between processing and storage space: As an operation newly acquired at the beginning of a stage becomes more efficient with practice, the amount of executive space devoted to the operating space diminishes and there is progressively more space left for the storage space. There are other differences between the two models. In particular, Pascual-Leone uses an energy metaphor, probably closer to current connectionist models, whereas Case uses a spatial metaphor, in which processing space consists in a number of slots (Case, 1985). Finally, Pascual-Leone defines several, independent sources of activation of schemes in working memory, whereas Case considers a single source of activation, assigned to different contents. In this sense, working memory can be considered unitary in Case's model but not in Pascual-Leone's. It should be remarked that Case's suggestion of a trade-off between storage and processing, and hence of a general, unitary pool of resources has also been seriously criticised by Halford (1993), who showed that it is contradictory with a number of empirical findings.

Similarities and Differences Between the Two Types of Models

Baddeley's model and the neo-Piagetian models may appear very different. In our opinion, however, they are complementary rather than contradictory.

First, they apply at different scales, "microscopic" versus "macroscopic". Baddeley's experimental approach focuses on the different processes at work within essentially single types of paradigms, and on the predictive power of these paradigms for other cognitive situations. The capacity of each subsystem is considered to be limited; however, Baddeley only

---

[5]The values predicted by the two models differ across the entire span of childhood, but we will not detail these differences here.

attempted to quantify these limits with regard to the Articulatory Loop. Relationships between WM and cognitive performance have been studied, but without attempting to formulate precise developmental predictions. In contrast, the objective of neo-Piagetian models is to provide hypotheses relative to general processes at work in a whole range of cognitive tasks, in order to predict developmental changes, together with individual differences in the case of Pascual-Leone, as well as to understand the underlying mechanisms responsible for development. As a result, they adopt a rather global point of view. For instance, Pascual-Leone's concept of M-power is meant as a general, content-free mechanism, whose growth accounts for cognitive development at large, and in particular for the existence of general developmental stages. As Halliday and Hitch emphasise (1988), such approaches strive to provide theories about causes of developmental change, whereas developmental studies within the Baddeley tradition tend to contribute a description of developmental differences without looking for explanations of the developmental process. As a result, neo-Piagetian models have focused on a quantitative assessment of limit in information-processing capacity, and on the increase in these limits with age, using tasks in which the influence of other factors is at least controlled to some extent (de Ribaupierre & Pascual-Leone, 1984).

A second difference seems to lie in the emphasis placed by Baddeley on the existence and the independence of several subsystems. However, as we have seen, WM is not unitary either in the case of Pascual-Leone's model: Items stored and maintained in WM may not all require M-activation, but can be weighed by other operators, too. This might explain the apparent contradiction between the large variability in performances reported in the experimental studies on working memory (e.g. Dempster, 1985) and the stability described by the neo-Piagetians. In the latter approach, stability is only postulated when the task is a relatively pure M-task; in contrast, in other cognitive tasks which call not only for attentional capacity but also for other processees, variability is the rule more than the exception (e.g. de Ribaupierre, 1993; de Ribaupierre & Pascual-Leone, 1984). We suggest that the mechanism of mental attention described by Pascual-Leone (i.e. M-operator, together with the I-operator and executive schemes) roughly corresponds to Baddeley's Central Executive and that information maintained by the slave subsystems corresponds to the schemes activated by other operators. Pascual-Leone's model not only distinguishes several silent operators, but also different types of schemes (Johnson, 1991; Pascual-Leone, Goodman, Ammon, & Subelman, 1978; Pascual-Leone & Johnson, 1991; de Ribaupierre, 1983), according to their (sensorial) modalities and their modes. The latter distinction refers to the way information is coded, and is not necessarily tied to particular types of content; modes are defined as infralogical or mereological (retaining spatio-temporal and/

or causal properties), logological (generic knowledge), and linguistic. Although this distinction is not made by Baddeley, one could regard the schemes maintained in the two subsystems as differing both in terms of modality and mode: Information maintained in the AL might correspond to verbal (modality) and linguistic or logological schemes whereas information stored in the VSSP might constitute visual and mereological schemes.

On the whole, however, for Case and Pascual-Leone, all schemes placed in the field of mental attention or in the processing space are considered functionally equivalent, as long as they are required in a task, are not activated directly by the input or by another operator, and need to be kept separate. Their equivalence results from the fact that they require the same amount of M-activation to apply, regardless of their content, whether verbal or spatial, simple or complex.[6] Measuring M-capacity requires a number of methodological precautions, to ensure that the task does not induce chunking strategies and is not too sensitive to individual differences (see, for instance, Pascual-Leone, 1970, 1978; de Ribaupierre & Pascual-Leone, 1984), that is, is not too sensitive to the influence of silent operators other than M. The main difficulty, in these approaches, consists indeed in assessing the number of schemes necessary in a task and/or used by a subject (e.g. de Ribaupierre, Neirynck, & Spira, 1989). For example, it is often not possible to equate the number of elements recalled with the number of schemes because of chunking strategies.

From an empirical point of view, the difference in focus between the two approaches to working memory influences the type of paradigm used: Typical studies in the Baddeley tradition use dual tasks, and rely on a paradigm of double dissociation to identify the contribution of different components of working memory to performance. In contrast, neo-Piagetians have tended to use a single task, or a battery of tasks (e.g. Morra, 1992, this issue) supposed to address the same underlying processes.

Despite the fact that neo-Piagetian models do not directly address the issue of different working memory subsystems, we believe that they can nevertheless accommodate the kind of empirical findings which led Baddeley to postulate different slave systems. The lack of interference obtained when two different tasks are used conjointly could simply reflect the fact that processing resources are large enough to handle both tasks simultaneously, either because the subjects' M-capacity is sufficient and/or because different silent operators in Pascual-Leone's sense may also contri-

---

[6]In this regard, schemes are like chunks, that is, they are independent items of information of "arbitrary size, and their status does not depend on their information value" (Halford, 1993, p. 124).

bute to performance. Indeed, the tasks used are generally simple; when they become more complex, interference effects are usually observed.[7] In Pascual-Leone's model, simple tasks often call for schemes which may be activated by other source than M-power and consequently do not compete for the same limited resources. Conversely, one can ask why there is any effect of dual-task interference at all. Pascual-Leone's model would predict interference in two cases: (a) when both tasks are difficult enough to require the contribution of M-operator, and their combined M-demand exceeds the subjects' M-power; (b) when one task is misleading with respect to the other. This is the case when the two tasks call for the same system. It is then necessary to inhibit, in each task, a number of irrelevant schemes which tend to be strongly activated by the concurrent task because they are in the same format. Monitoring both tasks simultaneously and selecting the relevant schemes while inhibiting the irrelevant ones at the proper moment require a particularly efficient I-operator and good executive schemes. It may even be the case that extra M-power is required to activate the relevant schemes.

In summary, there are a number of important differences between Baddeley's and Pascual-Leone's models. Our view is not that all of them can and have to be wiped out. Nevertheless, we contend that correspondences can be established between these two approaches. We have suggested that Baddeley's subsystems of WM, taken together, correspond to Pascual-Leone's second subset of activated schemes sometimes specifically labelled working memory, whereas the CE corresponds to the most restricted subset of highly activated schemes, namely the field of mental attention. We see two reasons for bringing more closely together these two models. First, from a general, epistemological perspective, it seems useful to draw links when it is possible between trends of studies which have largely ignored each other. Secondly, the two models may prove useful when it comes to interpret empirical results. Baddeley's model provides a finer account of the functioning of WM, particularly as regards possible between-task effects of interference; by focusing on general, underlying mechanisms at work in a large number of situations, Pascual-Leone's model contributes to insert WM studies in a more integrated picture of cognitive development.

---

[7]One of our anonymous reviewers called our attention to Klapp, Marshburn, and Lester's (1983) work, in which no interference effect was observed, even though the tasks were more complex. However, the argument that several operators may work in parallel to activate different sets of schemes applies in this case, too. If there is enough time to encode the memory preload, its content may then be activated by an operator other than M.

AN EMPIRICAL ILLUSTRATION

We will now try to illustrate, using results obtained in a neo-Piagetian task, the way in which these approaches are complementary rather than contradictory. The study presented here is part of a longitudinal project which aimed at studying developmental changes in attentional capacity, using a number of neo-Piagetian tasks. As mentioned in the Introduction, the initial objective was to examine neo-Piagetian developmental hypotheses, it is only in the course of the study that we realised that some results could just as well be accounted for by Baddeley's model.

Four cohorts of children, aged 5, 6, 8, and 10 at the first assessment, were followed over five years; they were examined once a year with attentional capacity tasks adapted from Pascual-Leone and Case, and with Piagetian tasks. In the last two years of the project, other working memory tasks were also introduced (verbal span, articulatory rate tasks). The present paper will focus on the changes observed in two related tasks (visual memory tasks called Peanut-P and Peanut-C), following a modification in the response mode. On Year 4, the Peanut tasks were computerised and subjects had to respond using a computer mouse. Presentation of results proceeds in three parts. First, cross-sectional comparisons of the two forms of the task are presented, which support the neo-Piagetian hypothesis of limits in attentional capacity. Longitudinal results are then described, with a focus on the changes observed following computerisation. It is argued that the task was thereby transformed into a dual paradigm, which was responsible for a severe reduction in performance. Finally, a finer analysis which contrasts two different scores is reported, in order to discuss the possible role played by the VSSP system in our tasks.

METHOD

Subjects

The initial sample consisted of 120 children (30 by age group), aged 5, 6, 8, and 10 at the onset of the study. Each age group is referred to as a cohort. Testing took place within two months of the subjects' birthday, and the interval between the annual testing sessions was approximately one year. The initial sample was representative of the Genevan primary school population with respect to gender, socioeconomic status, and national origin. Results presented here are based on 100 children who were examined each year (i.e. five times) with the task (respectively 27, 22, 28, and 23 for each age group); the overall attrition rate was thus 20% in this task over the five years.

Task

This short-term memory task was adapted from Case (1985) and has been used several times in Case's own research (Case, 1985; Case, Marini, McKeough, Dennis, & Goldberg, 1986). Children were presented with a clown figure (see Fig. 1, left), with a varying number of coloured dots painted on different body parts. The picture was then removed, and replaced with a blank clown figure. Children had to place coloured chips on the parts that were painted in the model. The figure was slightly modified in Year 4 (see Fig. 1, right) so as to increase the number of locations in which painted dots could be placed.

Two forms were constructed, which are considered as two separate tasks: (a) *Mr Peanut Purple (Peanut-P)*: all coloured dots and all chips were purple (red on Years 4 and 5). Children had to recall the position of each dot; (b) *Mr Peanut Coloured (Peanut-C)*: dots were of different colours; children had to recall the position and the colour of each dot.

Item complexity was defined on the basis of the number of coloured dots: Class 1 items contained one dot, Class 2 items contained two dots, etc. The complexity ranged from 1 to 5 or 6, depending on the version. There were five items for each level of difficulty; items were distributed randomly throughout the task. A number of conditions were met in constructing the task: no item contained two dots in symmetrical locations (e.g. in the two arms) nor two dots of the same colour; obvious patterns were avoided so as to minimise chunking; identical positions were not used on consecutive items.

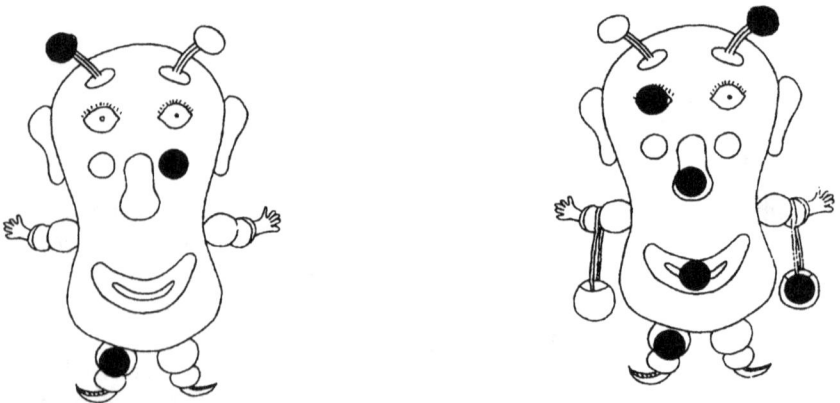

FIG. 1.   Peanut figure used in the longitudinal study. Left: figure used in Years 1–3, 14 possible locations; example of a Class 3 item. Right: figure used in Years 4–5, 16 possible locations; example of a Class 6 item.

Scoring. Items were scored as passed when all the correct positions (Peanut-P) or correct colours in the correct positions (for Peanut-C) had been recalled. An overall score was computed by dividing the number of correct items by 5 (i.e. by the number of items in each class of complexity). This score is comparable to a more traditional span measure: For instance, a score close to 1 means that subjects pass Class 1 items, but fail most items of Class 2 or higher. The number of correctly recalled dots, whether the item was passed or failed, was also recorded; it constitutes a finer score than the number of correct items. Finally, for Peanut-C, a colour score (number of correct colours independent of positions) and a position score (number of correct positions independent of colours) were used.

Procedure

Each child was tested individually in a quiet room, each year for 3–5 sessions of approximately 45 minutes, during which the full range of tasks used were administered in no predetermined order. However, the Peanut tasks were given in the same session, and the Peanut-P task was always presented before the Peanut-C task. Each Peanut task lasted from 15 to 30 minutes. Different versions, adapted in terms of the level of difficulty, were constructed for the different age groups and the different years of the project. Table 1 shows the different versions by year and by cohort. All

TABLE 1
Versions of Mr Peanut by Assessment Year and by Cohort

	Cohort 5	Cohort 6	Cohort 8	Cohort 10
Year 1	P1–P4	P1–P4	P1–P5	P1–P5
	C1–C3	C1–C3	C1–C4	C1–C5
Year 2	P1–P4	P1–P5	P1–P5	P1–P5
	C1–C3	C1–C4	C1–C5	C1–C5
Year 3	P1–P5	P1–P5	P1–P5	P1–P5
	C1–C4	C1–C4	C1–C5	C1–C5
Year 4	P2–P5	P2–P5	P2–P6	P2–P6
	C2–C5	C2–C5	C2–C6	C2–C6
Year 5	P2–P6	P2–P6	P2–P6	P2–P6
	C2–C6	C2–C6	C2–C6	C2–C6

Note. The table reports the classes of complexity administered (5 items per class); P = Peanut-P and C = Peanut-C. P1–P4 means that Classes 1–4 were given in the Peanut-P task.

items of the same complexity level were identical across versions, but followed a different order.

On Years 1–3, presentation was manual: Subjects were shown a Peanut figure on a sheet of paper, and had to recall by placing coloured chips on a blank figure. On Years 4–5, the procedure was computerised. The coloured figure appeared on the screen, followed by a blank figure; children had to move coloured dots on the screen to place them on the Peanut figure, using a computer mouse. In both types of presentation, exposure time was limited (1 second per coloured dot in the figure), but response time was free. New items were constructed for the computerised task, due to the addition of baskets on the arms. A supplementary training phase was also introduced to ensure that children could manipulate the mouse, and to show them how to move the coloured dots to different places and to correct errors.

RESULTS

As mentioned earlier, we focus here on three aspects of the results: (1) the difference between Peanut-P and Peanut-C; (2) the comparison of Years 1–3 versus Years 4–5, that is, the changes consecutive to the computerisa-

TABLE 2
Mean Number of Correct Items

Age	Peanut-P Years					Peanut-C Years				
	1	2	3	4	5	1	2	3	4	5
5	1.36 (0.32)					1.09 (0.41)				
6	1.63 (0.41)	1.90 (0.53)				1.38 (0.39)	1.46 (0.39)			
7		2.06 (0.47)	2.27 (0.47)				1.70 (0.37)	1.66 (0.48)		
8	2.61 (0.70)		2.89 (0.59)	2.14 (0.49)		1.94 (0.48)		2.01 (0.57)	1.55 (0.33)	
9		3.34 (0.67)		2.51 (0.52)	2.77 (0.47)		2.54 (0.60)		1.76 (0.32)	1.78 (0.30)
10	3.29 (0.60)		3.77 (0.62)		3.05 (0.63)	2.57 (0.51)		2.84 (0.61)		2.13 (0.49)
11		3.90 (0.67)		3.69 (0.60)			3.16 (0.58)		2.48 (0.50)	
12			4.32 (0.43)		4.14 (0.88)			3.38 (0.62)		2.74 (0.68)
13				4.17 (0.76)					2.90 (0.65)	
14					4.37 (0.87)					3.04 (0.77)

Note. Standard deviations are in parentheses.

tion of the task; (3) the comparison of the colour score and the position score for Peanut-C.

First, overall results are presented. Table 2 reports the mean number of correct items by chronological age and by year of testing, for both Peanut-P and Peanut-C. Recall that four cohorts (5, 6, 8, and 10) were examined. A vertical reading allows a cross-sectional analysis at each assessment point; that is, children were aged 5, 6, 8, and 10 on Year 1, and 6, 7, 9, and 11 on Year 2, and so on. Horizontal reading allows a comparison of results for children of the same age at different assessment years. For instance, three cohorts were examined when they were aged 8: cohort 8 on Year 1, cohort 6 on Year 3, and cohort 5 on Year 4. Longitudinal results, that is the results obtained by a given cohort each consecutive year, can be read in the diagonal (e.g. 5–1, 6–2, 7–3, etc., where the first digit stands for chronological age and the second for the year of assessment).

Two general comments are in order. First, there were clear differences between age groups, each year and for each task. Usually, the difference between cohorts 5 and 6 was smaller than the difference between cohorts 6 and 8, and than between cohorts 8 and 10. This was confirmed through analyses of variance[8] on the results of each year: The main effect of age was significant for each year, and contrast analyses showed that cohorts 5 and 6 either did not differ from each other or differed less than the other cohorts. Likewise, in an overall Age × Task × Year of Testing three-way analysis of variance, the main effect of Age was significant, $F(3,96) = 100.7$, $P < 0.01$. Scheffé tests showed that the difference between cohorts 5 and 6 was only significant for Peanut-C ($F(1,47) = 15.36$, $P < 0.05$), but not for Peanut-P ($F(1,47) = 14.29$). The other effects of this analysis of variance will be discussed later.

Secondly, there were effects of retest or practice on Years 2 and 3. Table 2 shows that, keeping age constant, performances were higher for children having had more encounters with the tasks. For instance, children aged 6 years on Year 2 had higher scores than children aged 6 on Year 1 (mean scores of respectively 1.9 vs. 1.63 for Peanut-P and 1.46 vs. 1.38 for Peanut-C); the same was true at Ages 7 (only for Peanut-P) and 8. Retest effects were stronger for Peanut-P. These differences were not all tested or did not all prove significant. Nevertheless, such retest effects were also observed in a parallel study in which 6-, 8-, and 10-year-olds were examined twice with the Peanut tasks over an interval of one month (for more

---

[8]Given the different versions administered to the different cohorts and over the course of the study, the design of analyses of variance was not always the same. For instance, when all age groups were considered together, only Class 1 to Class 3 items could be analysed on Years 1 and 2, even though the older subjects had items up to Class 5. Therefore, different analyses of variance were conducted each year on cross-sectional data, and for reasons of space only a few will be reported in some detail.

details, see de Ribaupierre & Spira, 1991; Spira & Keizer, 1991). They are probably due to more elaborate encoding and processing strategies (e.g. spatial chunks) which children can develop when they know the task better, this reflecting other processes besides attentional capacity *per se*.

Cross-sectional Comparison of Peanut-P and Peanut-C

A number of differences were hypothesised between the two tasks (see also de Ribaupierre et al., 1989). First, Peanut-P should be easier than Peanut-C, because of a lower informational load. Secondly, the use of spatial patterns or chunks is more likely in Peanut-P due to a greater homogeneity in the information to be encoded; if two or more purple dots can be encoded as a single chunk, the difficulty of the task is lowered further. In Peanut-C, it is necessary to recall positions and colours and to match them correctly; this requires the co-ordination of visuo-spatial and verbal encoding and is therefore hypothesised to draw on the resources of the Central Executive. In terms of Pascual-Leone's model, the necessity to match colours and positions demands probably an additional activation by M, monitored by executive schemes. Thirdly, although being nonverbal in nature, both tasks are assumed to require a visuo-spatial and a verbal encoding (the colours as well as the positions are nameable), particularly with respect to positions. The different positions can be named and they are spatially located; in addition, as already mentioned, there is a certain likelihood that subjects chunk several positions by creating spatial patterns. However, the relative importance of each type of encoding differs between the two tasks. Incidentally, it probably also varies among different types of subjects, but individual differences will not be analysed further in the present paper. With respect to Peanut-C, in which subjects had to retain not only positions but also colours, it is suggested that the relative weight of verbal encoding is greater for the encoding of colours than for positions. Reciprocally, the relative weight of spatial encoding is larger in encoding positions than colours. This point will be analysed more in detail in a later section.

We had a fourth hypothesis with respect to the difference between the two tasks, which had to do with the maximal performances possible. Neo-Piagetian models predict that performances are severely constrained by limits in the amount of information that can be processed. This should result in a relative invariance of performance across items of different complexity, once the processing limits are reached. In the Peanut tasks, this implies that subjects should recall approximately the same number of dots independently of class complexity. For instance, a subject whose upper limit corresponds to two units of information should pass items Class

1 and Class 2, and should not recall more than two correct dots on the more difficult items, regardless of whether items are of Class 3, 4 or 5. We assumed that this would apply to Peanut-C only; in this task, the number of correctly recalled dots should remain stable across classes, beyond a certain level of difficulty corresponding to the child's processing limits. In contrast, in Peanut-P, stability in performance was not expected, for the two reasons stated above, that is, the lower informational load and the greater facility to encode spatial patterns. Moreover, the opportunity for chunking increases with the number of dots. Consequently, the number of correctly recalled dots should no longer be invariant across classes, but should increase with complexity.

Results were consistent with these hypotheses. Table 2 shows that the number of correct items was higher for Peanut-P, attesting to its greater facility. All analyses of variance conducted on cross-sectional data showed a main effect of the task. In the Age × Task × Year of Testing three-way analysis of variance which was described earlier, the main effect of Task was significant, $F(1,96) = 791.02$, $P < 0.01$, as well as the Age × Task interaction, $F(3,96) = 16.15$, $P < 0.01$. Scheffé tests showed the Task effect to be significant for each age group and the Age effect significant in each task; however, the Task effect was larger for the older age groups, which was to be expected if older children apply more readily facilitating strategies. The difference between the two tasks is not due to an order effect: Indeed, the Peanut-C task was always administered after the Peanut-P one, and, given the effects of retest which were observed, it is likely that the difference would have been even larger had the two tasks been administered in a different order.

Figure 2 reports the mean number of *correctly recalled dots* by cohort, class complexity (C2–C6), and year (Years 1–5). It can be observed that performance increased steadily with class complexity in Peanut-P (top panel), this being replicated for each age and assessment. In contrast, performance tended to be stable in Peanut-C (bottom panel), or even to slightly diminish. When the overall difficulty of the task was relatively low, as for instance on Year 3 or Year 5 for cohorts 8 and 10 (these subjects were then respectively aged 10 and 12, and 12 and 14), performance increased up to Class 4, after which it remained stable. This was confirmed by analyses of variance conducted on the cross-sectional data obtained each year. For instance, on Year 5, the Age (4) × Task (2) × Class (5) three-way analysis of variance performed on the number of dots recalled per class (Class 2–6) showed a main effect of Age ($F(3,96) = 42.1$, $P < 0.01$), Task ($F(1,96) = 790.7$, $P < 0.01$), and Class ($F(4,384) = 188.3$, $P < 0.01$), as well as the following interactions: Class × Task ($F(4,384) = 153.6$, $P < 0.01$), Class ×Age ($F(12,384) = 12.3$, $P < 0.01$) and Age × Task × Class ($F(12,384) = 2.54$, $P < 0.01$). Of particular interest here is

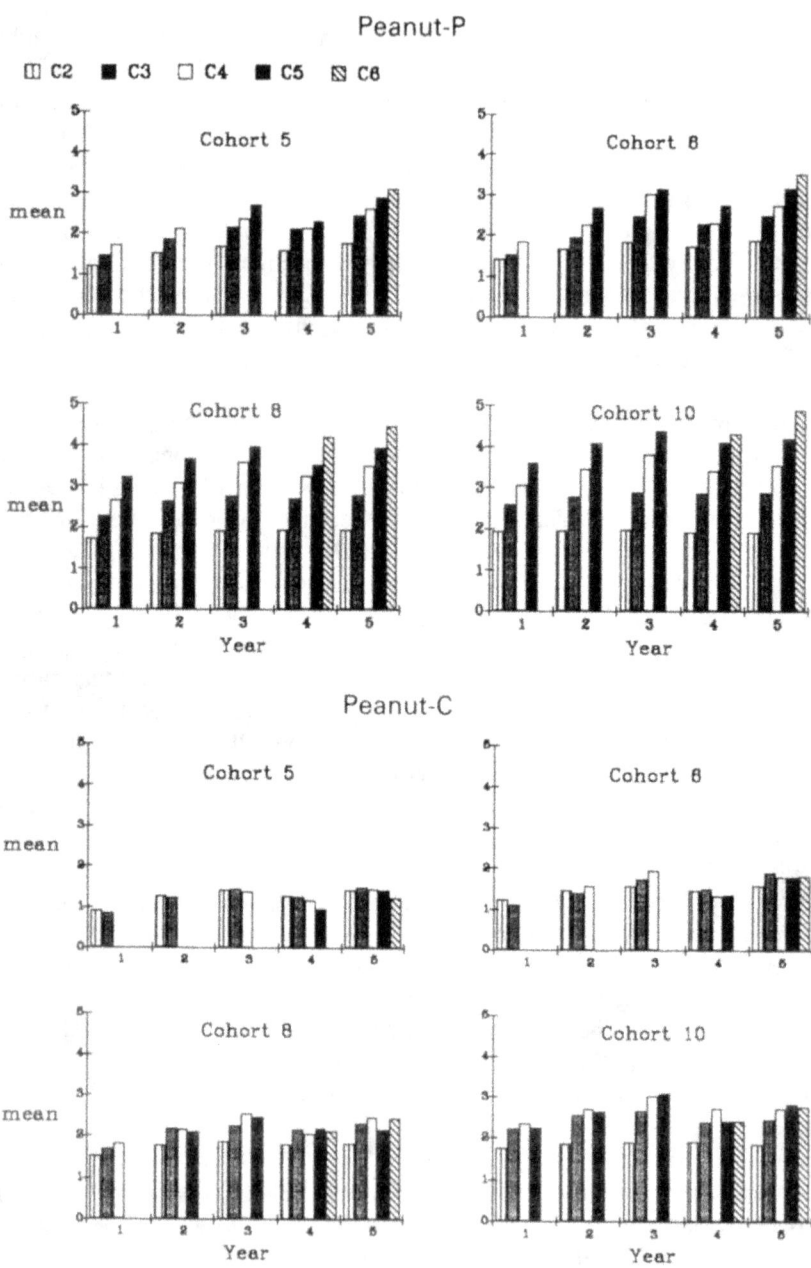

Peanut-P

Legend: C2 C3 C4 C5 C6

Cohort 5

Cohort 8

Cohort 8

Cohort 10

Peanut-C

Cohort 5

Cohort 8

Cohort 8

Cohort 10

FIG. 2. Mean number of correctly recalled spots by Cohort, Class, and Year (C2–C6: Class 2 to Class 6 items). Top panel: Peanut-P. Bottom panel: Peanut-C.

the Class × Task interaction. Scheffé tests showed that all between-class differences were significant in Peanut-P. In contrast, only the difference between the two easiest classes were significant in Peanut-C. This is, of course, due to the ceiling effect in Classes 2 and 3, particularly for the older cohorts: Subjects cannot obtain a score higher than 2 in Class 2 or higher than 3 in Class 3, even though they are capable of retaining more dots; therefore, they obtain higher scores in Class 4 items than in either of these two classes. Between-class differences were, however, not significant from Class 4 on. Similar effects were obtained each year: The Class × Task interaction was always significant (F ratios were $F(2,192) = 32.09$, $F(1,192) = 47.65$, $F(3,288) = 129.46$ and $F(3,288) = 97.04$ for Years 1, 2, 3, and 4 respectively) and Scheffé tests showed that only the easiest classes (up to Class 3) were different in Peanut-C, while all between-class differences were significant in Peanut-P.

The greater difficulty and stability obtained in Peanut-C is due to the necessity to match colours and positions. This was confirmed by means of a different score: the sum of correct colours and correct positions recalled (Co + Po), independent of whether they were correctly matched. This sum was further *divided by two*, to make it directly comparable to the number of dots in the stimulus. Results turned out somewhat differently in the three-way analyses of variance comparing this score for Peanut-C with the number of correctly recalled dots in Peanut-P. On Year 5 again, the Age × Task × Class three-way analysis of variance also showed a main effect of Age ($F(3,96) = 44.3$, $P < 0.01$), Task ($F(1,96) = 95.6$, $P < 0.01$), and Class ($F(4,384) = 526$, $P < 0.01$). All interactions proved significant, too. However, the analysis of the three-way interaction ($F(12,384) = 2.54$, $P < 0.01$) by means of Tukey tests showed that the two tasks no longer differed, except for the two older age groups in the more difficult classes (in Classes 4–6 for Cohort 8 and in Classes 5 and 6 for Cohort 10). All classes differed significantly from each other, in both tasks, in contrast with the analyses conducted on the number of correctly recalled dots. Similar effects were obtained on the first four years: on Years 3 and 4, a three-way interaction was also obtained ($F(9,288)$ were respectively 4.28, $P < 0.01$ and 3.06, $P < 0.01$), showing an effect of Task only in the older cohorts and the more difficult classes, whereas the Class effect was significant in both tasks. In Years 1 and 2, the three-way interaction was not significant; however, analyses of the two-way interactions obtained (Age × Task, Age × Class and Version × Class) showed that again the effect of Task showed only in the more difficult classes (it was not more pronounced in the older subjects), whereas the Class effect remained significant in both tasks. This means that subjects now retain as much information, if not even more, in Peanut-C than in Peanut-P; because it has been divided by two, the Co + Po score in Peanut-C has a higher information value than the number of correct positions in Peanut-P. Furthermore, the effect of Class observed with this score in Peanut-C shows that the ceiling in performance observed with the previous score originates in the necessity to match two heterogenous types of information (colours and positions).

It is argued that Pascual-Leone's model can better account for this difference in results than Baddeley's model. Positions and colours alone are probably activated not only by M-operator but also by other operators which allow for a less effortful encoding, resulting in an increase in performance across classes. However, the matching of colours and positions can only be handled by an M-activation, together with the executive schemes. Given the limits in M-power, the number of correctly recalled dots is invariant once the ceiling is reached. In reference to Baddeley's model, it can be suggested that the matching of colours and positions is handled by the Central Executive, whereas the retention of colours and positions alone could be managed by the Articulatory Loop system and/or the VSSP system. However, stability across classes could probably not be predicted.

LONGITUDINAL ANALYSIS:
YEARS 1–3 VS. YEARS 4–5

For reasons of space, the results which are reported in this section are based on the number of passed items only. Analyses conducted on the number of correctly recalled dots led to similar results. The overall proportion of passed items by task, cohort, and year of assessment is displayed in Fig. 3 (see also Table 2). It can be observed that the increase was relatively linear over the first three years, for the four cohorts. This linear increase is not congruent with the neo-Piagetian postulate of developmental stages lasting for two years. In view of the M-stages defined by Pascual-Leone for instance, Cohorts 6, 8, and 10 should have progressed from Year 1 to Year 2, but not from Year 2 to Year 3; Cohort 5 should have progressed from Year 2 to Year 3, but not from Year 1 to Year 2. We cannot claim, however, that the results invalidate the neo-Piagetian models because of the retest or practice effects which were mentioned above. The developmental curves observed over the first three years must therefore be understood as pointing to the difficulty of unconfounding learning and developmental changes.

With respect to the comparison of Baddeley's and neo-Piagetian models, results obtained on Year 4 are particularly interesting. Recall that on Year 4, the task was computerised. The consequence was a drastic change in performances, which were considerably lower on Year 4 than on Year 3 despite the interval of one year; for instance, for Cohort 10, performances on Peanut-C "regressed" by more than two years. An Age (4) × Year of Testing (2) × Task (2) three-way analysis of variance comparing Years 3

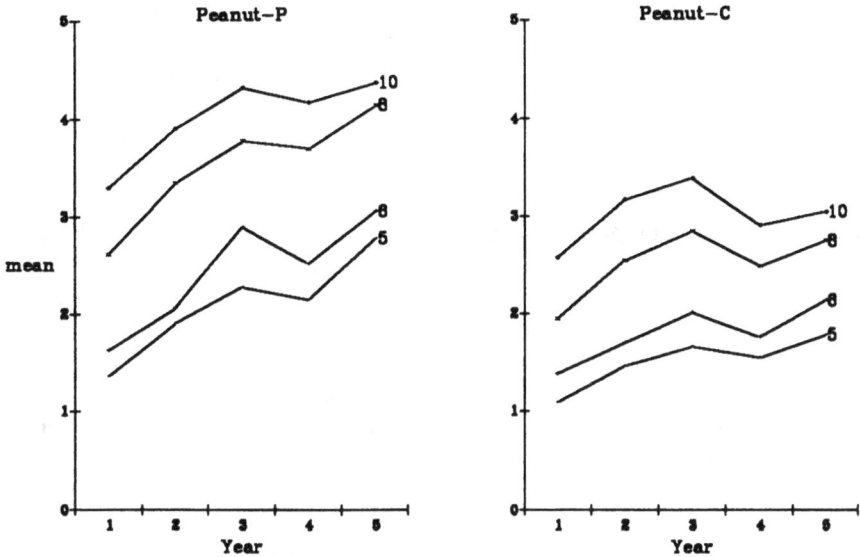

FIG. 3.   Mean number of passed items by Cohort and by Year. Left: Peanut-P; Right: Peanut-C.

and 4 only showed a main effect of Age ($F(3,96) = 93.4$, $P < 0.01$), Task ($F(1,96) = 526.6$, $P < 0.01$), and Assessment ($F(1,96) = 27.6$, $P < 0.01$); there was also a significant Age × Task interaction, ($F(3,96) = 9.60$, $P < 0.01$).

Additional analyses using structural equations modelling were conducted on the data for the whole sample, to test further the difference between the two tasks, and to assess the extent of developmental change. They will only be briefly summarised here (for details, see de Ribaupierre & Bailleux, 1992, 1993). In our case, structural equations modelling makes it possible not only to work at the level of latent variables instead of observed means, but also to overcome the difficulties introduced by the changes in the versions administered over the years; recall that the versions differed across age groups in terms of the number of classes used. First, confirmatory factor analyses were used to test the hypothesis that different processes were tapped in the manual task on Years 1–3 on the one hand, and in the computerised task on Years 4–5 on the other. Two models were contrasted: a one-factor model for the five years; and a two-factor model opposing Years 1–3 and Years 4–5. Note that the hypothesis that all years load on a single factor not only implies that the same processes are tapped, but also that a very high stability exists from year to year. Results indicated that a one-factor model was satisfactory for Peanut-P: Although it was not very good ($\chi^2(5) = 11.67$, $P = 0.04$), it was not significantly different from the two-factor model ($\chi^2(4) = 10.30$, $P = 0.036$). For Peanut-C, however, a two-factor model ($\chi^2(4) = 3.96$, $P = 0.41$) was both very good and significantly better than the one-factor model ($\chi^2(5) = 11.67$, $P = 0.04$). The difference observed between the two tasks is consistent with the suggestion that the computerisation introduced more changes in Peanut-C than in Peanut-P. Secondly, latent growth curve analyses were used to estimate the developmental trends in the number of passed items on each task (e.g. McArdle & Epstein, 1987; Rudinger, Andres, & Rietz, 1991). Again, differences were found between the two tasks. The slope of the change was steeper in Peanut-P than in Peanut-C whether in the first three years or from Year 4 to Year 5; it was also more linear in Peanut-P from Year 1 to Year 3. The absolute decrease in performance from Year 3 to Year 4 was larger for Peanut-P; however, when compared to the level in performance observed in previous years, subjects "regressed" relatively more in Peanut-C and did not "recover" as well. In the latter task, their performances on Years 4 and 5 were identical to those of Years 2 and 3, respectively; in Peanut-P, despite the drop on Year 4, the level on Year 5 was the highest of the five years.

Our current hypothesis is that underlying processes are altered by the change in the response mode. In Baddeley's terms, the concurrent monitoring of a computer mouse can be considered to draw heavily on the VSSP system, just like the Peanut task itself; as a consequence, less processing resources are left for retrieving information. In addition, the Central Executive is probably also called for, to co-ordinate the two tasks. In Pascual-Leone's terms, the monitoring of the mouse calls for an activation by M, unless it is completely automatised. In addition, there might be an incompatibility between the displacement of the mouse and the displacement of the dot, particularly with respect to the up and down movement (on a horizontal vs. a vertical plane). This renders the monitoring of the mouse a misleading task, requiring the intervention of the I-operator. The difference in slope in the two Peanut tasks may be due to the relatively higher involvement of M-power in the Peanut-C task, which was discussed earlier.

Colours vs. Positions

If the monitoring of a mouse is considered not only to require supplementary resources, but also to constitute a spatial concurrent task, interfering with the placement of the dots on the screen, the interference should be stronger for the position score. To investigate this, partial scores were compared for Peanut-C: correct colours independent of positions and correct positions independent of colours.

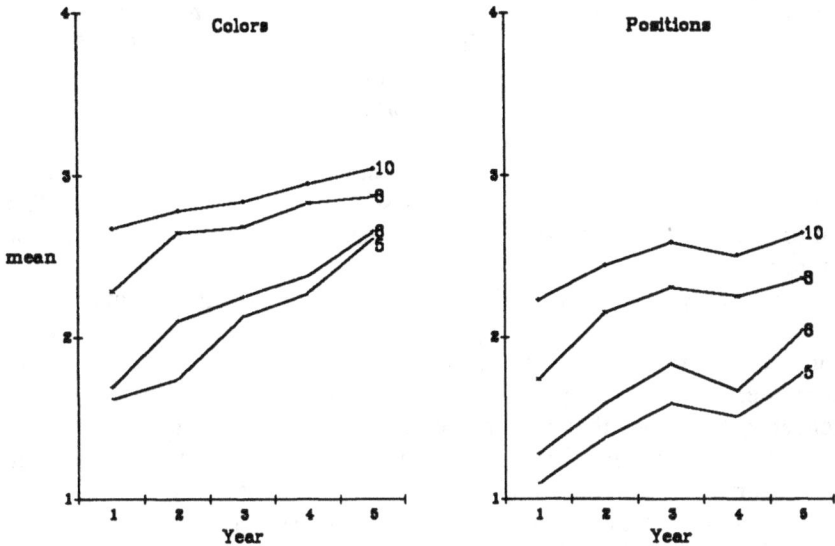

FIG. 4.   Peanut-C: Mean number of correct colours (left) and positions (right) by Year and by Cohort.

Figure 4 reports the mean number of colours and of positions recalled, by Year and by Cohort. As expected, the drop from Year 3 to Year 4 was greater for the Position score.

In order to compare the developmental changes in both scores over the five years, an Age (4) × Year of Testing (5) × Type (2, Position vs. Colour) three-way analysis of variance was made. All effects were significant, including the three-way interaction, $F(12,384) = 3.99$, $P < 0.01$. Because effect of assessment may be confounded with changes in version over the years, four separate analyses of variance, in which the number of classes was kept constant, were also conducted on each pair of consecutive assessments. The focus being here on the change from Year 3 to Year 4, detailed results are given for these two years only. The four-way analysis of variance (4 Age groups × 2 Years of testing × 2 Types × 3 Classes, for Class 2 to 4) showed a main effect of Age ($F(3,96) = 55.1$, $P < 0.01$), Assessment ($F(1,96) = 6.74$, $P < 0.01$), Type ($F(1,96) = 343.2$, $P < 0.01$), and Class ($F(2,192) = 652$, $P < 0.01$). Of interest here is the Type × Year interaction ($F(1,96) = 12.7$, $P < 0.01$). Further analysis of this interaction by means of Scheffé tests showed that the effect of Type was significant each year, more colours being recalled than positions, and the effect of Year significant for both types of responses, but more marked for the position score. Also, the Year effect was opposite: Progression for colours versus regression for positions. A Type × Year of testing interaction was also obtained in the other analyses, except when comparing Years 2 and 3: $Fs(1,96)$ were 10.8, $P < 0.01$ when comparing Years 1–2 and 9.65, $P < 0.01$ for Years 4–5, but only 1.96 for Years 2–3. This shows that the change from year to year was usually less important, although still significant, for colours than for positions. The other interactions obtained in these four analyses were: Age × Type, Age × Class, and Class × Type; they are all due to a ceiling effect in the lower classes and/or the colour score. The difference between the two scores remained, nevertheless, significant for all age groups.

These analyses are congruent with the hypothesis that computerisation has a more disruptive effect on positions than on colours recalled. Even if subjects continue to encode positions in the form of patterns in the computerised task, they probably cannot retrieve them as easily nor rehearse them once they start responding, because of the spatial interference created by the monitoring of the mouse. A further argument in favour of the importance of encoding strategies for positions is found in analyses on individual curves: It was observed that the subjects who "regressed" most from Year 3 to Year 4 showed, on average, a higher rate of progression from Year 1 to Year 3. This seems true for the number of correctly placed dots in Peanut-P and the number of positions in Peanut-C, but not for the number of colours (de Ribaupierre & Bailleux, 1993).

DISCUSSION

The main objective of this paper was to argue that it is theoretically interesting to combine two approaches to Working Memory which have developed within radically different perspectives, namely, neo-Piagetian models such as Pascual-Leone's and Case's on the one hand, and Baddeley's model, on the other. It was not to discriminate between these models. Results obtained in a neo-Piagetian task, Mr Peanut, used in a longitudinal study of attentional capacity in children aged 5 to 14, were presented as empirical evidence. The original intent of our longitudinal study was to study developmental changes in attentional capacity from a neo-Piagetian perspective; it is only midway in the project that we realised that our data could be interpreted within Baddeley's model as well. Therefore, the results reported here were essentially meant as an illustration of the argument, rather than as a decisive, empirical demonstration. The latter requires further experimentation (see later); until then, some of our conclusions remain necessarily speculative.

Neo-Piagetian models, in particular Pascual-Leone's model, provided a number of predictions for the present study. The stability in scores which was observed in Peanut-C across different classes of complexity, beyond a certain level, is totally congruent with the hypothesis that limits in M-power exert constraints on cognitive performance. These limits were, however, lower than those observed by Case: In the manually presented task, they ranged from around 1 unit (defined here as the number of correctly recalled dots) at 5–6 years of age to 3 units at 12 years of age, rather than 4 around 10 years of age as predicted by Case. Incidentally, there is also a rather large variability among the results reported in the different studies conducted by Case and collaborators in which this task was used (Case, 1985; Case et al., 1986; Dennis, 1991). This is probably due to differences in the experimental procedure and demonstrates the difficulty to define what is a unit or chunk from the subject's point of view (see also Flavell, 1984; de Ribaupierre et al., 1989). In the Peanut tasks, a chunk does not coincide with a dot and does not contain the same information value in Peanut-P and in Peanut-C. Pascual-Leone's very elaborated method of task analysis is an attempt to take into account the difference between a situational unit and a subjective chunk (for details on task analysis, see for instance, Alp, 1992; Case, 1992; Pascual-Leone et al., 1978; de Ribaupierre & Pascual-Leone, 1979). It was, however, not applied in the present case.

The developmental curves did not show the existence of stages lasting for two years. Indeed, the increase was relatively linear from year to year for the first three years, that is, before the task was computerised. We argued, however, that our results are not sufficient to refute the neo-Piagetian postulate of the existence of stages, but rather that they attest to a combination of learning and developmental aspects. This is almost unavoidable in longitudinal studies in which the same tasks are used repeatedly; *a contrario*, if different tasks are used, it is difficult to claim that the very same processes are studied (de Ribaupierre, 1993). Pascual-Leone's model can indeed account for such effects: In his model, learning operators come into play mostly during the even year of a stage, enabling, in particular, the acquisition and consolidation of more sophisticated executive schemes (Pascual-Leone & Goodman, 1979). In consequence, changes with age may be linear when they result from a combination of the growth in M-power and of effects of learning. It should also be noted that, contrary to Case's hypothesis (Case, 1985), performances did not tend to an asymptote around the age of 10–11: The difference between the older cohorts was always significant, whether they were aged 8 and 10 (Year 1), 10 and 12 (Year 3), or 12 and 14 (Year 5).

Other results were probably less directly predictable albeit explainable from a neo-Piagetian perspective, namely the drop in performance when subjects had to respond using a computer mouse. This is not a developmental effect. There is indeed no reason to think that developmental changes in this task should undergo regression, as has been sometimes observed in other developmental tasks yielding U-shape curves. On the basis of our theoretical analyses, it was argued that a double encoding, verbal and spatial, is at work in the Peanut tasks. The monitoring of the mouse presumably calls for spatial processes, interfering with the spatial aspects of the Peanut task itself. One could of course claim that the interference is due to poor skills in manipulating a computer mouse; if individual differences were certainly important in this respect—some children had a computer at home, others not—it is sufficient to observe a child using a mouse for the very first time to realise that this is probably not the main factor at work. On the basis of Pascual-Leone's perspective, we suggested that the use of a mouse requires additional activation by M unless thoroughly automatised, and also constitutes a misleading task which calls for better executive schemes and the intervention of the I-operator.

The diminution in performance on Year 4 was also, and perhaps more directly, explainable in terms of Baddeley's model. The Peanut tasks draw upon the resources of both the Articulatory Loop and the VSSP system whereas the Central Executive is probably needed for co-ordinating the verbal, visual, and spatial information. Baddeley and other researchers within the same line of studies provided numerous experimental demonstrations of interference effects when two concurrent tasks rely on the same subsystem. Their results can thus directly be used to understand the change in performance following the computerisation of the task. The use of the mouse is assumed to rely on the VSSP system, like, in part, the Peanut task itself. It is therefore not surprising that performing simultaneously two VSSP tasks lowers the scores despite the one year interval.[9] The finding that the diminution was more marked for the number of positions than the number of colours recalled was a supplementary argument in favour of the mouse task being a concurrent spatial task. Although both types of information can be named, verbal encoding is indeed likely to play a relatively larger role in encoding colours than positions whereas spatial encoding is more important for positions. Thus, if the monitoring of the mouse constitutes a spatial interference, its impact should be higher on the positions score than on the colours score. This is precisely what was found.

It should be underscored that the results presented here do not provide a conclusive, empirical picture of the processes at work in the Peanut tasks, but serve to illustrate our thesis that the two types of models are

---

[9]Note that, in our study, the concurrent task was performed during the retrieval phase. In most studies, the concurrent task is introduced during the encoding phase and continued or not into the rehearsal phase; in some studies it is even extended to the retrieval phase. Morris (1987) claimed that VSSP is only disrupted by a concurrent task introduced during the encoding phase, and not during the rehearsal phase. Results are, however, still unclear as to when an interfering task is most effective (e.g. Hue & Erickson, 1988).

complementary rather than contradictory. The computerised task was originally introduced for reasons of convenience (stricter conditions of presentation, automatic recording of response, etc.), and was not necessarily meant to be contrasted with the manual task. It is therefore very difficult, in the present study, to assess the extent of interference created by the use of the mouse. A number of additional experiments and converging operations are necessary.

First, the comparison was longitudinal; it is likely that the interference was somewhat compensated by a developmental change. One could argue that the results reported in the present paper are artefactual, hence our conclusions unwarranted, due to a confound between age and method. Note, however, that these two effects work in opposite directions: Whereas the modification in the response mode leads to a regression in performance, changes with age should be accompanied by enhanced peformances. Performance increased in the first three years of the study; an increase was again observed from Year 4 to Year 5. One can therefore be rather confident that the drop in performance observed on the fourth year is a reliable result. A cross-sectional study is nevertheless needed, comparing two groups of children, one with a manual presentation, the other with a computerised presentation using a computer mouse as a mode of response.

Secondly, a much more direct test of the role of verbal and spatial encoding is needed, by systematically introducing selectively interfering tasks. Tasks such as articulatory suppression and easy spatial tasks (e.g. drawing circles or eight-like shapes on a sheet of paper) should be given concurrently with the Peanut tasks. Our hypothesis is that both types of concurrent tasks should produce disruption in performance. Combining two types of concurrent tasks with different modes of response should allow a comparison of interference effects, at the time of encoding and/or retrieval. We also intend to compare a sequential presentation with the simultaneous one; presenting the coloured dots sequentially should prevent subjects from creating spatial patterns and reinforce the role of verbal encoding. A number of these additional experiences are presently in progress in our group.

To sum up, despite its drawbacks, this study illustrated that a same set of empirical findings are compatible with two very different models of working memory, showing that these models might be complementary rather than contradictory. Pascual-Leone's neo-Piagetian model, and to some extent Case's model, provided the ground for the longitudinal study itself; it could also account for the drop in performance observed on the fourth year, by means of general mechanisms such as the M- and I-operators. Baddeley's model of WM, and perhaps still more the numerous empirical studies conducted in this direction, provided more specific explanations of the interference effect; it has been shown repeatedly that two tasks calling on a same subsystem, as we assumed was the case for the Peanut task and for the monitoring of the mouse task, should indeed lead to a diminution in performance. Our propositions of similarities between the two types of models, however, remain still highly speculative and we do not want to convey the idea that Baddeley's and neo-Piagetian approaches are totally superposable. There remain a number of important divergences between them, both at an epistemological and an empirical level. Finally, we would like to point out that we deliberately restricted ourselves to the comparison of two theoretical models, albeit two predominant ones, whereas there exist a number of other approaches to working memory. There will undoubtedly pass some time before the field of working memory, which is in full expansion, can be considered unified.

REFERENCES

Alp, I.E. (1992). *A task analysis of the imitation sorting task*. Paper presented at the Vth European Conference on Developmental Psychology, Seville, 6–9 September.

Baddeley, A.D. (1986). *Working memory*. Oxford University Press.

Baddeley, A.D. (1988). Imagery and working memory. In M. Denis, J. Engelkamp, & J.T.E. Richardson (Eds.), *Cognitive and neuropsychological approaches to mental imagery* (pp. 169–180). Dordrecht: Martinus Nijhoff.

Baddeley, A.D. (1992). Is working memory working? The fifteenth Bartlett lecture. *The Quarterly Journal of Experimental Psychology, 44A*, 1–31.

Baddeley, A.D., & Hitch, G.J. (1974). Working memory. In G.A. Bower (Ed.), *Recent advances in learning and motivation* (Vol. 8, pp. 47–90). New York: Academic Press.

Bjorklund, D.F., & Harnishfeger, K.K. (1990). The resources construct in cognitive development: Diverse sources of evidence and a theory of inefficient inhibition. *Developmental Review, 10*, 48–71.

Case, R. (1974). Structures and strictures: Some functional limitations on the course of cognitive growth. *Cognitive Psychology, 6*, 544–573.

Case, R. (1985). *Intellectual development. Birth to adulthood*. New York: Academic Press.

Case, R. (1987). Neo-piagetian theory: Retrospect and prospect. *International Journal of Psychology, 22*, 773–791.

Case, R. (1992). Neo-piagetian theories of intellectual development. In H. Beilin & P.B. Pufall (Eds.), *Piaget's theory: Prospects and possibilities* (pp. 61–104). Hillsdale, NJ: Lawrence Erlbaum Associates Inc.

Case, R., Kurland, D.M., & Goldberg, J. (1982). Operational efficiency and the growth of short-term memory span. *Journal of Experimental Child Psychology, 33*, 386–404.

Case, R., Marini, Z., McKeough, A., Dennis, S., & Goldberg, J. (1986). Horizontal structure in middle childhood: Cross-domain parallels in the course of cognitive growth. In I. Levin (Ed.), *Stage and structure. Reopening the debate* (pp. 1–39). Norwood, NJ: Ablex.

Chapman, M. (1987). Piaget, attentional capacity and the functional implications of formal structure. In H.W. Reese (Ed.), *Advances in child development and behavior* (Vol. 20, pp. 289–334), Orlando, FL: Academic Press.

Dasen, P.R., & de Ribaupierre, A. (1987). Neo-piagetian theories: cross-cultural and differential perspectives. *International Journal of Psychology, 22*, 793–832.

Dempster, F.N. (1985). Short-term memory development in childhood and adolescence. In C.J. Brainerd & M. Pressley (Eds.), *Basic processes in memory development* (pp. 209–248). New York: Springer.

Dempster, F.N. (1992). The rise and fall of the inhibitory mechanism: Toward a unified theory of cognitive development and aging. *Developmental Review, 12*, 45–75.

Dennis, S. (1991). Stage and structure in the development of children's spatial representations. In R. Case (Ed.), *The mind's staircase* (pp. 229–245). Hillsdale, NJ: Lawrence Erlbaum Associates Inc.

Engle, R.W., Cantor, J., & Carullo, J.J. (1992). Individual differences in working memory and comprehension: A test of four hypotheses. *Journal of Experimental Psychology: Learning, Memory, and Cognition, 18*, 972–992.

Fischer, K.W. (1980). A theory of cognitive development: The control and construction of hierarchies of skills. *Psychological Review, 87*, 477–531.

Fischer, K.W., & Lamborn, S.D. (1989). Mechanisms of variation in developmental levels: cognitive and emotional transitions during adolescence. In A. de Ribaupierre (Ed.), *Transition mechanisms in child development* (pp. 33–67). Cambridge University Press.

Flavell, J.H. (1984). Discussion. In R.J. Sternberg (Ed.), *Mechanisms of cognitive development* (pp. 188–209). New York: W.H. Freeman.

Flavell, J.H., & Wellman, H.M. (1977). Metamemory. In R.V. Kail & J.W. Hagen (Eds.), Perspectives on the development of memory and cognition (pp. 3–33). Hillsdale, NJ: Lawrence Erlbaum Associates Inc.

Halford, G.S. (1982). *The development of thought*. Hillsdale, NJ: Lawrence Erlbaum Associates Inc.

Halford, G.S. (1993). *Children's understanding: The development of mental models*. Hillsdale, NJ: Lawrence Erlbaum Associates Inc.

Halliday, M.S., & Hitch, G.J. (1988). Developmental applications of working memory. In G. Claxton (Ed.), *Growth points in cognition* (pp. 193–222). London: Routledge.

Henry, L.A. (1991). Development of auditory memory span: The role of rehearsal. *British Journal of Developmental Psychology, 9*, 493–511.

Hitch, G.J., Halliday, M.S., Dodd, A., & Littler, J.E. (1989a). Development of rehearsal in short-term memory: Differences between pictorial and spoken stimuli. *British Journal of Developmental Psychology, 7*, 347–362.

Hitch, G.J., Halliday, M.S., & Littler, J.E. (1989b). Item identification time and rehearsal rate as predictors of memory span in children. *The Quarterly Journal of Experimental Psychology, 41A*, 321–337.

Hitch, G.J., Halliday, M.S., Schaafstal, A.M., & Schraagen, J.M. (1988). Visual working memory in young children. *Memory and Cognition, 16*(2), 120–132.

Hitch, G., Woodin, M.E., & Baker, S. (1989c). Visual and phonological components of working memory in children. *Memory and Cognition, 17*, 175–185.

Hue, C.W., & Erickson, J.R. (1988). Short-term memory for Chinese characters and radicals. *Memory and Cognition, 16*, 196–205.

Hulme, C., Thomson, N., Muir, C., & Lawrence, A. (1984). Speech rate and the development of short-term memory span. *Journal of Experimental Child Psychology, 38*, 241–253.

Hulme, C., & Tordoff, V. (1989). Working memory development: The effects of speech rate, word length, and acoustic similarity on serial recall. *Journal of Experimental Child Psychology, 47*, 72–87.

Johnson, J. (1991). Constructive processes in bilingualism and their cognitive growth effects. In E. Bialystok (Ed.), *Language processing in bilingual children* (pp. 193–21). Cambridge University Press.

Klapp, S.T., Marsburn, E.A., & Lester, P.T. (1983). Short-term memory does not involve the "working memory" of information processing: The demise of a common assumption. *Journal of Experimental Psychology: General, 112*, 240–264.

Logie, R.H., & Baddeley, A.D. (1990). Imagery and working memory. In P.J. Hampson, D.E. Marks, & J.T.E. Richardson (Eds.), *Imagery: Current developments* (pp. 103–128). London: Routledge.

Logie, R.H., & Marchetti, C. (1991). Visuo-spatial working memory; Visual, spatial or central executive?. In R.H. Logie & M. Denis (Eds.), *Mental Images in human cognition* (pp. 105–115). Amsterdam: North Holland.

McArdle, J.J., & Epstein, D. (1987). Latent growth curves within developmental structural equations models. *Child Development*, *58*, 110–133.

Morra, S. (1992). *Testing for capacity of working memory components*. Paper presented at the Vth European Conference on Developmental Psychology, Seville, 6–9 September.

Morris, N. (1987). Exploring the visuo-spatial scratch pad. *The Quarterly Journal of Experimental Psychology*, *39A*, 409–430.

Moscovitch, M., & Umilta, C. (1990). Modularity and neuropsychology: Modules and central processes in attention and memory. In M.E. Schwartz (Ed.), *Modular processes in dementia* (pp. 1–59). Cambridge, MA: MIT Press.

Nicolson, R. (1981). The relationship between memory span and processing speed. In M. Friedman, J.P. Das, & N. O'Connor (Eds.), *Intelligence and learning* (pp. 179–184). New York: Plenum.

Pascual-Leone, J. (1970). A mathematical model for the transition rule in Piaget's developmental stages. *Acta Psychologica*, *32*, 301–345.

Pascual-Leone, J. (1978). Compounds, confounds and models in developmental information-processing: A reply to Trabasso and Foellinger. *Journal of Experimental Child Psychology*, *26*, 18–40.

Pascual-Leone, J. (1984). Attention, dialectic and mental effort: Toward an organismic theory of life stages. In M.L. Commons, F.A. Richards, & C. Armon (Eds.), *Beyond formal operations* (pp. 182–215). New York: Praeger.

Pascual-Leone, J. (1987). Organismic processes for neo-Piagetian theories: A dialectical causal account of cognitive development. *International Journal of Psychology*, *22*, 531–570.

Pascual-Leone, J., & Goodman, D.R. (1979). Intelligence and experience: A neo-Piagetian approach. *Instructional Science*, *8*, 301–367.

Pascual-Leone, J., Goodman, D.R., Ammon, P., & Subelman, I. (1978). Piagetian theory and neo-Piagetian analysis as psychological guides in education. In J. McCarthy Gallagher & J.A. Easley (Eds.), *Knowledge and development* (Vol. 2, pp. 243–289). New York: Plenum.

Pascual-Leone, J., & Ijaz, I. (1989). Mental capacity testing as a form of intellectual-developmental assessment. In R.J. Samuda, S.L. Kong, J. Cummins, J. Pascual-Leone, & J. Lewis (Eds.), *Assessment and placement of minority students* (pp. 143–171). Toronto: Hogrefe.

Pascual-Leone, J., & Johnson, J. (1991). Psychological unit and its role in task analysis: A reinterpretation of object permanence. In M. Chandler & M. Chapman (Eds.), *Criteria for competence: Controversies in the assessment of children's abilities*. Hillsdale, NJ: Lawrence Erlbaum Associates Inc.

de Ribaupierre, A. (1983). Un modèle néo-piagétien: la Théorie des Opérateurs Constructifs de Pascual-Leone. *Cahiers de Psychologie Cognitive*, *3*, 327–356.

de Ribaupierre, A. (1993). Structural invariants and individual differences: On the difficulty of dissociating developmental and differential processes. In R. Case & W. Edelstein (Eds.), *The new structuralism in cognitive development: Theory and research on individual pathways (Contributions to Human Development)* (pp. 11–32). Basel: Karger.

de Ribaupierre, A., & Bailleux, C. (1992, September). *Developmental change in a spatial task of attentional capacity: A comparison of two modes of response*. Paper presented at the Vth European Conference on Developmental Psychology, Seville, 6–9 September.

de Ribaupierre, A., & Bailleux, C. (1993, June). *Development of attentional capacity in childhood: A longitudinal study*. Paper given at the Conference on research on memory development: State-of-the art and future directions, Ringberg, Germany.

de Ribaupierre, A., Neirynck, I., & Spira, A. (1989). Interactions between basic capacity and strategies in children's memory: Construction of a developmental paradigm. *Cahiers de Psychologie Cognitive*, *9*, 471–504.

de Ribaupierre, A., & Pascual-Leone, J. (1979). Formal operations and M-Power: A neo-Piagetian investigation. In D. Kuhn (Ed.), *Intellectual development beyond childhood (New Directions in Child Development)* (pp. 1–43). San Francisco: Jossey-Bass.

de Ribaupierre, A., & Pascual-Leone, J. (1984). Pour une intégration des méthodes en psychologie: approches expérimentale, psycho-génétique et différentielle. *L'Année Psychologique*, *84*, 227–250.

de Ribaupierre, A., & Spira, A. (1991, March). *Attentional capacity and cognitive development from 5 to 14: Overall presentation and some methodological problems*. Paper presented at the European Science Foundation Conference on Longitudinal research: Challenges for the future, Budapest.

Rudinger, G., Andres, J., & Rietz, C. (1991). Structural equation models for studying intellectual development. In D. Magnusson, L.R. Bergman, G. Rudinger, & B. Törestad (Eds.), *Problems and methods in longitudinal research: Stability and change* (pp. 274–307). Cambridge University Press.

Salthouse, T.A., & Babcock, R.L. (1991). Decomposing adult age differences in working memory. *Developmental Psychology*, *27*, 763–776.

Schumann-Hengsteler, R. (1989, July). *Memory development: The analysis of a popular picture-game*. Poster presented at the Tenth Biennial Meetings of ISSBD, Jyväskylä, Finland.

Schumann-Hengsteler, R., Demmel, U., & Seitz, K. (1992). *Visuo-spatial working memory in children and adults*. Paper presented at the Vth European Conference on Developmental Psychology, Seville, 6–9 September.

Spira, A., & Keizer, I. (1991, July). *Developmental changes versus retest effects in a working memory task*. Paper presented at the 11th meeting of the International Society for the Study of Behavioral Development, Minneapolis.

Van der Linden, M. (1989). *Les troubles de la mémoire*. Liège: Mardaga.

Wilson, J.T.L., Scott, J.H., & Power, K.G. (1987). Developmental differences in the span of visual memory for pattern. *British Journal of Developmental Psychology*, *5*, 249–255.

INTERNATIONAL JOURNAL OF BEHAVIORAL DEVELOPMENT, 1994, *17* (1), 37–56

The Relationship between Speech Rate and Memory Span in Children

Lucy A. Henry

Department of Psychology, University of Reading, UK

Evidence of a linear relationship between speech rate and memory span in children has been obtained in several studies (e.g. Hulme, Thomson, Muir, & Lawrence, 1984). This evidence is used to support an explanation of the development of memory span based on the working memory model (Baddeley, 1990). The model argues that speech rate is related to the amount recalled and that developmental increases in speech rate allow faster rehearsal with age and, hence, greater recall. However, the linear relationship between speech rate and memory span has generally been reported in terms of group means for speech rate and memory span rather than individual level correlations between the two variables. The present studies replicate the group relationship, but find that correlations between individual subject's speech rates and memory spans, when the effects of age are partialled out, are no longer significant. Nor was the size of the word length effect related to the difference in speech rate between short and long words. It is argued that the group mean relationship between speech rate and memory span is clear and replicable, but that the speech rates of individual children are not good predictors of those children's memory spans. The implications of these results for the working memory explanation of span development are discussed.

INTRODUCTION

The working memory model (Baddeley, 1986, 1990) has provided a persuasive account of the development of memory span with age. However, much of the evidence supporting it is correlational. In addition,

Requests for reprints should be sent to Lucy A. Henry, Department of Psychology, University of Reading, Reading RG6 2AL, UK.

I would like to thank Sue Gathercole, Rod Nicolson, Graham Hitch, and an anonymous reviewer for their very helpful comments on an earlier version of this manuscript. I would also like to express my thanks to all of the staff and pupils of the schools that took part in this research.

most of this evidence concerns data from group means as opposed to individual subjects. This paper explores the correlational evidence supporting the working memory explanation of memory span development in detail, examining both group data and individual data.

The working memory model (Baddeley, 1986, 1990) involves three major components: a central executive which is a controlling attentional system; a visuo-spatial sketch pad that maintains visuo-spatial material in a rote manner; and a phonological loop system that maintains verbal material. The phonological loop system is the main focus of the current paper as it has been used to explain the development in memory span. The phonological loop consists of a passive speech input store that decays very rapidly. This is known as the phonological store, and auditory material gains direct access to it. However, as the inputs decay so rapidly, the "articulatory rehearsal loop" is used to recycle the material back into the phonological store. This process ("rehearsal"), if repeated continually, prevents the material in the phonological store from decaying. The duration of the phonological store is argued to be only 1.5 to 2 seconds (Baddeley, Thomson, & Buchanan, 1975; Schweikert & Boruff, 1986), so that subjects with fast rehearsal rates are able to retain more (Baddeley, et al., 1975). Another key finding is that longer words that take longer to articulate during rehearsal are less well recalled than short words (Baddeley et al., 1975; Baddeley, Lewis, & Vallar, 1984).

The model has been applied very successfully to the development of auditory memory span (Baddeley, 1986, 1990; Halliday & Hitch, 1988; Hulme et al., 1984). Children develop faster speech rates with age, allowing them to rehearse more rapidly and, hence, recall more. This account is supported by several studies that have found a relationship between speech rate and memory span in children of a variety of ages (Hitch, Halliday, & Littler, 1989b; Hitch, Halliday, Dodd, & Littler, 1989a; Hulme & Tordoff, 1989; Hulme et al., 1984; Nicolson, 1981; Roodenrys, Hulme, & Brown, 1993). The basic method used in these studies was to measure speech rate and memory span for words of differing lengths in children of differing ages as well as adults. Speech rate was generally measured by asking subjects to repeat groups of words (often pairs or triads) or read lists of words orally as fast as possible (the results were the same). All of the studies found that one linear function described the data from all age groups. In other words, speech rate was a function of memory span for words of differing lengths in subjects of varying ages. Baddeley (1986) does point out that speech rate is unlikely to be a full explanation for memory span or the development of memory span; factors such as temporal discrimination and retrieval will play a role. However, the working memory explanation does suggest that speech rate is a key factor in the development of memory span.

Recent evidence, such as demonstrations that word frequency effects cannot entirely be accounted for in terms of speech rate (Gregg, Freedman, & Smith, 1989; Henry & Millar, 1991), has led to some modifications in the model to take into account a long-term memory component. Hulme, Maughan, & Brown (1991) and Roodenrys et al. (1993) argued that linear functions with different intercepts relate speech rate and memory span for words and nonwords in adults and children. They interpreted the differences in intercepts as reflecting the long-term memory component, suggesting that long-term memory representations aid retrieval of partially decayed phonological traces. Henry and Millar (1993) make a very similar point about long-term memory aiding retrieval, and also suggest that long-term memory is important both in terms of lexical knowledge and familiarity with retrieving output procedures. The more frequently and recently words have been accessed, the easier it is to retrieve them. In addition to this long-term memory modification, Henry (1991a,b; Henry & Millar, 1993) has questioned whether children at the youngest ages really do use articulatory rehearsal, and has suggested that the relationship between speech rate and auditory memory span may be explained in terms of speed of verbal output rather than speed of articulatory rehearsal in nonrehearsing subjects.

However, the evidence relating speech rate to memory span has generally been based on group correlations. These refer to correlations between data aggregated at the group level. This involves averaging speech rate and memory span at each age level for each word type and then looking at the relationships between these summary measures. Several authors have pointed out that correlations at the group level may differ quite considerably from correlations at the individual level and that these two types of relationships may have quite different theoretical interpretations (Brown & Kirsner, 1980; Kilty, 1970; Kraemer, 1978; Robinson, 1950). One of the main points raised in these studies was that group correlations cannot be used as substitutes for individual correlations. In view of this, it seemed important to investigate the relationship between speech rate and memory span using both group and individual correlations. Many of the developmental studies did not report individual level correlations. Of those that did, most found consistently lower correlations than those suggested by the group relationships. Nicolson (1981) found correlations of 0.71, 0.51, and 0.66 at ages 8, 10, and 12 respectively which were good support for the notion that individual level correlations were robust. However, although Hulme et al. (1984) found correlations of 0.67 and 0.72 with triads and single words respectively, and Raine, Hulme, Chadderton, and Bailey (1991) found correlations of 0.62 and 0.55 with short and long words, it does not appear that the effects of age were partialled out in either study which makes the correlations hard to interpret. Cohen and

Heath (1990) found a lower correlation of about 0.5 at ages 10 to 11 years. This was very similar in size to the correlation of 0.57 found by Kail (1992) with subjects aged 9 and 19 years and those found by Roodenrys et al. (1993) with 5-and 10-year-olds. Finally, Standing and Curtis (1989) testing children aged 7 to 17 years found a correlation of 0.57 which reduced to a much more modest 0.29 when the effects of age were partialled out.

Partialling out the effects of age is important. Memory span is highly correlated with age (Dempster, 1981), as is speech rate (Kail, 1992; see also correlations reported in Raine et al., 1991). Few studies have tested a range of ages and quoted correlations with the effects of age partialled out (Standing & Curtis, 1989). The resulting correlation certainly appears to be modest, although significant. This is in contrast to the very strong linear relationship between speech rate and memory span found when group means are used. This implies that the relationship between speech rate and memory span at the group level is much more robust than the relationship at the level of individuals. Clearly, this is to be expected, given that individual variation is removed by averaging. However, for the working memory model to provide a good account of individual differences in memory span, *some* correlations between speech rate and memory span at the level of individuals and with the effects of age partialled out should be expected.

Therefore, the two studies reported here compared, in detail, the issue of group versus individual correlations between speech rate and memory span in samples of young children. In addition, the results were compared with and without partialling out the effects of age. By providing a full analysis of the data using alternative correlational methods, it was hoped that two key theoretical questions could be addressed: (1) whether speech rate was a good predictor of memory span over age groups; *and* (2) whether speech rate was a good predictor of individual subjects' memory spans.

EXPERIMENT 1

This study aimed to test whether speech rate and memory span were correlated at the level of individual subjects, and whether these correlations would remain once the effects of age were partialled out. Speech rate was assessed using repetitions of single words, pairs of words, and triads in order to determine whether the relationship varied with the memory load. Repeating three words can be considered a "span" load for many 5-year-olds and may, therefore, confound the speech rate measure with a memory component.

Method

Subjects. Subjects were 36 children divided equally into three age groups: 12 had a median age of 5 years 5 months (range 5;0 to 5;9), 12 had a median age of 7 years 7 months (range 7;0 to 7;10), and 12 had a median age of 11 years 2 months (range, 10;10 to 11;6). The children came from two neighbouring Local Education Authority Schools in Oxfordshire. Age groups were balanced for sex.

Materials and Apparatus. Seven short, high-frequency words were selected from the Carroll, Davies, and Richman (1971) Grade Three frequency norms. They were dog, hat, man, ball, book, cup, and door. Their mean frequency rating was 462.6 instances per million.

A taperecorder and two microphones were used to record the entire session, including testing of memory span and speech rate. The tapes were used to transcribe memory span performance and to time speech rates using a stopwatch.

Design. Children aged 5, 7, and 11 years were tested. Speech rate was measured as the number of words a subject could say in 1 second and was assessed using groups of 1, 2, and 3 words. Memory span was measured using the standard progressive span procedure.

Procedure. Each child was given the memory span test first. It was introduced as a game and with the two younger age groups the Experimenter and the child each played the part of a "teddy". The Experimenter instructed the child that her teddy would say some words and the child's teddy was to try and say the same words back in just the same way. Two or three practice trials at list lengths of two items were administered in order to make sure the child was clear about the procedure. All children found the instructions easy to follow.

Testing began with lists of two words and progressed up to the longest list that the subject could repeat on at least two out of three trials without error in the correct serial order. Memory span equalled this final list length, plus a bonus of 0.5 if one list at the next list length was correctly repeated. All span lists were constructed randomly for each subject separately. Children were instructed to say "blank" if they forgot one or more of the words during recall.

Next, the speech rate measures for groups of 1, 2, and 3 words were obtained. The subject was instructed to listen to the word(s) that the Experimenter (or the Experimenter's teddy) said, and then say the same word(s) as fast as they could until the Experimenter said "stop". The Experimenter counted 10 repetitions and then gave the instruction to stop.

Each subject repeated each of the 7 words 10 times individually as well as repeating three pairs of words and three triads of words 10 times over. The order of presentation for the 7 individual words was randomised for each subject. The words in the pairs and triads were randomly selected from the pool separately for each subject, and randomly ordered. No word within a pair or triad was repeated. Single words, pairs, and triads were tested in sequence and the order that subjects received them was counterbalanced. Care was taken to ensure that the subject could remember word pairs and triads before timing the 10 repetitions. Some 5-year-olds had difficulty in remembering the triads.

Speech rates were timed from the audiotapes using a stopwatch and converted into words per second.

Results

Speech Rate. Table 1 gives mean speech rate in words per second for children aged 5, 7, and 11 years. The data were subjected to an Age (3) × Group size (1, 2, or 3 words) × Order (6) analysis of variance. Order had no effect in the initial analysis so was excluded, leaving Age (2) × Speech Rate (3), the former was between subjects and the latter was within subjects.

There were significant main effects of Age, $F(2,33) = 6.55$, $P < 0.005$, and of Group Size, $F(2,66) = 11.64$, $P < 0.0001$. Newman–Keuls tests showed that speech rate for individual words and pairs was faster than for triads ($P < 0.01$). Single words and pairs did not differ. Children aged 5 and 11 years differed significantly in speech rate ($P < 0.01$), but this was the only significant age comparison.

Memory Span. Mean memory spans at each age level with standard deviations are given in Table 1. A one-way analysis of variance revealed a significant main effect of Age, $F(2,33) = 4.80$, $P < 0.02$. Newman–Keuls

TABLE 1
Mean Memory Spans and Speech Rates for Children Aged 5, 7, and 11 Years (Standard Deviations in Parentheses): Experiment 1

Age	Speech Rate			Memory Span
	Single Words	Pairs	Triads	
5	2.02 (0.68)	2.09 (0.53)	1.71 (0.52)	3.29 (0.52)
7	2.44 (0.79)	2.49 (0.53)	2.18 (0.55)	3.88 (0.51)
11	3.10 (0.83)	2.85 (0.62)	2.64 (0.74)	4.00 (0.68)

TABLE 2
Full Correlation Matrix for Experiment 1 Including Speech Rate for Single Words (SR1),
Pairs of Words (SR2), and Triads (SR3)

Measures	2	3	4	Age
1. Span	0.320	0.434**	0.397*	0.434**
2. Speech rate (singles) SR1		0.823**	0.795**	0.498**
3. Speech rate (pairs) SR2			0.847**	0.496**
4. Speech rate (triads) SR3				0.473**

*$P < 0.05$; **$P < 0.01$.

tests revealed significant age differences between 5-year-olds and the other two age groups ($P < 0.05$) which themselves did not differ.

Correlational Evidence. Of central interest were the correlations between speech rate and memory span. Table 2 gives a full correlation matrix. Age was significantly related to all three measures of speech rate and to span ($P < 0.01$). In addition, the correlations between memory span and two of the speech rate measures were significant: speech rate for pairs of words ($P < 0.01$) and speech rate for triads ($P < 0.05$). However, when the effects of age were partialled out, neither of the correlations between speech rate and memory span remained significant: pairs, $r = 0.30$, n.s.; triads, $r = 0.24$, n.s.

Discussion

The correlations between speech rate and memory span, before age was removed, were modest, and slightly lower than previous studies that have reported correlations in the region of 0.6. This provides support for the notion that the speech rates of individuals predict their memory spans. However, there were, on the whole, larger relationships between age and both span and speech rate. After partialling out the effects of age, there were no significant correlations between speech rate and memory span, although they were all positive and in the correct direction. These results indicate that the strong prediction of the working memory hypothesis, that individual speech rates should relate to individual memory spans regardless of age, was not supported. These findings are similar to those of Standing and Curtis (1989) who found that a moderate correlation between speech rate and memory span (0.57) was considerably reduced when age was partialled out (0.29). The size of their correlation was small and in the region of those found in the present study.

Speech rates for individual words and pairs were faster than speech rate for traids. This suggested that speech rate may be slightly slowed when there is a memory load. Hulme et al. (1984) also found that speech rate for individual words was faster than that for triads, and their rates are very comparable to those found in this study. Age differences were present in speech rate, but not marked between children near in age. Five- and 11-year-olds differed, but 5- and 7- and 11-year-olds did not. This is apparently contrary to the findings of earlier studies (Hitch et al., 1989a,b; Hulme & Tordoff, 1989; Hulme et al., 1984), but in several of these studies, a large age range is used, and comparisons between means for different ages are not reported. Therefore, main effects of age may reflect the difference between only the youngest and oldest age groups and mask the fact that age groups between these do not actually differ.

The linear relationship found in many studies (Hitch et al., 1989a,b; Hulme & Tordoff, 1989; Hulme et al., 1984; Nicolson, 1981; Roodenrys et al., 1993) between speech rate and memory span is based on using group means for each of these variables with several word types. The data here cannot be examined in the same way because there is only one type of word for each age group. The next experiment investigates the relationship between speech rate and memory span more thoroughly using several word types and a larger sample.

EXPERIMENT 2

This study aimed to replicate the results of Experiment 1 and explore in more detail the relationships between speech rate and memory span for words of differing lengths and frequencies. Two word lengths were tested, one- and three-syllable words. The frequency manipulation was introduced because there has been little work investigating whether the relationship between speech rate and memory span holds equally for words that are familiar and unfamiliar in children, although this has been investigated for nonwords (Roodenrys et al., 1993).

Method

Subjects. A total of 60 subjects participated in this study: 20 had a median age of 5 years 1 month (range 4;11–5;3), 20 had a median age of 7 years 3 months (range 7;0–7;9), and 20 had a median age of 10 years 1 month (range 9;0–10;10). All came from the same Local Education Authority School in Berkshire. In each age group, half of the subjects were males and half females.

Materials and Apparatus.   Four sets of words, with eight words in each set were assembled. Short high frequency words (e.g. door, book) had a mean frequency rating of 351.4 (s.d. = 285.8), long high frequency words (e.g. family, animal) had a mean rating of 353.1 (s.d. = 337.4). Short low frequency words (e.g. hose, lung) had a mean rating of 11.6 (s.d. = 9.5), long low frequency words (e.g. boundary, skeleton) had a mean rating of 12.6 (s.d. = 11.2). All frequency ratings were taken from the Grade Three frequency norms of Carroll et al. (1971). Short and long words were matched for frequency in order to provide a stringent test of word length effects, independent of the effects of word frequency. A full list of the words and their frequency ratings is given in the Appendix.

A taperecorder and two microphones were used to record the speech rate sessions.

Design.   The design of this study was Age (5, 7, 10) by Word Length (short, long) by Word Frequency (high, low) by Order (4 counterbalanced orders). This design was the same for the span and speech rate phases of the study.

Procedure.   Children were tested in two sessions. Each session tested speech rate for two types of words, and memory span for two types of words. The order of receiving each word type was counterbalanced. In each session, two tests of speech rate were followed by two tests of memory span. Both speech rate and memory span were tested in the same way as in Experiment 1 with the following exceptions. Subjects repeated single words and pairs only, five times each (all 8 words singly and 4 pairs of words encompassing all 8 words from the pool). In addition, the Experimenter stressed several times, instead of just once, that the child was to repeat the words as fast as possible. This was because, in Experiment 1, it was noted that some subjects repeated single words rather slowly. The order of the words and word pairs was fixed for each subject within a word type, although the order of receiving word types varied according to the counterbalancing. There were four possible orders arranged according to a Latin Square in the following order: short high frequency (1); short low frequency (2); long high frequency (3); long low frequency (4). On incorrect trials in the memory span test, the number of words in the correct serial position was recorded. This allowed for a more sensitive scoring method which gave credit for partial success on incorrect lists. Subjects received 0.5 points if they were fully correct on a trial, as in the first experiment. An extra credit of 0.25 was also available for each trial that was incorrect. This was allocated in line with the proportion of correct items in the correct serial position. For example: This subject succeeds up to list length 4, then proceeds with three trials at list length 5 as follows:

Trial 1, correct, score 0.5.
Trial 2, 2/5 items correct, score 2/5 × 0.25 = 0.10.
Trial 3, 4/5 items correct, score 4/5 × 0.25 = 0.20.

The total score is calculated as (4 + 0.5 + 0.1 + 0.2) = 4.80. This scoring reflects the fact that this subject made two incorrect attempts at the list length of 5, as well as one entirely correct attempt. The logic of the scoring is that 0.25 is available as extra credit for each failed attempt to reflect the performance of subjects who remember something. It also serves to allow more variation in span scores so that correlations between speech rate and memory span would be more likely.

Results

Analysis of Speech Rate.   The mean speech rates for each type of word, for single words, and pairs of words are given in Table 3 (untransformed scores). In comparison with the speech rates from the first study, they are somewhat higher which suggests that the greater emphasis in the instructions on speed did lead to faster articulation.

Because the standard deviations were markedly smaller for long words than short words (i.e. standard deviations were strongly proportional to means), the data were subjected to a log transform prior to analysis of variance (Howell, 1986). Two four-way ANOVAs were conducted on the data for single words and word pairs separately, including the factors of Age (3), Order (4), Word Length (2), and Word Frequency (2).

The analysis on single words showed highly significant main effects of Age, $F(2,48) = 21.84$, $P < 0.0001$; Word Length, $F(1,48) = 1013.74$, $P < 0.001$, and Word Frequency, $F(1,48) = 177.50$, $P < 0.0001$. The main effect of age was explored using Newman–Keuls tests which indicated that 5-year-olds and 10-year-olds differed significantly in speech rate ($P < 0.01$), but that this was the only significant difference. The main effects of length and frequency indicated that long words were slower to recite than short words and low frequency words were slower to recite than high frequency words. There was also a significant interaction between Word Frequency and Order, $F(3,48) = 6.32$, $P < 0.001$. Analysis of simple effects indicated that the effect of frequency was highly significant for each of the four orders used [$F(1,48) = 86.23$; 16.14; 68.77; and 25.83, respectively for each order, $P < 0.0001$ in each case]. The interaction reflected the fact that the effect was larger for the two orders in which high frequency words were presented first (orders 1 and 3).

The analysis on pairs of words was very similar. It showed the same highly significant main effects of Age, $F(2,48) = 27.35$, $P < 0.0001$; Word Length, $F(1,48) = 1911.54$, $P < 0.0001$; and Word Frequency, $F(1,48) =$

107.08, $P < 0.0001$. There was also an interaction between Word Length and Frequency, $F(1,48) = 39.11$, $P < 0.0001$. Analysis of simple effects indicated that the effect of frequency was significant for both short, $F(1,92) = 13.43$, $P > 0.0001$, and long words, $F(1,92) = 138.16$, $P < 0.0001$. The interaction was due to the effect of frequency being much larger for long than short words.

Therefore, to summarise, the analysis of speech rates confirmed that speech rate increased between the ages of 5 and 10 years and that: (a) low frequency words have slower speech rates than high frequency words; (b) long words have slower speech rates than short words. One difference between pairs of words and single words was that there was a strong interaction between length and frequency for pairs only, reflecting the fact that frequency effects were stronger with long than short words.

Analysis of Memory Span.   The mean memory spans are given in Table 4. A four-way ANOVA was conducted on the span data including the factors of Age (3), Order (4), Word Length (2), and Word Frequency (2).

There were highly significant main effects of Age, $F(2,48) = 46.37$, $P < 0.0001$; Word Length, $F(1,48) = 195.30$, $P < 0.0001$; and Frequency, $F(1,48) = 59.52$, $P < 0.0001$. The main effect of age was explored using Newman–Keuls tests which indicated that there were significant age differences between 5-year-olds and both 7- and 10-year-olds : $Ps < 0.01$),

TABLE 3

Mean Speech Rates for Words of Differing Lengths and Frequencies at ages 5, 7, and 10 Years (Standard Deviations in Parentheses)

Age/No. words	Word Type[a]			
	Short (High Freq.)	*Short (Low Freq.)*	*Long (High Freq.)*	*Long (Low Freq.)*
5 single words	2.75 (0.70)	2.42 (0.64)	1.32 (0.16)	1.13 (0.11)
5 pairs of words	2.41 (0.44)	2.28 (0.48)	1.23 (0.16)	1.03 (0.11)
Mean	2.58	2.35	1.28	1.08
7 single words	3.13 (0.72)	2.80 (0.66)	1.54 (0.23)	1.34 (0.18)
7 pairs of words	2.73 (0.52)	2.61 (0.58)	1.45 (0.24)	1.18 (0.17)
Mean	2.93	2.71	1.50	1.26
10 single words	3.68 (0.75)	3.38 (0.72)	1.96 (0.27)	1.69 (0.25)
10 pairs words	3.32 (0.55)	3.15 (0.57)	1.84 (0.24)	1.58 (0.21)
Mean	3.50	3.27	1.90	1.64

[a]Rates are given in words per second and calculated for repetitions of single words and pairs of words.

TABLE 4
Mean Memory Spans for Words of Differing Lengths and Frequencies at ages 5, 7, and 10 Years (Standard Deviations in Parentheses)

	Word Type[a]			
Age	Short (High Freq.)	Short (Low Freq.)	Long (High Freq.)	Long (Low Freq.)
5	3.57 (0.59)	3.34 (0.73)	3.07 (0.53)	2.66 (0.42)
7	4.69 (0.53)	4.27 (0.44)	3.70 (0.47)	3.37 (0.43)
10	5.31 (0.78)	4.73 (0.64)	4.43 (0.66)	3.92 (0.68)

[a]Spans are given for standard scoring (standard) and for scoring allowing partial credit on failed lists (alternative).

but that 7-year-olds and 10-year-olds did not differ in span. The main effects of length and frequency indicated the usual word length effect whereby short words were better recalled than long words and a frequency effect—high frequency words were better recalled than low frequency words.

There were two interactions: an interaction between Word Length and Age, $F(2,48) = 3.32$, $P < 0.05$; and an interaction between Word Length and Order, $F(3,48) = 3.19$, $P < 0.05$. Analyses of simple main effects were used to explore these interactions. The effect of Word Length was highly significant at each level of age: $F(1,48) = 32.54$, $P < 0.0001$ at age 5; $F(1,48) = 89.58$ $P < 0.0001$ at age 7; and $F(1,48) = 73.22$, $P < 0.0001$ at age 10. As is apparent, the interaction occurred because the size of the effect was smaller at age 10. As is apparent, the interaction occurred because the size of the effect was smaller at age 5 than at the other two ages, although still very highly significant. The effect of Word Length was also highly significant for each order of presentation, $F(1,48) = 22.95$, 37.68, 72.82, and 62.96, respectively for each order, $P < 0.0001$ in each case. The interaction reflceted larger effects of word length with orders 3 and 4 which beagn with long words, than orders 1 and 2 which began with short words.

The Correlation Between Speech Rate and Memory Span. There are a number of ways of looking at the relationship between speech rate and memory span. Figure 1 illustrates the group correlation, using speech rate for pairs of words. There is a clear linear relationship between speech rate and memory span when the data are plotted in this way. The correlation between these mean values of speech rate and memory span was high, $r(10) = 0.83$, $P < 0.01$, and the full regression equation was:

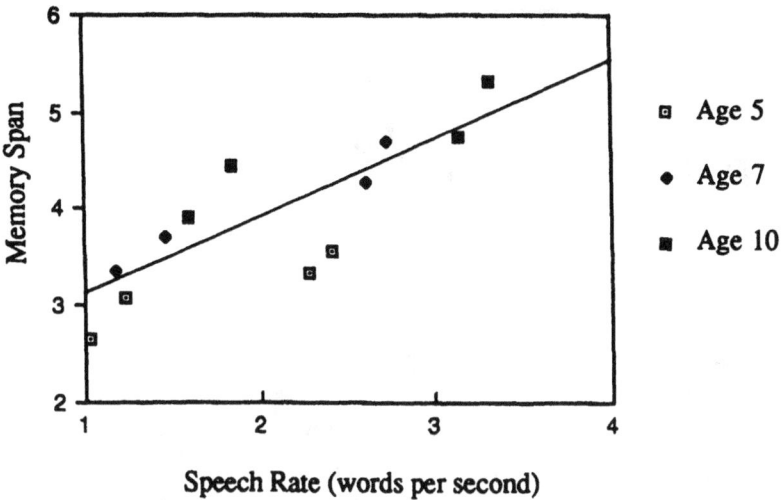

Speech Rate (words per second)

FIG. 1.   The relationship between speech rate and memory span given in terms of age group means for four types of words: short high frequency; short low frequency; long high frequency; long low frequency. Each word type is represented in the reverse of the above order along the regression line. Children are aged 5 (open squares), 7 (diamonds), and 10 years (closed squares).

$$\text{Memory span} = 0.82 \text{ (Speech Rate)} + 2.24$$

Therefore, group means for speech rate were good predictors of group means in memory span.

The correlations between speech rate and memory span for individual subjects were also examined. For this analysis, data were pooled over word types and the mean speech rates (based on pairs of words) correlated with the mean memory spans. Table 5 gives these values, as well as the correlations of each variable with age. Speech rate was significantly related

TABLE 5
Correlations Between Speech Rate, Memory Span, and Age. Speech Rates and Memory Spans are Pooled Over Word Types

	Speech Rate	Age
Memory span	0.60**	0.76**
Speech rate		0.70**

**All correlations are significant at below the $P < 0.01$ level.

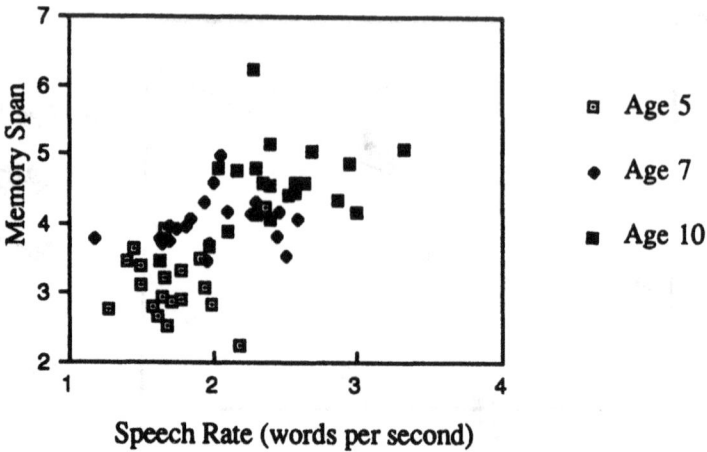

FIG. 2. The relationship between speech rate and memory span for individual subjects. Each point shows an individual child's mean speech rate plotted against that child's mean speech rate over the four word types. Children are aged 5 (open squares), 7 (diamonds), and 10 years (closed squares).

to memory span ($r = 0.60$, $P < 0.0001$). However, both speech rate and memory span were more strongly related to age than to each other. When the effects of age were partialled out, the relationship between speech rate and memory span was no longer significant ($r = 0.15$, n.s.). These results were essentially the same when each word type was analysed separately. As in Experiment 1, the speech rate measures were highly related to each other (rs between 0.795 and 0.896, all $Ps < 0.0001$). The span measures were also highly related to each other (rs between 0.684 and 0.798, all $Ps < 0.0001$), which suggests that they were reliable.

Figure 2 shows a scatter plot of all of the individual data points for speech rate and memory span averaged over all four word types. Children of each age are represented with different symbols. It is clear from this plot that, although there is an overall relationship between speech rate and memory span when all ages are combined, this relationship does not hold true when individual ages are investigated. There was considerable variation in span and speech rate scores within age, but despite this range, none of the within-age correlations were significant (0.18, 0.24, and 0.21, respectively for 5-, 7-, and 10-year-olds) which simply confirms the results of the partial correlations.

Another method of looking at the relationship between speech rate and memory span that is "free" of the effects of age is to compare the difference in speech rate between long and short words with the size of the word length effect. Some subjects may be able to articulate long words faster, in comparison to short words, than others. Given the relationship proposed between speech rate and memory span, subjects with larger differences in speech rate between long and short words should also show larger differences in memory span for short and long words.[1] This should provide a measure of the individual variation in the size of the word length effect in relation to the size of the difference in speech rate for long and short words, and this relationship should not be confounded with age. In fact, there was no such relationship. The correlation was −0.03 (n.s.). Thus, there was no evidence that subjects with larger word length effects showed larger differences in speech rate between short and long words.

Discussion

In this study, the overall group relationship between speech rate and memory span that has been found by many others (Hitch et al., 1989a,b; Hulme & Tordoff, 1989; Hulme et al., 1984; Nicolson, 1981) was replicated. When group means for word types at different ages were plotted, there was a clear linear relationship between speech rate and memory span. In addition, this function related words of differing lengths and frequencies. However, it was argued that averaging over groups may mask individual relationships that are far from orderly (e.g. Brown & Kirsner, 1980) and that individual level correlations should be examined as well as group correlations. In the current study, these correlations were lower, in the range of 0.4 to 0.6, but still moderate. These two findings, together, suggest that speech rate is a good predictor of memory span.

However, the correlations between age and both speech rate and memory span were higher than the correlations between speech rate and memory span. It is certainly possible to argue that in assessing whether speech rate predicts memory span for individual subjects, the effects of age should be taken into account first. One of the main difficulties in examining the relationship between speech rate and memory span over a large age range is that there may be many factors contributing both to the development of memory span and speech rate. One example may be that greater facility with speech output planning enhances speech rate *as well as* memory span. One way of minimising this type of effect is to partial out the effects of age. When this was done, the correlations between speech rate and memory span were reduced to a nonsignificant level. The working

---

[1]Some authors have used the correlation between overall speech rate and the size of the word length effect (e.g. Caplan et al., 1992). However this does not capture whether the difference in speech rate between long and short words is related to the size of the word length effect.

memory view does not demand that speech rate should entirely account for variations in memory span. However, the lack of any significant relationship between speech rate and memory span after the effects of age were partialled out is contrary to the notion that speech rate is a strong predictor of individual differences in memory span for children in this age range.

One problem with this interpretation is that partialling out the effects of age necessarily removes most of the variance in speech rate because it is, itself, highly correlated with age. This rather circular argument makes interpretation difficult. One suggested alternative was to examine whether subjects with larger word length effects also showed larger differences in speech rate between short and long words. This should be a relatively "pure" indication of the relationship between speech rate and memory span, as it is not reliant on absolute size of span or rate of speech, both of which are strongly related to age. However, although these scores may have included more "noise" as they represented the differences between two other scores, this analysis also indicated that the correlation was virtually zero.

GENERAL DISCUSSION

Averaging over age groups, speech rate was strongly related to memory span. Simple correlations between speech rate and memory span for individuals were lower, but also significant. These results suggested that speech rate was a good predictor of memory span. However, the speech rates of individual children did not predict their memory spans once the effects of age had been partialled out. In fact, age was more strongly related to span than speech rate. In addition, the size of the word length effect in speech rate did not relate to the size of the word length effect in memory span. These latter results were not consistent with a strong version of the working memory explanation for the development of memory span. At the very least, the model would predict that the size of the word length effect should be related to an extent to the difference in articulation rate between short and long words.

There is no easy way to evaluate the respective merit of these different results. Clearly, speech rate is not necessarily a good predictor of an individual child's memory span. If one circumvents the difficulties of whether to partial out the effects of age or not and investigates within ages, the correlations were very low. However, despite the low power within age (20 subjects per age in Experiment 2), there is reason to believe that this result holds true at least for the younger ages. Cowan (1992) found no correlation between speech rate during recall and memory span in 4-year-olds. A very similar result was found by Gathercole, Adams, and Hitch (in press) in a large sample. Therefore, although the individual correlations appear to be strong in adults ($r = 0.69$ in Baddeley et al., 1975; $r = 0.80$ in Standing & Curtis, 1989), they are not necessarily strong in younger children. One explanation for this is that the youngest children may not use rehearsal, at least in the form that older children and adults use it (Henry, 1991a; Hitch et al., 1991). Even older children may use rehearsal inconsistently or make errors during rehearsal (e.g. stumbling over words). Flavell, Beach, and Chinsky (1966) found that only 65% of 10-year-olds used rehearsal on more than three trials in a picture serial recall task. Henry (1991b) found little evidence of articulatory suppression affecting auditory memory span in children aged 8–9 years, suggesting that the use of rehearsal may not have been widespread. Therefore, if children are using rehearsal inconsistently or making errors as they rehearse, a strong relationship between speech rate and memory span at the level of individual subjects would not necessarily be expected.

In addition, other factors are implicated in the development of memory span which are likely to reduce any individual relationship between speech rate and memory span. Individuals vary on many attributes that affect memory span. For example, Hulme et al. (1991) and Henry and Millar (1993) have emphasised the role of long-term memory representations. Therefore, there are many other factors involved in the development of memory span, over and above the contribution of speech rate. The current results, although not inconsistent with current models of the development in memory span, draw attention to the empirical limits on using speech rate to predict memory span. The significance of the group relationship between speech rate and memory span may be that much of the "noise" apparent in the individual results is cancelled out when data is averaged across subjects. It could also be that speech rate is linked with memory span at this group level because increases in speech rate reflect greater ease at speech output planning or in retrieving items for output.

Even if a model based on decay and speed of rehearsal (or speech of verbal responding) model is retained, one other finding remains troublesome for the notion that speech rate is related to memory span. Cowan (1992) found that speech rate was not related to memory span in 4-year-olds, but that the total recall duration was. Children with higher memory spans were more able to maintain the memory trace during recall: ". . . more capable subjects speak at the same rate as less capable subjects, but respond for a longer time". In fact, subjects responded for between 2 and 5 seconds, well above the proposed 2 second limit to the phonological store. Cowan (1992) puts forward a decay-and-reactivation process to account for these results. However, it could be that the phonological trace does endure for considerably longer than 2 seconds. Longoni, Richardson, and Aiello (1993) found that phonological information could be maintained for at least 10 seconds. This type of result would have important implications for the notion of rehearsal, particularly the question of whether rehearsal is necessary for the recall of relatively short lists of auditorily presented items. Penney (1989) argues that rehearsal is not so critical for auditorily presented items, because rehearsal is primarily useful for maintaining order information, and successive auditory items are strongly associated with each other so that order information is well preserved.

In conclusion, the main point of the present work was to contrast the use of group and individual correlational evidence in evaluating the relationship between speech rate and memory span in young children. The group relationship was replicated, but the simple correlations between speech rate and memory span were much lower, and age was a better predictor of memory span than speech rate. These results underline the importance of considering correlational evidence with care in evaluating current models of the development of memory span with age.

REFERENCES

Baddeley, A.D. (1986). *Working memory*. Oxford University Press.

Baddeley, A.D. (1990). *Human memory*. Hove, Sussex: Lawrence Erlbaum Associates Ltd.

Baddeley, A.D., Lewis, V., & Vallar, G. (1984). Exploring the articulatory loop. *Quarterly Journal of Experimental Psychology, 36A*, 233–252.

Baddeley, A.D., Thomson, N., & Buchanan, M. (1975). Word length and the structure of short-term memory. *Journal of Verbal Learning and Verbal Behavior, 14*, 575–589.

Brown, H.L., & Kirsner, K. (1980). A within subjects analysis of the relationship between memory span and processing rate in short-term memory. *Cognitive Psychology, 12*, 177–187

Caplan, D., Rochon, E., & Waters, G.S. (1992). Articulatory and phonological determinants of word length effects in span tasks. *Quarterly Journal of Experimental Psychology, 45A*, 177–192.

Carroll, J.B., Davies, P., & Richman, B. (1971). *The American heritage word frequency book*. New York: American Heritage.

Cohen, R.L., & Heath, M. (1990). The development of serial short-term memory and the articulatory loop hypothesis. *Intelligence, 14*, 151–171.

Cowan, N. (1992). Verbal memory span and the timing of spoken recall. *Journal of Memory and Language, 31*, 668–684.

Dempster, F.N. (1981). Memory span: Sources of individual and developmental differences. *Psychological Bulletin, 89*, 63–100.

Gathercole, S.E., Adams, A.-M., & Hitch, G.J. (in press). Do young children rehearse? An individual differences analysis, *Memory and Cognition*.

Gregg, V.H., Freedman, C.M., & Smith, D.K. (1989). Word frequency, articulatory suppression and memory span. *British Journal of Psychology, 80*, 363–374.

Halliday, M.S., & Hitch, G.J. (1988). Developmental applications of working memory. In G. Claxton (Ed.), *Growth points in cognition*. New York: Routledge, Chapman & Hall, Inc.

Henry, L.A. (1991a). The effects of word length and phonemic similarity in young children's short-term memory. *Quarterly Journal of Experimental Psychology, 43A*, 35–52.

Henry, L.A., & Millar, S. (1991). Memory span increase with age: A test of two hypotheses. *Journal of Experimental Child Psychology*, *51*, 459–484.

Henry, L.A., & Millar, S. (1993). Why does memory span improve with age? A review of the evidence for two current hypotheses. *European Journal of Cognitive Psychology*, *5*, 241–287.

Hitch, G.J., Halliday, M.S., Dodd, A., & Littler, J.E. (1989a). Development of rehearsal in short-term memory: differences between pictorial and spoken stimuli. *British Journal of Developmental Psychology*, *7*, 347–362.

Hitch, G.J., Halliday, M.S., & Littler, J.E. (1989b). Item identification time and rehearsal as predictors of memory span in children. *Quarterly Journal of Experimental Psychology*, *41A*(2), 321–327.

Hitch, G.J., Halliday, M.S., Schaafstal, A.M., & Hefferman, T.M. (1991). Speech, "inner speech" and the development of short-term memory: The effects of picture labelling on recall. *Journal of Experimental Psychology*, *51*, 220–234.

Hulme, C., Maughan, S., & Brown, G.D.A. (1991). Memory for familiar and unfamiliar words: Evidence for a long-term memory contribution to short-term memory span. *Journal of Memory and Language*, *30*, 685–701.

Hulme, C., Thomson, N., Muir, C., & Lawrence, A. (1984). Speech rate and the development of short-term memory. *Journal of Experimental Child Psychology*, *38*, 241–253.

Hulme, C., & Tordoff, V. (1989). Working memory development: The effects of speech rate, word length, and acoustic similarity on serial recall. *Journal of Experimental Child Psychology*, *47*, 72–87.

Kail, R. (1992). Processing speed, speech rate, and memory. *Developmental Psychology*, *28*, 899–904.

Kilty, K.M. (1970). Consistency between and within subjects. *Perceptual and Motor Skills*, *31*, 701–702.

Kraemer, J.C. (1978). Individual and ecological correlation in a general context. *Behavioral Science*, *23*, 67–72.

Longoni, A.M., Richardson, J.T.E., & Aiello, A. (1993). Articulatory rehearsal and phonological storage in working memory. *Memory and Cognition*, *21*, 11–22.

Nicolson, R. (1981). The relationship between memory span and processing speed. In M.P. Friedman, J.P. Das, & N. O'Connor (Eds.), *Intelligence and learning*. New York: Plenum.

Penney, C.G. (1989). Modality effects and the structure of short-term verbal memory. *Memory and Cognition*, *17*, 398–422.

Raine, A., Hulme, C., Chadderton, H., & Bailey, P. (1991). Verbal short-term memory span in speech-disordered children: Implications for articulatory coding in short-term memory. *Child Development*, *62*, 415–423.

Robinson, W.S. (1950). Ecological correlations and the behavior of individuals. *American Sociological Review*, *15*, 351–357.

Roodenrys, S., Hulme, C., & Brown, G. (1993). The development of short-term memory span: Separable effects of speech rate and long-term memory. *Journal of Experimental Child Psychology*, *56*, 431–442.

Schweikert, R., & Boruff, B. (1986). Short-term memory capacity: Magic number or magic spell? *Journal of Experimental Psychology: Learning, Memory and Cognition*, *12*, 419–425.

Standing, L., & Curtis, L. (1989). Subvocalization rate versus other predictors of the memory span. *Psychological Reports*, *65*, 487–495.

APPENDIX

Words used in Experiment 2 and their Frequencies[a]

Short High (Frequency)		Short Low (Frequency)		Long High (Frequency)		Long Low (Frequency)	
door	489	hose	11	vegetables	119	audience	26
book	418	rook	0	indian	575	sandpiper	3
cup	105	hem	4	elephant	105	gramophone	0
man	1012	lung	27	grandfather	224	headquarters	5
pig	103	moat	4	radio	84	boundary	16
hat	239	bait	19	family	386	barrister	0
ball	335	gale	5	dinosaur	187	skeleton	23
chair	110	cane	23	animal	1145	conductor	28
Mean	351.4		11.6		353.1		12.6
s.d.	(285.8)		(9.5)		(337.4)		(11.2)

[a]Grade 3 norms from Carroll et al. (1971).

INTERNATIONAL JOURNAL OF BEHAVIORAL DEVELOPMENT, 1994, 17 (1), 57-71

Developmental Aspects of Phonemic and Visual Similarity Effects: Further Evidence in Italian Children

Anna M. Longoni and T.G. Scalisi

Department of Psychology, Università La Sapienza, Rome, Italy

Phonemic and visual similarity effects were investigated in Italian children of different ages. In Experiment 1, two groups of children (mean age 5;1 and 10;3 years) were asked to recall either pictures of common objects with phonemically similar or dissimilar names, or the spoken names of the pictures. Although a similarity effect was present in older children for both words and drawings, in younger children only a tendency in the expected direction occurred. The lack of a phonemic similarity effect for spoken words was attributed to the presence of a ceiling effect. In addition, results showed a significant superior recall for words in younger children and for drawings in older ones. An additional group of 5-year-old children was tested, increasing the list length to four items. Results indicated a significant similarity effect for words but not for drawings, together with a superior recall for words. These findings, in agreement with previous results, suggest that phonological memory traces contribute to performance of younger children only when material to be recalled is in the auditory modality, whereas in older children phonological coding is independent in the input modality. In Experiment 2 the performance of 5- and 10-year-old children was compared for immediate recall of two different sets of visually similar and dissimilar drawings. Results showed a significant effect of visual similarity in younger children only, for both sets of drawings, extending previously obtained results (e.g. Hitch, Halliday, Schaaftal, & Scrhaagen, 1988) to different materials and to Italian subjects. In Experiment 3, the visual similarity effect was investigated with a delayed recall procedure in a 5-year-old group. Four delay intervals (0, 5, 10, 15 seconds) and two activities during delay (articulatory suppression and a tapping task) were considered. Results obtained indicated that the visual similarity effect is present at all delay intervals for both activities during delay; and are discussed in terms of alternative interpretations of the visual similarity effect.

Requests for reprints should be sent to Professor Anna M. Longoni, Dipartimento di Psicologia, Università La Sapienza Via dei Marsi 78, 00185 Roma, Italy.

This research was made possible by a CNR grant. The authors are grateful to Laura Castagna, Anna Giulia Decagno, and Carmela Tanese for collecting the data.

INTRODUCTION

Several studies have suggested that immediate recall of pictures and spoken words is mediated by different memory codes in children of different ages. One method of examining memory codes is by testing for the phonemic similarity effect (PSE) and the visual similarity effect (VSE). These effects consist in a tendency to show poorer recall for phonemically similar items (words or drawings of common objects with phonemically similar names) and for visually similar drawings. Both effects have been interpreted as indicating that recall is based on decaying memory traces (Conrad, 1965, 1967; Hitch et al., 1988): At the moment of recall the subject examines partially decayed traces and it is easier to make errors if traces share common features because they do not provide discriminative information about an item. Decaying speech-based codes are thought to be responsible for PSE and decaying visual codes for VSE.

Research on PSE, first investigated by Conrad (1971) in groups of children aged 3–11 years, has shown that the age of first occurrence of PSE depends on presentation modality (see Table 1). In fact, when children are tested on immediate serial recall of spoken words, better recall for phonemically dissimilar words is found in children from 4 to 10 years old (Hulme, 1987; Hulme & Tordoff, 1989). On the other hand, when items to be recalled are drawings of familiar objects, the PSE is usually present only in children older than 5 years (Brown, 1977; Conrad, 1971; Halliday, Hitch, Lennon, & Pettipher, 1990; Hayes & Shulze, 1977; Halliday, 1983; Hitch, Woodin, & Baker, 1989; Venneri, Nichelli, Cubelli, & Cossu, 1991). The only exception to these findings is represented by Hulme's study (1987), reporting an impaired recall for black on white line drawings with phonemically similar names even in 4-year-old children.

The visual similarity effect has been studied using alphabetic letters and drawings of familiar objects as materials. The pattern of results emerging from these studies (see Table 1) indicates that visual similarity between items impairs memory performance in younger children (5-year-olds) in serial matching tasks (Brown, 1977, experiment 2; Hayes & Shulze, 1977) and in immediate recall tasks (Hitch et al., 1988, experiment 1). In contrast, memory performance in older children (10-year-olds) is unaffected by the visual similarity of the material, provided they are free to articulate (Hitch et al., 1989). Results coming from studies on PSE and VSE suggest that, on the whole, in serial recall tasks younger children rely on modality-dependent attributes of memory traces. If an auditory presentation is used (spoken words), recall relies on speech-based codes and a phonemic similarity effect emerges. If visual presentation is used (pictures) children appear to be relying on visual codes even if a verbal code is available (the name of the object); thus visually dissimilar pictures will be recalled better than similar ones, but pictures with phonemically similar

TABLE 1

Phonemic and Visual Similarity Effects Obtained in the Literature, as a Function of the Task and the Subject Characteristics

Reference	Children (age)	Country	School	Task	Type of stimuli	Similarity effect
Phonemic similarity effect (visual modality)						
Conrad (1971)[a]	3–5	UK	Nursery	Serial matching	Coloured pictures	n.s.
	5–6, 6–7, 7–8	UK	Primary			Significant
Brown (1977, exp. 2)	4	USA	Nursery	Serial matching	Letters	n.s.
Hayes & Shulze (1977, exp. 1)	5	USA	Primary	Serial matching	Line drawings	n.s.
Hitch & Halliday (1983)	10	UK	Primary	Serial recall (span)	Line drawings	Significant
Hulme (1987)	4	UK	Nursery	Serial matching	Line drawings	Significant
	7, 10	UK	Primary			Significant
Hitch et al. (1989, exp. 1)	5	UK	Primary	Serial recall	Line drawings	n.s.
	11	UK	Primary			Significant
Halliday et al. (1990, exp. 2)	5	UK	Primary	Serial recall (span)	Line drawings	n.s.
	10	UK	Primary			Significant
Venneri et al. (1991)	4–5	Italy	Nursery	Serial recall (span)	Line drawings	n.s.
	6, 7, 8	Italy	Primary			Significant
Phonemic similarity effect (auditory modality)						
Hulme (1984)	4	UK	Nursery	Serial recall (span)	Object names	n.s.
	5–10	UK	Primary			Significant
Hulme (1987)	4	UK	Nursery	Serial recall	Object names	Significant
	7, 10	UK	Primary			Significant
Hulme & Tordoff (1989)	4	UK	Nursery	Serial recall	Object names	Significant
	7, 10	UK	Primary			Significant
Visual similarity effect						
Brown (1977, exp. 1)	4	USA	Nursery	Serial matching	Pictures[b]	Significant
Brown (1977, exp. 2)	4	USA	Nursery	Serial matching	Letters	Significant
Hayes & Shulze (1977, exp. 1)	4	USA	Nursery	Serial matching	Line drawings	Significant
Hitch et al. (1988, exp. 1)	5	UK	Primary	Serial recall	Line drawings	Significant
	10	UK	Primary			n.s.
Hitch et al. (1989, exp. 1)	5, 11	UK	Primary	Serial recall	Line drawings	Significant
Hitch et al. (1989, exp. 2)	4	UK	Nursery	Serial matching (span)	Line drawings	n.s.
	5, 7, 11	UK	Primary			n.s.

[a]Conrad's groups are divided on the basis of mental ages.
[b]Stimuli are drawings showing cats.

and dissimilar names will be remembered equally well. In contrast, encoding of pictures by older children seems to be dependent on whether or not they are free to articulate. Normally, they encode pictures verbally leading to the absence of VSE and the presence of PSE; however, in articulatory suppression conditions levels of recall are sensitive to visual similarity rather than to phonemic similarity (Hitch et al., 1989). These results have been interpreted by Hitch, Halliday, Dodd, and Littler (1989) in the framework of the working memory model of Baddeley and Hitch (1974) and Baddeley (1990). According to this model, two separate components, the articulatory loop and visuo-spatial scratch pad, are specialised in the retention of information in a phonological or visuo-spatial form.

The investigations reported in the foregoing, with the exception of one study (Venneri et al., 1991), refer to English-speaking children and to a limited set of phonemically and visually similar stimuli: Typically words or drawings with monosyllabic phonemically similar names (rat, cat, mat, hat, bat, man, bag, tap) and drawings of long objects, each with its major axis positioned in the same oblique orientation. The aim of the present study is to acquire further evidence concerning phonemic and visual similarity effects in Italian children of different ages using different stimulus materials. Evidence of this nature bears on the stability of PSE and VSE in relationship to cultural differences, and the robustness of these effects with respect to changes in stimulus material. In Experiments 1 and 2, phonemically similar and dissimilar spoken words and drawings were presented to groups of 5- and 10-year-old children. We expected to find a significant PSE for spoken words in both age groups, and a significant PSE for drawings only, in the older group. In Experiment 3, visually similar and dissimilar drawings were presented to groups of 5- and 10-year-old children. We used two kinds of similar drawings: oblong and round objects. We expected to replicate Hitch et al.'s (1988) findings, i.e. the occurrence of a VSE in younger children for both kinds of drawings and its absence in the older group. Experiment 4 investigated whether the visual similarity effect reflects decaying memory traces. One way of testing this is to interpose a brief delay between the presentation and recall of each sequence of drawings. One obvious prediction from the decay hypothesis is that, if children do not visually rehearse during the interval, the visual trace should decay and the visual similarity effect will eventually disappear.

EXPERIMENT 1

Method

Subjects.   These were 20 children in each of two age groups drawn from two schools located in a middle class area in Rome. The 5-year-old group had a mean age of 5;1 years (range: 4;3–5;10) and the 10-year-old group a mean age of 10;3 years (range: 9;6–11;0).

Materials. These were two sets of black and white line drawings of familiar objects and two sets of spoken words (the names of the objects) matched for frequency. Each drawing was mounted on a 10cm × 10cm card. The drawings were all familiar objects which pilot work had established were uniquely named by 5- and 10-year-olds. The materials, reported in Appendix 1, were distributed as follows:

5 drawings with phonemically similar 2-syllable names in Set 1;
5 drawings with phonemically dissimilar 2-syllable names in Set 2;
5 spoken words (names of objects in Set 1) in Set 3;
5 spoken words (names of objects in Set 2) in Set 4.

Design. The type of material was manipulated as a within-subjects factor. Each trial was constructed by random sampling from the corresponding set of items. Trials were blocked by type of material, and the order of blocks was counterbalanced across subjects. A trial consisted of a sequence of three items for 5-year-olds and five items for 10-year-olds. Each child received 12 trials of drawings (six from Set 1 and six from Set 2) and 12 trials of spoken words (six from Set 3 and six from Set 4).

Procedure. Children were tested individually in a quiet room. They were first asked to name each of the drawings. Any failures to give the designated name were corrected and retested. The children were then allowed to practice on the two recall tasks, using shorter sequences than in the experimental trials. This involved sequences comprising two items for the 5-year-olds and three items for the 10-year-olds. The presentation rate was one item per 2 seconds. In the visual presentation each drawing was shown face up and then turned face down at a separate location in a horizontal row going from the right to the left side of the experimenter. The children were instructed to remain silent during presentation and then to repeat the names of the pictures in the same order as they were shown. In the 5-year-old group recall was prompted by the experimenter, who pointed to each overturned drawing in turn, proceeding from right to left, and asked the child to name it. After the first one or two trials, the verbal component of the prompt was omitted. Children were allowed to say "I don't know" if they were unsure of the correct answer. In the auditory presentation condition, the names of the drawings were spoken to the child who attempted to repeat the sequence immediately after hearing it. Training was terminated when recall was accurate on two consecutive trials.

In the main part of the experiment the foregoing procedure was repeated except that sequence length was now increased to three for the 5-year-olds and five for the 10-year-olds. All the experimental testing was carried out in two sessions lasting approximately 10 minutes each. In each session, subjects were given two blocks of trials, one in the visual and one in the auditory presentation modality.

Results

Items were scored correct only if they were recalled in the correct position. Table 2 shows the recall performance of the 5-year-old group (G1) and the 10-year-old group (G2). Because the groups received different list lengths, statistical analyses were conducted separately. A two-way analysis of variance with repeated measures was carried out for each group. In the 5-year-old group, the analysis revealed a significant main effect of Modality $[F(1,19) = 47.2; P < 0.001]$ corresponding to an advantage for the Auditory Modality (mean numbers correct 2.74 vs. 1.76) and a nearly significant Modality × Similarity interaction $[F(1,19) = 3.93; P = 0.059]$ reflecting a slightly larger Modality effect for Dissimilar items (differences between Auditory and Visual condition 1.12 vs. 0.82). The Duncan's test revealed that the Modality effect was significant for both Similar and Dissimilar items, whereas there was no Similarity effect for either the Visual or the Auditory modality. In the 10-year-old group there were significant effects of Similarity $[F(1,19) = 32.71; P < 0.001]$ with more correct items in the Dissimilar condition (2.50 vs. 1.95); Modality $[F(1,19) = 8.39; P < 0.01]$ with more correct items for Visual presentation (2.37 vs. 2.08); and a Modality × Similarity interaction $[F(1,19) = 6.36; P < 0.02]$. The similarity effect was larger for auditory presentation but was significant when each modality was considered in isolation (Duncan's test).

TABLE 2

Mean Numbers of Items Correctly Recalled (and Standard Deviations) for Phonemically Similar and Dissimilar Items as a Function of Presentation Modality and Age (Experiments 1 and 2)

	Group 1 (G1) 5 Years (3 Items)		Group 2 (G2) 10 Years (5 Items)		Group 3 (G3) 5 Years (4 Items)	
	Visual	Auditory	Visual	Auditory	Visual	Auditory
Similar	1.85 (0.55)	2.67 (0.45)	2.23 (0.48)	1.67 (0.61)	1.62 (0.75)	1.44 (0.39)
Dissimilar	1.68 (0.71)	2.80 (0.40)	2.51 (0.37)	2.49 (0.49)	1.59 (0.81)	2.59 (1.01)

Discussion

The results on the phonemic similarity effect confirm that 5-year-old children do not rely on a speech-based code in memory for drawings, unlike 10-year-olds who do. These findings are in agreement with previously reported results both with English-speaking (Hitch & Halliday 1983; Hitch et al., 1989; Halliday et al., 1990) and Italian children (Venneri et al., 1991) and in disagreement with Hulme (1987) who reported a significant PSE in 4-year-old children for spoken words. The hypothesis that speech-based codes are automatically activated predicts a PSE in both age groups. However, a significant similarity effect for spoken words was found only in the older group. In the younger group, there was a difference in the expected direction but did not reach significance. However, it is possible that the lack of a phonemic similarity effect is due to a ceiling effect as young children's performance was very close to the maximum possible score. Experiment 2 addresses this.

Results also indicate a significant advantage for words in the younger group and for drawings in the older group. This finding is consistent with the hypothesis that young children rely on modality-dependent memory codes: speech-based when stimuli are spoken words; based on visual details when stimuli are drawings. For spoken words, but not for drawings, memory codes are compatible with the verbal response. Consequently, one may expect better performance to be associated with words. For older children, on the other hand, verbal recoding implies that both memory codes are available in the visual modality, whereas only the speech code is available in the auditory modality. This could explain why drawings are better recalled than words.

In order to check for a possible ceiling effect in the 5-year-old group, Experiment 2 was run in which four-item lists were presented to an additional group of 5-year-old children.

EXPERIMENT 2

Method

Subjects.   A total of 12 5-year-old children (mean age: 5;0 years; range: 4;2–5;9) took part in the experiment.

Materials and Procedure.   Children were tested following exactly the same procedure as in Experiment 1, except that four-item lists were presented.

Results

Mean numbers of items correctly recalled and standard deviations are presented in Table 2. A two-way analysis of variance revealed a significant main effect on Similarity [$F(1,11)$ = 10.99; P = 0.007] and a Modality × Similarity interaction [$F(1,11)$ = 15.05; P = 0.003] indicating that the Similarity effect was significant only in the Auditory modality ($P < 0.05$, Duncan's test).

Discussion

Results of Experiment 2 confirm that, provided performance of subjects avoids ceiling effects, a PSE is present in young children when stimuli are spoken words. They also confirm the absence of the effect with visual material. The superiority for spoken words with respect to drawings, found in Experiment 1, is confined in Experiment 2 to dissimilar words, presumably reflecting the emergence of the PSE. Taken together, the results of Experiments 1 and 2 confirm the robustness of the PSE and suggest that cultural differences, such as the system of formal education, do not influence the relationship between PSE and input modality in children of different ages.

In Experiment 3 the visual similarity effect is studied in Italian children of different ages, using materials different from the ones used previously. In one set of similar drawings the items all had a round shape. In the other, they all had long shapes and were tilted at the same angle. There were two sets of visually dissimilar drawings, each matched to one of the similar sets in terms of the length of the names of drawings, which can effect recall (Hitch et al., 1988).

EXPERIMENT 3

Method

Subjects.   These were 20 children in each of two age groups drawn from two schools located in a middle class area in Rome. The 5-year-old group had a mean age of 5;2 years (range: 4;4–6;0) and the 10-year-old group a mean age of 10.4 (range: 9;3–11;0).

Materials.   These were 20 black and white line drawings (see Appendix 2) consisting of the following four sets of items:

Set 1: 5 objects having similar round shapes and 2-syllable names.
Set 2: 5 objects having similar long shapes and 3-syllable names; each drawing had its major axis in the same oblique orientation as the others.

Set 3: 5 objects having dissimilar shapes and 2-syllable names.
Set 4: 5 objects having dissimilar shapes and 3-syllable names.

Each drawing was mounted on a 10cm × 10cm card. The drawings were all familiar objects that pilot work had established were uniquely named by 5- and 10-year-olds.

Design.   Type of material was manipulated as a within-subject factor, such that there were six trials for each type of material per subject. Each trial was constructed by random sampling from the corresponding set of drawings. Trials were blocked by type of material, and the order of blocks was counterbalanced across subjects. A trial consisted of a sequence of three items for 5-year-olds and five items for the 10-year-olds.

Procedure.   The training, presentation, and recall procedures all followed exactly the procedure adopted in Experiment 1 for the visual presentation modality. The only difference was that 5-year-old children were tested in three sessions.

Results

Table 3 summarises the recall performance of the two experimental groups in terms of mean numbers of items correctly recalled. The Similarity effect was tested by performing two different within-subjects ANOVAs for each group, one on long objects and one on round objects scores. In the 5-year-old group these analyses revealed a significant Similarity effect both for Long [$F(1,19) = 4.94$; $P < 0.03$] and Round objects [$F(1,19) = 4.94$; $P < 0.03$] indicating in both cases an advantage for the Dissimilar material. In the 10-year-old group the Similarity effect was not significant for either Long [$F(1,19) = 2.21$] or Round objects [$F(1,19) = 0.04$].

TABLE 3
Mean Numbers of Items Correctly Recalled (and Standard Deviations)
for Visually Similar and Dissimilar Items in Different Age Groups
(Experiment 3)

		5 Years (3 Items)	10 Years (5 Items)
Similar	(long)	1.87 (0.60)	2.31 (0.47)
Dissimilar	(3 syllables)	2.12 (0.46)	2.30 (0.45)
Similar	(round)	2.00 (0.59)	2.53 (0.26)
Dissimilar	(2 syllables)	2.26 (0.44)	2.51 (0.38)

Discussion

A significant visual similarity effect was found only in younger children for both sets of drawings. These results, therefore, extend to different materials and to Italian subjects, the same age differences in memory for visually similar and dissimilar drawings reported in previous work (Hitch et al., 1988, 1989).

The results are consistent with the hypothesis that older children, unlike the younger ones, translate visual items in speech-based codes and use these codes to hold the information in the short-term store. In contrast, younger children rely on visually based codes and must be assumed to recode the stimuli only at the moment of giving the spoken answer.

Experiment 4 was a preliminary investigation of the hypothesis that the VSE is based on trace decay using a delayed recall paradigm. In this situation, it was expected that, with a delay between presentation and recall, performance would decline and the VSE would attenuate because it is supposed to be sustained by a decaying visual trace. This statement does not entail a specific prediction with regard to the shape of the decay function: Rather, it asserts that after a certain delay the VSE should disappear.

Regarding the duration of visual short-term memory traces, it has been stated that they are shorter than auditory ones (Crowder & Morton, 1969; O.C. Watkins & M.J. Watkins, 1980). The duration of the auditory memory trace has been estimated as being 20 seconds at the most (Cowan, 1984). Given the lack of an established estimate of the length of the time interval necessary to rule out the contribution of the hypothetical visual store, we investigated a variable interval between 0 seconds and 15 seconds. Two kinds of activities had to be performed during the delay. One of them was articulatory suppression and was chosen to prevent phonological recoding of the items during delay. The other was a "tapping" task. This condition, being very low in attentional demands, was considered as functionally equivalent to an empty interval but served to control children's behaviour during delay.

EXPERIMENT 4

Method

Subjects.   A total of 32 5-year-old children (mean age: 4;9 years; range: 4;5–5;3) attending nursery school took part in the experiment.

Materials.   Drawings from Set 2 and Set 4 of Experiment 3 (long objects and 3-syllable controls) were used.

Design. Type of materials (similar objects and control items) and delay intervals (0, 5, 10, 15 seconds) were manipulated as within-subjects factors, such that there were five trials for each type of material and delay interval per subject. A trial consisted of a sequence of four items and was constructed by random sampling from the corresponding set of drawings. Trials were blocked by type of material, and the order of blocks was counterbalanced across subjects. Activity during delay (Tapping or Articulatory Suppression) was manipulated as a between-subject factor. Sixteen children were assigned at random to the Tapping group and 16 to the Articulatory Suppression group.

Procedure. The first part of the training session consisted in naming and recall practice and was the same as in Experiment 1 (visual modality). In the second part, the subjects were allowed to practise the activities (Articulatory Suppression or Tapping) to be performed under delayed recall. Subjects in the Articulatory Suppression condition were asked to repeat, during delay, the word *farfalla* (butterfly). Subjects in the Tapping condition were requested to perform a tapping task consisting in beating rhythmically the middle finger on the table. Practice was repeated until the child understood the task.

In the main part of the experiment each child was tested individually in two sessions lasting approximately 15 minutes each on separate days. In each trial, the subject was presented with a four-item list[1] and was asked to recall at a given cue (the experimenter raised a hand). The recall cue occurred at variable intervals after the last item to be remembered. During delay, children performed either the Articulatory Suppression or the Tapping task.

Results

Mean numbers of items correctly recalled by Tapping and Articulatory Suppression groups are reported in Table 4. An analysis of variance was performed with the Task (Tapping and Articulatory Suppression) as between-subjects factor and Delay Interval and Visual Similarity as repe-

---

[1]A pilot study was run in order to determine which list length was more convenient to use in a delayed recall paradigm. Four children were tested with four-item lists and four children with three-item lists, all drawings being dissimilar. Two delay intervals, 5 and 10 seconds, and 2 intervening activities, "articulatory suppression" and "tapping" were considered as *within-subjects* variables. Results indicated that list length did not produce a main effect nor interacted with any of the considered variables. We opted for a length of four thinking that, in view of the problems which emerged in Experiment 1 with a length of 3 items, it would differentiate better between conditions.

TABLE 4
Mean Numbers of Items Correctly Recalled and Standard Deviations as a Function of
Visual Similarity and Delay Intervals in Articulatory Suppression and Tapping Groups
(Experiment 4)

Delay Intervals (sec):		Articulatory Suppression Group				Tapping Group			
		0	5	10	15	0	5	10	15
Similar	Means	1.12	0.87	0.75	0.85	1.26	1.08	1.00	1.12
	s.d.	0.75	0.51	0.32	0.32	0.88	0.81	0.76	0.59
Dissimilar	Means	1.39	0.97	1.07	1.22	1.42	1.19	1.40	1.32
	s.d.	0.63	0.53	0.62	0.65	0.79	0.87	0.67	0.74

ated measures. The analysis revealed significant main effects of the factors Similarity [$F(1,30) = 12.5$; $P < 0.01$] and Delay [$F(3,90) = 4.52$; $P < 0.01$]. The interaction Similarity $\times$ Delay was not significant [$F(3,90) = 1.06$; $P = 0.37$] nor were the remaining main effects and interactions. The main effect of the factor Delay Interval was further analysed by means of a trend analysis that revealed that only the quadratic trend was significant [$F(1,30) = 20.57$; $P < 0.001$]. In fact, the performance at the different delay intervals shows an initial decrease between 0 and 5 seconds and an increase between 10 and 15 seconds.

Discussion

The results of Experiment 4 show that: (a) there is no difference between the "articulatory suppression" and the "tapping" group; (b) there is a significant effect of delay in both groups; (c) the visual similarity effect persists at all delay intervals in both tapping and articulatory suppression conditions. The lack of difference between the two groups indicates that young children do not phonologically rehearse during delay, phonological recoding of items occurring only at output. The main effect of delay is accounted for by a significant quadratic trend, corresponding to an initial drop of performance between 0 seconds and 5 seconds, followed by a flat performance between 5 seconds and 10 seconds, and a subsequent increase between 10 seconds and 15 seconds. Delayed recall is poorer than immediate recall at all delay intervals, but it does not follow a monotonically decreasing function. This time course is problematic for a clear interpretation in terms of decay and, in principle, other processes could be responsible for the observed time function. One of our referees suggested that the initial drop in performance could reflect task switching. However, this variability in level of performance was not associated with any reduction of the VSE: The interaction similarity $\times$ delay was not at all significant. The persistence of VSE across delays is not easily handled by a decay hypothesis, unless it is assumed either that the two groups adopted a visual rehearsal strategy during delay, or that short-term visual traces last longer than 15 seconds. It is, however, consistent with the encoding hypothesis proposed by Nairne (1988) to explain the PSE. According to this explanation the features of a trace are degraded by subsequent input at the time of presentation and the amount of "overwriting" is influenced by the similarity of the successive input. Because the Nairne framework does not use decay as an operative source of forgetting, we expect the VSE to be independent of delay intervals.

CONCLUDING REMARKS

The findings of the present investigation with regard to Experiments 1, 2, and 3 are easily summarised. First, under conditions of auditory presentation the phonemic similarity effect is present at both age 5 and age 10. Secondly, under conditions of visual presentation the phonemic similarity effect is present only in the older group. Thirdly, the visual similarity effect is present only in the younger group. Taken together, these findings provide comprehensive additional evidence on the development of memory codes used in immediate serial recall tasks. Young children rely on modality-dependent codes, which are probably automatically activated and therefore do not use a speech-based code in memory for drawings. Older children use speech-based memory codes for drawings as well as words. This pattern of findings appears to be independent of cultural differences and the precise experimental stimulus materials used.

It has been stated that it is obvious that adults remember things in terms of verbal descriptions when they are able to do so (Hulme, 1987), but it is not obvious why the shift from a visual memory code to a phonemic one should take place sometime after the age of 5 years. One possible reason is that as the child achieves familiarity with reading and, in particular, with the process of phonologically recoding a visual stimulus, this process becomes generalised to memory tasks. Italian children start their formal education in reading at 6 years, and according to this hypothesis we would expect a phonemic similarity effect to emerge during the first year of schooling. In agreement with this hypothesis Venneri et al. (1991) reported a significant PSE in 6-year-old Italian children. It would be interesting to investigate the relationship of first occurrence of PSE with reading achievement.

In addition to these assumptions regarding the developmental changes in the use of memory codes it has also been hypothesised that memory codes involved in VSE are subject to rapid decay, unless refreshed by rehearsal process. Results of Experiment 4, concerning the time course of VSE in a delayed recall paradigm raise problems for this hypothesis. However, the exact temporal characteristics of the VSE will need to be established in further research.

REFERENCES

Baddeley, A.D. (1990). *Human memory: Theory and practice.* Hillsdale, NJ: Lawrence Erlbaum Publishers Inc.

Baddeley, A., & Hitch, G. (1974). Working memory. In G. Bower (Ed.), *Recent advances in learning and motivation* (Vol. VII, pp. 47–90). New York: Academic Press.

Brown, M. (1977). Examination of visual and verbal coding processes in preschool children. *Child Development, 48,* 38–45.

Conrad, R. (1965). Order errors in immediate recall of sequences. *Journal of Verbal Learning and Verbal Behavior, 4,* 161–169.

Conrad, R. (1967). Interference or decay over short retention interval? *Journal of Verbal Learning and Verbal Behavior, 6,* 49–54.

Conrad, R. (1971). The chronology of the development of covert speech in children. *Developmental Psychology. 5,* 598–405.

Cowan, N. (1984). On short and long auditory stores. *Psychological Bulletin, 96,* 341–370.

Crowder, R.G., & Morton, J. (1969). Precategorical acoustic storage (PAS). *Perception and Psychophysics, 5,* 365–373.

Halliday, S., Hitch, G., Lennon, C., & Pettipher, G. (1990). Verbal short-term memory in children: The role of the articulatory loop. *European Journal of Cognitive Psychology, 2,* 23–37.

Hayes, D., & Schulze, A. (1977). Visual encoding in preschoolers' serial retention. *Child Development, 66,* 1066–1070.

Hitch, G., & Halliday, S. (1983). Working memory in children. *Philosophical Transactions of the Royal Society .V., B302,* 325–340.

Hitch, G., Halliday, S., Dodd, A., & Littler, J. (1989). Development of rehearsal in short-term memory: Differences between pictorial and spoken stimuli. *British Journal of Developmental Psychology, 7,* 347–362.

Hitch, G., Halliday, S., Schaaftal, A., & Scrhaagen, M. (1988). Visual working memory in young children. *Memory and Cognition, 16,* 120–132.

Hitch, G., Woodin, M.E., & Baker, S. (1989). Visual and phonological components of working memory in children. *Memory and Cognition, 17(2),* 175–185.

Hulme, C. (1984). Developmental differences in effects of acoustic similarity in memory span. *Developmental Psychology, 20,* 650–652.

Hulme, C. (1987). The effects of acoustic similarity on memory in children: A comparison between visual and auditory presentation. *Applied Cognitive Psychology, 1,* 45–51.

Hulme, C., & Tordoff, V. (1989). Working memory development: the effects of speech rate, word length, and acoustic simlarity on serial recall. *Journal of Experimental Child Psychology, 47,* 72–87.

Longoni, A.M., Richardson, J.T.E., & Aiello, A. (1993). Articulatory rehearsal and phonological storage in memory. *Memory and Cognition, 21,* 11–22.

Nairne, J.S. (1988). A framework for interpreting recency effects in immediate serial recall. *Memory and Cognition, 16,* 343–352.

Venneri, A., Nichelli, P., Cubelli, R., Corrado, G., & Cossu, G. (1991). La comparsa degli effetti di similarità fonologica e di lunghezza di parola nei bambini da 4 a 8 anni. *Giornale Italiano di Psicologia, XVIII(5),* 779–798.

Watkins, O.C., & Watkins, M.J. (1980). The modality effect and echoic persistence. *Journal of Experimental Psychology: General, 109,* 251–278.

APPENDIX 1
Materials used in Experiments 1 and 2

Set 1: 5 drawings with phonemically similar 2-syllable names:

Borsa   Corna   Porta   Orso   Torta

Set 2: 5 drawings with phonemically dissimilar 2-syllable names.

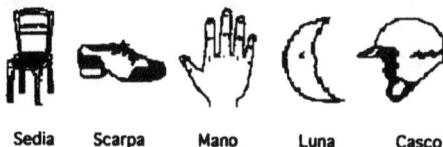

Sedia   Scarpa   Mano   Luna   Casco

Set 3: 5 spoken words (names of drawings in Set 1).
Set 4: 5 spoken words (names of drawings in Set 2).

APPENDIX 2
Materials used in Experiment 3

Set 1: Visually similar round objects (2-syllable names):

Palla   Faccia   Disco   Mela   Sole

Set 2: Visually similar long objects (3-syllable names):

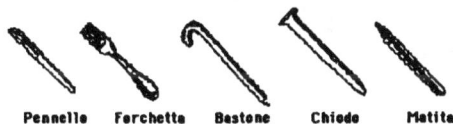

Pennello   Forchetta   Bastone   Chiodo   Matita

Set 3: Visually dissimilar objects (3-syllable names):

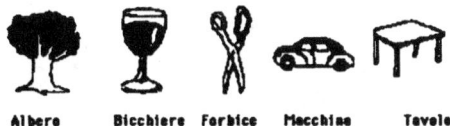

Albero   Bicchiere   Forbice   Macchina   Tavolo

Set 4: Visually dissimilar objects (2-syllable names):

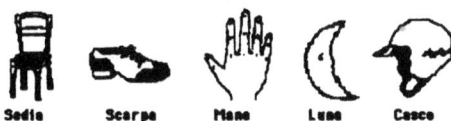

Sedia   Scarpa   Mano   Luna   Casco

INTERNATIONAL JOURNAL OF BEHAVIORAL DEVELOPMENT, 1994, *17* (1), 73-89

The Development of Short-term Visual Memory in Young Children

Peter Walker
University of Central Lancashire, England

Graham J. Hitch
Lancaster University, England

Alison Doyle
University of Ulster at Jordanstown, Northern Ireland

Tracey Porter
Manchester University, England

A probed memory task was used to investigate children's short-term visual memory for an object's spatial location or colour. In Experiment 1, 5-year-olds recognised the location of one of three coloured shapes that had appeared in a random spatio-temporal order. Two aspects of the children's performance confirmed their reliance on visual memory. First, performance was impaired when the shapes were visually similar. Secondly, the serial position curve was characteristic of visual memory, with a final-item recency effect and no primacy effect. Experiment 2 assessed 5- and 7-year-old children's memory for a shape's colour or its spatial location. Although there was developmental improvement in memory for spatial location, that was confined to pre-recency items, there was no effect of age with regard to the recall of colour. The results go against Hasher and Zacks' (1979) proposal that, in contrast to colour, spatial location would not show developmental improvement because it is remembered automatically. The concept of an object file, that was devised specifically to explain how different visual features of an object are represented (Kahneman & Treisman, 1984), is considered as a potential explanation of both the serial

Requests for reprints should be sent to Peter Walker, Faculty of Health, University of Central Lancashire, Preston PR1 2HE, UK.

Alison Doyle contributed to the present study while she was on placement in the Department of Psychology, Manchester University, UK. Tracey Porter undertook Experiment 1 in partial fulfilment of the requirements for an M.Sc. degree.

position curve and the distinctive behaviour of different visual features. It is suggested that although 5-year-olds are as adept as 7-year-olds at creating and immediately accessing an object file, they are less able to access information about the visual features of objects whose files are no longer current.

INTRODUCTION

Current accounts of short-term memory distinguish speech-based and visuo-spatial forms of representation. The model of working memory, for example, identifies a phonological store, supported by articulation, and a visuo-spatial sketch pad (see Baddeley, 1990). Obviously, tests that make reference to how information is distributed in space make demands on the sketch pad (den Heyer & Barrett, 1971; Meudell, 1972; Murray & Newman, 1973). However, the operation of visual memory can also be highlighted by taking steps to preclude the involvement of speech, as when subjects are required to suppress their articulation or non-nameable visual patterns are the to-be-remembered stimuli. In addition, there are some subject populations for whom short-term memory for visual stimuli is unlikely to draw on speech (Goodglass, Denes, & Calderone, 1974; O'Connor & Hermelin, 1978; Warrington & Shallice, 1972). Young children (5- to 6-year-olds) form one such group (see Hitch, Halliday, Schaafstal, & Schraagen, 1988; Hitch, Woodin, & Baker, 1989) as at this age the tendency to verbally recode visual stimuli is not developed (Conrad, 1971).

The distinction between speech-based and visuo-spatial memory processes touches on an important developmental issue. Hasher and Zacks (1979) propose that spatial location is one of a small number of stimulus features that is encoded and retained automatically. They further propose that as a consequence of being automatic, memory for spatial location should not show any developmental enhancement. However, this aspect of their original hypothesis has not fared well in the face of experimental tests, with the evidence remaining equivocal according to a recent review by Schumann-Hengsteler (1992). Although on occasions young children have been surprisingly adept at remembering the association between an item and its spatial location, so that performance has not improved with age (Ellis, Katz, & Williams, 1987), it is now clear that such improvement can occur, and can sometimes be quite marked (Mandler, Seegmiller, & Day, 1977; Park & James, 1983; Pezdek, Roman, & Sobolik, 1986; von Wright, Gebhard, & Karttunen, 1975). The prerequisites for this to occur are not known.

Schumann-Hengsteler (1992) examined 4- to 10-year-olds' performance on a task that required them to view a display of several pictorial elements for 4 seconds and then immediately reconstruct the display. The children had to select the relevant pictorial elements from a larger set before placing them in their remembered positions. Her scoring of performance endeavoured to distinguish three facets of memory. First, memory for the items themselves, as reflected in subjects' ability to select the correct pictorial elements from the larger set. Secondly, memory for the spatial distribution of the items, as revealed by subjects' ability to restrict their placements to locations that had previously been occupied. Thirdly, memory for the specific item-location associations, as reflected in subjects' ability to place a correctly remembered item in its appropriate location. With regard to item memory, her results revealed a steady improvement across the age range tested. Consistent with Hasher and Zacks' (1979) proposal, memory for the spatial distribution of the items showed no developmental improvement at all, although memory for the item-location associations did improve over the 4 to 8 years range. The absence of developmental improvement in memory for the spatial distribution of the items is clearly interesting, and deserves further investigation. However, it is memory for the item-location associations that relates most closely to what others have considered to be the essence of memory for spatial location. The modest developmental improvement observed agrees with the general pattern emerging from previous work. However, as Schumann-Hengsteler (1992) acknowledges, her own measure of memory for the item-location associations did not completely distinguish this from memory for the items themselves. The same problem of interpretation arises in relation to other developmental studies of visual memory (see, for example, Hitch et al., 1988, 1989).

Several studies of visual short-term memory have successfully distinguished memory for individual visual features from memory for associations between features (Stefurak & Boynton, 1986; Treisman, 1977). Recognising the same distinction, Kahneman and Treisman (1984) identified a special mechanism for preserving information about the conjunctions of features that define a particular object. They propose that one product of attending to a visual object is a temporary file representing information about the object's visual features along with its spatial and temporal position. Given the emerging interest in the concept of an object file (see Kahneman, Treisman, & Gibbs, 1992) memory for feature associations deserves consideration in the context of questions about memory development.

The present study re-examines the development of memory for spatial location using a technique which isolates memory for the association between an object's shape and its location. This is achieved using a variant of the probed location memory task used by Atkinson, Hansen, and Bernbach (1964). In particular, after a short sequence of to-be-remembered items has been presented, with each item appearing at a different location, one of the shapes is re-presented to probe subjects' memory, and the alternative locations with which it could have been associated are limited in number (3), are known, and are constantly on display. In this way the need to remember the individual shapes and locations is circumvented, leaving the recovery of their associations as the only demand placed on subjects. It is known from pilot studies that even with sequences of just three stimuli, performance lies below ceiling. There is no need, therefore, to burden children with longer sequences in order to guarantee intermediate levels of performance capable of showing sensitivity to experimental manipulations. Memory for colour is also considered. Colour is a visual feature that is excluded from Hasher and Zacks' (1979) list of features that are retained automatically, and to that extent it provides a useful contrast with spatial location. Colour also is limited to just three alternatives.

To-be-remembered stimuli are presented sequentially so that the effects of serial position can provide converging evidence for the involvement of visual memory and can, at the same time, permit examination of the potential restriction of developmental improvement to particular aspects of short-term visual memory. Previous studies of short-term visual memory have consistently observed a distinctive serial position curve characterised by a pronounced recency effect, often confined to the final item, and the absence of primacy (e.g. D.E. Broadbent & M.H.P. Broadbent, 1981; Hitch et al., 1988, 1989; Locke & Deck, 1978; Phillips & Christie, 1977). This contrasts with verbal memory, which is normally associated with both primacy and recency effects. There are indications that developmental improvements in probed location memory are confined to pre-recency items (Keely, 1971; Siegel & Allik, 1973).

Most studies of memory development that have exploited the probed location memory procedure have used fixed spatio-temporal orders of presentation, typically the most straightforward left-right pattern, and have therefore been unable to dissociate spatial and temporal positions (see Atkinson et al., 1964; Berch, 1978; Bernbach, 1978; R.M. Brown, N.L. Brown, & Caci, 1981; Calfee, Hetherington, & Waltzer, 1966; Hagen & Kingsley, 1968; Keely, 1971; Siegel & Allik, 1973). Hence, it is difficult to be confident that subjects' performance was based on memory for the direct association between an item and its spatial location. It would be possible, for example, to remember the temporal order of the items separately from the spatio-temporal sequence and then cross-reference these two sources of information to derive the location of the probe. In order to avoid such problems of interpretation here, the spatio-temporal sequence for each trial was determined on a random basis.

EXPERIMENT 1

As a preliminary to the main study, Experiment 1 used the probed location memory task to isolate children's memory for the association between an item and its spatial location with the aim of confirming that such memory is predominantly, if not exclusively, mediated by visual representations.

Hitch et al. (1988, 1989) have shown that 5- to 6-year-olds rely on visual memory when immediately recalling the positions of drawings of common objects. Their children were presented with short sequences of picture cards which were placed face down in an array. The experimenter touched the back of each card in turn and thereby prompted the recall of the picture in each location. Of particular interest here are two features of the results. First, the serial position curve showed a strong recency effect and no primacy, a well-documented characteristic of visual short-term memory. Secondly, performance was sensitive to the visual similarity of the shapes of the pictures.

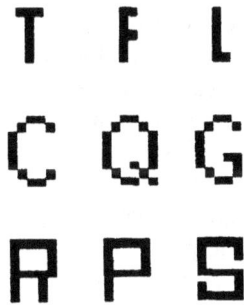

FIG. 1.   The nine letters used in Experiment 1.

Experiment 1 also used a similarity manipulation to confirm the significance of visual memory for probed location memory. Visual similarity was manipulated in two ways, by varying the shape and colour of the stimuli. Hitch et al. (1988, 1989) manipulated shape similarity by altering the overall orientation of the principal axis of each picture. In the present experiment, shape similarity was varied by using stimuli in which the character of the local elements of the to-be-remembered shapes is altered. Walker, Hitch, and Duroe (1993) found that the same stimuli gave rise to a visual similarity effect when adults were prevented from verbal recoding by articulatory suppression. The colour similarity manipulation is novel in this context.

Method

Stimuli.   Nine letters were used as stimuli, designed so that they comprised three relatively distinct subsets of visually similar letters (see Fig. 1). The letters within a subset were endowed with a style that either exaggerated the visual features they already shared or provided them with similar features. To give an indication of the sizes of the letters, the letter S measured 15mm by 22mm. The spatial locations at which the letters were presented were marked out with a horizontal array of white outline squares. These squares measured 35mm by 35mm and their adjacent edges were separated by 10mm. An additional square, in which each probe stimulus appeared, was positioned 40mm below the centre of this row. All the squares were presented continuously throughout. To-be-remembered letters were presented in colour (red, green, and blue), but the probe letter always appeared in white. All stimuli were viewed from a distance of 50cm.

Design and Procedure.   The experiment was conducted using a BBC (model B) microcomputer linked to a colour monitor (Microvitec 452). Short sequences of three letters were presented, each one appearing in a different spatial location in a randomly determined spatio-temporal sequence. A trial was initiated by the experimenter pressing the SPACE bar and the first letter was presented after a blank interval of 2sec. Each letter appeared for 1.5sec and a blank interstimulus interval (ISI) of 0.5sec separated successive letters. After a blank interval of 1.0sec subjects were presented with a single probe that was always one of the three letters that had just been presented. The probe was selected randomly, but with the constraint that for each subject the three temporal serial positions were tested equally often. Subjects responded to a probe letter by pointing to the spatial location in which it had just appeared. The three letters in a sequence were equally likely to be taken from the same subset or one each from the three different subsets. For a shape-similar list one of the subsets of letters was selected at random, with no attempt to use each subset equally often. For a shape-dissimilar list one member from each subset was selected at random, with no attempt to use each letter an equal number of times. When the letters for a trial had been selected in this way, their temporal order of presentation was randomly determined. Orthogonal to the manipulation of shape similarity, the colour similarity of the list items was also manipulated. Thus, for each level of shape similarity, it was equally likely that the three letters would each appear in a different one of the three colours, or each one in the same, randomly determined colour. The crossing of shape similarity and colour similarity created four experimental conditions and each subject completed six trials in each condition. Prior to the experimental trials, all subjects completed a number of

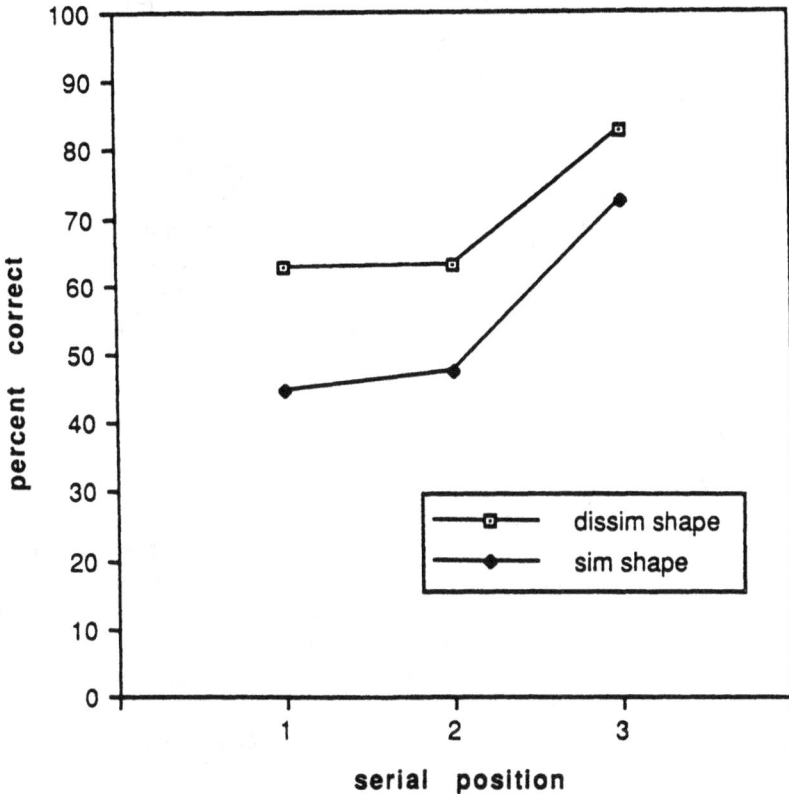

FIG. 2. Accuracy against serial position for probed location memory of visually similar and visually dissimilar letter sequences in Experiment 1. The data are collapsed over the two levels of colour similarity.

preliminary trials which confirmed that under the conditions of the main experiment they could name the letters without error.

Subjects. A total of 34 children participated in the experiment, their ages ranging from 4;10 to 5;11, with a mean of 5;5, and they were drawn from two urban primary schools in the Manchester area.

Results

The accuracy data were submitted to an analysis of variance, with Shape Similarity, Colour Similarity, and Serial Position as within-subjects factors. This analysis confirmed that although there were significant main effects of shape similarity, $F(1,33) = 21.02$, and serial position, $F(2,66) = 33.66$, there were no other significant effects. The results are illustrated in Fig. 2, where the data have been collapsed across the two levels of colour similarity. Planned comparisons revealed that performance at the final serial position was superior to performance at the initial two positions, $F(1,99) = 67.00$. Performance across the initial two positions did not vary significantly, $F(1,99) < 1.0$. In addition, there was a suggestion of differential effects of shape similarity according to serial position. Thus, there was a significant effect of shape similarity at the first two positions, but not at the final position, $F(1,99) = 9.15$, 7.00, and 3.11, for successive serial positions, respectively. In comparable experiments with adult subjects, Walker et al. (1993) observed that the effects of visual similarity are restricted to pre-recency items.

Discussion

Two separate aspects of children's performance converge on the view that they relied on visual memory. First, their performance was impaired when the shapes of the stimuli were similar. This is consistent with previous evidence on young children's immediate memory for pictures (Hayes & Schulze, 1977; Hitch et al., 1988, 1989). The present results show that the visual similarity effect generalises to non-pictorial, symbolic stimuli suggesting that young children's tendency to rely on visual short-term memory is very pervasive. Secondly, the serial position curves show a final-item recency effect and no primacy. This shape is characteristic of visual short-term memory in both children (e.g. Hitch et al., 1988, 1989; Bernbach, 1967) and adults (e.g. D.E. Broadbent & M.H.P. Broadbent, 1981; Locke & Deck, 1978; Phillips & Christie, 1977).

It is interesting to note that Walker et al. (1993) observed the same sensitivity to the visual similarity of the letters illustrated in Fig. 2 when adults were engaged in articulatory suppression. It appears from this, and the serial position effects, that visual short-term memory has remarkably similar characteristics in children and adults. The major developmental difference seems to be that adults are generally more likely to avoid reliance on visual short-term memory by using verbal recoding.

It could be argued that the absence of a colour similarity effect in the present experiment is evidence against the view that young children were relying on visual short-term memory. However, this negative result is difficult to interpret because it is not logically necessary to remember colour in order to remember the association between a shape and a location. Thus, the absence of an effect of colour indicates either that subjects ignored colour during encoding or that colour is stored independently of the shape-location association in visual short-term memory.

The distinctive serial position curve identified here with visual memory contrasts with the curve that is normally associated with verbal memory, in which both primacy and recency effects appear. There is evidence from the probed location memory task itself that phonological coding gives rise to both primacy and recency (see Bernbach, 1967; Locke & Deck, 1978). Nevertheless, a number of developmental studies of probed location memory have yielded a primacy effect in the absence of phonological coding (Berch, 1978; R.M. Brown et al., 1981; Hagen & Kingsley, 1968; Keely, 1971; Siegel & Allik, 1973). It appears, however, that this primacy effect has arisen from the first item's spatial distinctiveness rather than its temporal status as the first item (Berch, 1978; R.M. Brown et al., 1981; Hagen & Kingsley, 1968).

EXPERIMENT 2

Having shown that the probed location memory task successfully isolates the retention of item-location associations in children's short-term visual memory, the second experiment addresses the issue of possible developmental trends in spatial memory by studying children at two different ages. In addition, the experiment also explores memory for shape-colour associations because, according to Hasher and Zacks (1979), colour contrasts with location by being a visual feature that is not retained automatically. Because of this it was considered to provide a useful comparison with location memory.

FIG. 3.   The geometric shapes used in Experiment 2.

Method

Stimuli.   Three geometric shapes were used as stimuli and they are illustrated in Fig. 3. The sizes of the stimuli can be appreciated by noting that the overall dimensions of the cross were 7mm horizontally by 17mm vertically. On every trial each of the three shapes appeared in a different colour, viz. red, green, and blue. The locations in which stimuli appeared were marked out in the same way as in Experiment 1.

Design and Procedure.   The procedure of the preceding experiment was used here. On each trial the three shapes were presented in a randomly determined temporal order, with each shape appearing in a different colour. One of the shapes reappeared, in white, as the probe and remained visible until the subject's decision was registered on the computer. Each serial position was tested on 8 occasions, and every subject completed the 24 trials in a single block. The particular spatio-temporal sequence used on a trial was selected at random from the six sequences that were possible. There was no attempt to balance the overall frequency with which individual shapes and colours were associated with the different serial positions and spatial locations. Similarly, the assignment of colour to shape was determined randomly and independently for each trial. There were two versions of the task, given to separate groups of subjects, distinguished on the basis of the decision subjects had to make. In the first version subjects had to point with their finger to the location at which the test shape had appeared. In the second version they had to name the colour in which the test shape had appeared. The experimenter entered each decision into the computer.

Subjects. A total of 72 children participated in the experiment, an equal number being allocated to each of four groups. For each of two of the groups the average age of the children was 5;4 years (with a range of 4;11–6;0 years in both cases). For each of the other two groups the average age was 7;6 years (with ranges of 7;0–7;11 years and 7;0–8;0 years). At

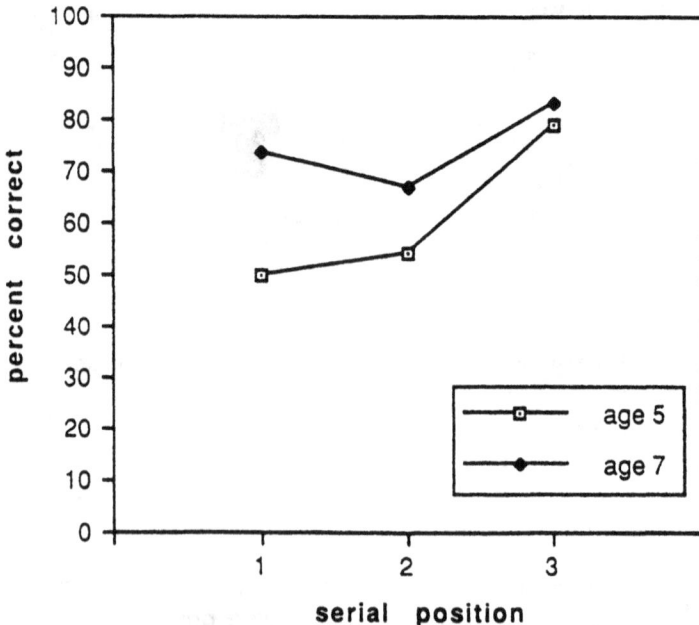

FIG. 4.   Accuracy against serial position for probed location memory by 5- and 7-year-olds in Experiment 2.

both age levels, one group was assigned to the probed location memory task, while the other group was assigned to the colour memory task. The children were drawn from four urban primary schools in the Manchester area.

Results

The accuracy data were first submitted to an analysis of variance with Age and Task as between-subjects factors, and Serial Position as a within-subjects factor. The interaction between Age and Task was significant, $F(1,68) = 5.77$, whereas the interaction between Age, Task, and Serial Position was not significant, $F(2,136) < 1$. An Age × Serial Position analysis of variance was completed for each task separately in order to better appreciate the differential impact of age on the two tasks.

Remembering the spatial location of a probed shape. The results from this version of the task are illustrated in Fig. 4. The main effect of serial position was significant, $F(2,68) = 19.24$, as was the main effect of age, $F(1,34) = 7.95$. The interaction between these two factors was also significant, $F(2,68) = 3.37$. Comparisons that focused on the effect of serial position for each age group separately, revealed that performance at the final serial position was superior to performance across the initial two positions, $F(1,68) = 34.67$ and 8.23, for the younger and older children, respectively. For neither age group was there a significant difference in performance across the initial two serial positions, $F(1,68) = 0.62$ and 1.71. (Although there is a suggestion of a primacy effect emerging with increasing age, in comparable situations the performance of adults has not shown a significant primacy effect, see Walker et al., 1993.) Comparisons that focused on the effect of age at each serial position revealed a significant difference at the first serial position, a marginally significant difference at the second serial position, and an insignificant difference at the final serial position, $F(1,102) = 13.44$, 3.77, and 0.42, respectively. In conclusion, there was improvement in performance with age that did not involve memory for the final item.

Remembering the colour of a probed shape. The results from this version of the task are illustrated in Fig. 5. The main effect of serial position was significant, $F(2,68) = 27.59$, while the main effect of age was insignificant, $F(1,34) < 1$. The interaction between these two factors was not significant, $F(2,68) < 1$. Comparisons that focused on the effect of serial position for each group separately, revealed that performance at the final serial position was superior to performance across the initial two positions, $F(1,68) = 34.72$ and 20.43 for the younger and older groups, respectively. For neither age group was there a significant difference in performance across the initial two serial positions, $F(1,68) < 1$ for both groups. Comparisons that

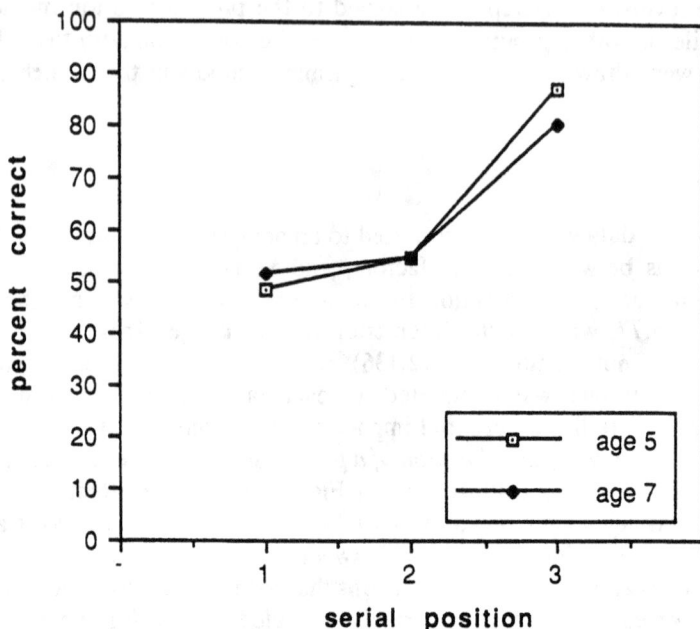

FIG. 5. Accuracy against serial position for probed colour memory by 5- and 7-year-olds in Experiment 2.

focused on the effect of age at each serial position failed to reveal any significant differences, $F(1,102) = 0.16, 0.00$, and 1.00, for successive serial positions, respectively. It is clear, therefore, that for this version of the task the two age groups performed equivalently.

Similar analyses that incorporated the results from both tasks, separately for each age group, confirmed that the younger children performed equivalently on both versions of the task. The older children, however, were better able to remember the spatial location than the colour of the probed shape.

Error Analysis.   Because a response was required on every trial a trivial interpretation of the recency effect has to be considered. It is possible that the relatively high hit rate for the final item reflects a strategy of selecting this item whenever subjects are uncertain of the correct item. One way of evaluating this interpretation is to examine the distribution of error responses from those trials where the test item relates to a serial position other than the final one. According to the foregoing interpretation these error responses should themselves be most frequently directed at the location of the final item. However, when subjects made an error response to the first item, they selected the second item on a total of 150 occasions and the final item on 85 occasions. When they made an error response to the second item, they selected the first item on a total of 154 occasions and the final item on 93 occasions. It is clear, therefore, that if anything there is a bias against responding in error with the final item, possibly reflecting subjects' good memory for this item.

Discussion

Performance in the probed location memory task has been found to improve with age, something that has also been observed by Atkinson et al. (1964); Hagen and Kingsley (1968); Keely (1971); and Siegel and Allik (1973). This result is also consistent with the observations of Schumann-Hengsteler (1992) with her picture reconstruction task. However, the result is inconsistent with Hasher and Zacks' (1979) proposal that spatial memory would not show developmental improvement on account of it being remembered automatically. As Schumann-Hengsteler's work indicates, however, it may be important in this regard to distinguish memory for an item's location from memory for spatial location *per se*. Finally, the results pertaining to memory for colour also contradict Hasher and Zacks' proposal. Although colour was excluded from their list of features remembered automatically, we see here that it shows no improvements with age.

In contrasting the results for location and colour, it is acknowledged that there are differences in the manner in which subjects were asked to respond. To convey their decision about location, subjects pointed to one of the continuously presented alternatives, whereas to convey their decision about colour subjects named the colour without the alternatives being on display. However, we do not see any obvious way in which these differences can explain the contrasting effects of age.

It is interesting that the improvement in probed location memory with age was confined to performance on pre-recency items, with performance on the final item remaining consistent across the two age groups. In fact, our assessment of adults performing in comparable situations (Walker et al., 1993) suggests that the level of performance on the final item remains relatively static over an even bigger age range. Support for this is provided by Keely (1971) and Siegel and Allik (1973) in their replications of the Atkinson et al. (1964) study. Keely investigated probed location memory, with various categories of stimulus, in 4-, 8-, and 14-year-olds. She observed a pronounced recency effect that often incorporated the last two items but that was occasionally confined to the final item. There were quite marked and consistent improvements with age with regard to memory for the pre-recency items, and this contrasted with the lack of developmental improvement in memory for the final item, despite the fact that performance was below ceiling. Similarly, when Siegel and Allik examined probed location memory in 6-, 8-, and 11-year-old children, as well as adults, they also found that memory for the final item(s) was remarkably consistent across all ages. There was, however, a progressive and marked improvement with age at all other, pre-recency positions.

The differential effects of age reinforce the view that remembering the final and earlier items is mediated by distinct mechanisms. For example, although probed feature-memory for the final item was comparable for shape-location and shape-colour associations, for the earlier items this was less so. Furthermore, to the extent that improvements with age are normally taken to reflect improved strategies for remembering, visual memory for the final item may contrast with memory for the earlier items by being essentially passive (see Walker & Marshall, 1982, for evidence of this). Finally, it is noteworthy that when studying probed location memory in 4-year-olds, Calfee, Hetherington, and Waltzer (1966) found a further contrast in the way final and earlier items are remembered: Only memory for the earlier items proved to be sensitive to list length.

GENERAL DISCUSSION

Given the nature of the probed feature-memory task, the present results confirm that the typical visual serial position curve can reflect the forgetting of feature associations rather than the forgetting of the individual features themselves. Moreover, the occurrence of recency when either colour or location were probed indicates that it may well be the associations between all of an item's features that are vulnerable to the presentation of succeeding stimuli, so that memory for the final item is special in that the associations between all of its features are still intact. Consistent with this interpretation, we have observed the same effects of serial position when directly probing the association between an item's colour and its spatial location (Hitch, Walker, & Porter, 1990). Bernbach (1967) observed the same effects of serial position when he tested young children's memory for the locations at which colours had appeared. In his experiment, moreover, the colour-location association was tested in the reverse direction, with subjects having to point to the appropriate colour in response to a probe that referred to a particular spatial location. Thus, a theoretical picture builds up in which the representation of the most recent stimulus in visual short-term memory is fairly accurate and complete in the sense that the associations between its different features are accurately and directly represented. Because subjects here are dealing with a very small subset of features which they know well, the much poorer performance for earlier items would appear to reflect the absence of direct representation of the feature associations (their feature conjunctions) rather than the loss of information about the individual features themselves.

The present results show that the distinction between memory for feature conjunctions and memory for individual features is important in visual short-term memory in children, consistent with conclusions based on studies with adults (Treisman, 1977; Stefurak & Boynton, 1986). Kahneman and Treisman (1984) have recognised the need for a mechanism to ensure that an object's feature conjunctions are preserved, especially as in early visual processing different features are separately represented. They propose that one product of attending to a visual object is a temporary representation, an object file, in which all its visual features are related to its spatio-temporal coordinates. Kahneman et al. (1992) recently explored the way in which object files can contribute to the processing of a new stimulus. They found evidence that only one object file is referred to when a new stimulus appears, and this file normally relates to the most recent stimulus. If object files are referred to in tasks such as immediate probed recall then the completeness of memory for the feature associations of the final item, but not preceding items, would be explained. Moreover, following this line of argument a little further, the present results would suggest that young children can derive information about feature associations from the most recent object file just as effectively as older children, but are somewhat less able to access the memory traces of object files that are no longer current. According to Kahneman et al. (1992), an object's spatial features play a particularly important role in accessing the object's file, whereas surface features such as colour have little significance in this regard. Thus, it seems that the object file concept has the potential to explain differential development for different feature conjunctions. The present results suggest that, for the age range studied here, there is developmental change in the efficiency of accessing object files but not in their contents.

Our data go against Hasher and Zacks' (1979) proposals regarding the development of memory for spatial location and colour that derive from their ideas regarding the automaticity of encoding of different features. However, although automaticity is an interesting notion, Hasher and Zacks do not make clear why some features and not others should be dealt with automatically, and to this extent their approach is theoretically sterile. The concept of an object file promises a richer theoretical framework for studying visual short-term memory and its development.

REFERENCES

Atkinson, R.C., Hansen, D.N., & Bernbach, H.A. (1964). Short-term memory with young children. *Psychonomic Science, 1*, 255–256.

Baddeley, A.D. (1990). *Human memory: theory and practice.* Hillsdale, NJ: Lawrence Erlbaum Associates Inc.

Berch, D.R. (1978). The role of spatial cues in the probe-type serial memory task. *Child Development, 49*, 749–754.

Bernbach, H.A. (1967). The effect of labels on short-term memory for colors with nursery school children. *Psychonomic Science, 7*, 149–150.

Broadbent, D.E., & Broadbent, M.H.P. (1981). Recency effects in visual memory. *Quarterly Journal of Experimental Psychology, 33A*, 1–15.

Brown, R.M., Brown, N.L., & Caci, M. (1981). Serial position effects in young children: Temporal or spatial? *Chlid Development, 52*, 1191–1201.

Calfee, R.C., Hetherington, E.M., & Waltzer, P. (1966). Short-term memory in children as a function of display size. *Psychonomic Science, 4*, 153–154.

Conrad, R. (1971). The chronology of the development of covert speech in children. *Developmental Psychology, 5*, 398–405.

Ellis, N.R., Katz, E., & Williams, J.E. (1987). Developmental aspects of memory for spatial location. *Journal of Experimental Child Psychology, 44*, 401–412.

Estes, W.K. (1973). Phonemic coding and rehearsal in short-term memory for letter strings. *Journal of Verbal Learning and Verbal Behavior, 12*, 360–372.

Goodglass, H., Denes, G., & Calderone, M. (1974). The absence of covert verbal mediation in aphasia. *Cortex, 10*, 264–269.

Hagen, J.W., & Kingsley, P.R. (1968). Labeling effects in short-term memory. *Child Development, 39*, 113–121.

Hasher, L., & Zacks, R.T. (1979). Automatic and effortful processes in memory. *Journal of Experimental Psychology: General, 108*, 356–388.

Hayes, D.S., & Schulze, S.A. (1977). Visual encoding in preschoolers' serial retention. *Child Development, 48*, 1066–1070.

den Heyer, K., & Barrett, B. (1971). Selective loss of visual and verbal information in STM by means of visual and verbal interpolated tasks. *Psychonomic Science, 25*, 100–102.

Hitch, G.J., Halliday, M.S., Schaafstal, A.M., & Schraagen, J.M.C. (1988). Visual working-memory in young children. *Memory and Cognition, 16*, 120–132.

Hitch, G.J., Walker, P., & Porter, T. (1990). *Similarity effects in short-term visual memory for spatial location.* Paper presented to meeting of the European Society for Cognitive Psychology, Como, Italy.

Hitch, G.J., Woodin, M.E., & Baker, S. (1989). Visual and phonological components of working memory in children. *Memory and Cognition, 17*, 175–185.

Kahneman, D., & Treisman, A. (1984). Changing views of attention and automaticity. In R. Parasuraman & J.R. Pomerantz (Eds.), *Varieties of attention.* New York: Academic Press.

Kahneman, D., Treisman, A., & Gibbs, B.J. (1992). The reviewing of object files: Object-specific integration of information. *Cognitive Psychology, 24*, 175–219.

Keely, K. (1971). Age and task effects in short-term memory of children. *Perception and Psychophysics, 9*, 480–482.

Locke, J.L., & Deck, J.W. (1978). Retrieval failure, rehearsal deficiency, and short-term memory loss in the aphasic adult. *Brain and Language, 5*, 227–235.

Mandler, J.M., Seegmiller, D., & Day, J. (1977). On the coding of spatial information. *Memory and Cognition, 5*, 10–16.

Meudell, P.R. (1972). Short-term visual memory: Comparative effects of two types of distraction on the recall of visually presented verbal and nonverbal material. *Journal of Experimental Psychology, 94*, 244–247.

Murray, D.J., & Newman, F.M. (1973). Visual and verbal coding in short-term memory. *Journal of Experimental Psychology, 100*, 58–62.

O'Connor, N., & Hermelin, B. (1978). *Seeing and hearing and space and time.* London: Academic Press.

Park, D.C., & James, C.Q. (1983). Effect of encoding instructions on children's spatial and colour memory: Is there evidence for automaticity? *Child Development, 54*, 61–68.

Pezdek, K., Roman, Z., & Sobolik, K.G. (1986). Spatial memory for objects and words. *Journal of Experimental Psychology: Learning, Memory and Cognition, 12*, 530–537.

Phillips, W.A., & Christie, D.F.M. (1977). Components of visual memory. *Quarterly Journal of Experimental Psychology, 29*, 117–133.

Schumann-Hengsteler, R. (1992). The development of visuo-spatial memory: How to remember location. *International Journal of Behavioral Development, 15*, 455–471.

Siegel, A.W., & Allik, J.P. (1973). A developmental study of visual and auditory short-term memory. *Journal of Verbal Learning and Verbal Behavior, 12*, 409–418.

Stefurak, D.L., & Boynton, R.M. (1986). Independence of memory for categorically different colors and shapes. *Perception and Psychophysics, 39*, 164–174.

Treisman, A. (1977). Focused attention in the perception and retrieval of multidimensional stimuli. *Perception and Psychophysics, 22*, 1–11.

Walker, P., Hitch, G.J., & Duroe, S. (1993). The effect of visual similarity on short-term memory for spatial location: Implications for the capacity of visual short-term memory. *Acta Psychologica, 83*, 203–224.

Walker, P., & Marshall, E.L. (1982). Visual memory and stimulus repetition effects. *Journal of Experimental Psychology: General, 111*, 348–368.

Warrington, E.K., & Shallice, T. (1972). Neuropsychological evidence of visual storage in short-term memory tasks. *Quarterly Journal of Experimental Psychology, 24*, 30–40.

von Wright, J.M., Gebhard, P., & Karttunen, M. (1975). A developmental study of the recall of spatial location. *Journal of Experimental Child Psychology, 20*, 181–190.

INTERNATIONAL JOURNAL OF BEHAVIORAL DEVELOPMENT, 1994, *17* (1), 91–107

The Relationship between Memory Span and Measures of Imitative and Spontaneous Language Complexity in Preschool Children

Joanna Blake, Wendy Austin, Marsha Cannon, Amanda Lisus, and Annabel Vaughan

Department of Psychology, York University, Canada

Preschool children, aged 2 to 5 years, were given a memory task that required them to repeat a list of animal names and a sentence imitation task. A sample of their spontaneous speech was also recorded. Word span was found to predict sentence imitation scores across the whole preschool age range. Word span and chronological age (CA), together, also predicted the mean length of utterance in spontaneous speech in younger preschool children. In a replication with children aged 2 to 3 years, word span predicted mean length or utterance (MLU) better than both CA and mental age (MA). These results extend previous findings regarding the relationship between word span and language imitation to younger preschool children. They also support the notion of a memory constraint on early spontaneous language. Increasing mastery of linguistic rules appears to obviate a memory constraint on spontaneous language, at least with these measures.

INTRODUCTION

It has often been suggested that children's early progress in producing complex sentences is constrained by a limited programming or memory span. As early as 1964, Brown and Bellugi proposed that utterance length

Requests for reprints should be sent to J. Blake, Department of Psychology, York University, North York, Ontario, M3J 1P3, Canada.

The research reported in this paper was funded in part by grants to the first author from the Natural Sciences and Engineering Research Council of Canada and the Faculty of Arts of York University. Some of these data were presented at the Biennial Meeting of the Society for Research in Child Development, Kansas City, April 1989. We are indebted to Helen Downie, Roman Konarski, and Mary-Lynn Stordy for their assistance with the data collection, transcription, and analysis. We would also like to thank the staff and children of the Canadian Infacare, Friendship Lodge, Hydrokids, Pelmo Park, Tender Loving Care, Woodbine, and York University daycare centres for their participation in the study.

is controlled by a span limitation that grows less restrictive with age as a consequence of both neurological growth and practice. Brown (1973) pointed to a more specific limit on the number of semantic relations the child is able to programme into a single sentence, although he then stressed that the basis for this limit was linguistic rather than memorial. Linguistic and memorial factors may be viewed as interacting to determine the complexity of early sentences. As Ramer (1977, p. 159) states, "productive and memory abilities are developing concurrently with linguistic knowledge, allowing for the realization of greater utterance length which is needed to express or perform with newly acquired linguistic information".

The notion that young children may not be able to express their linguistic knowledge because of a limited programming span motivated the view that their two-word utterances represent more complex underlying structure or meaning than can be overtly expressed (Bloom & Lahey, 1978; Brown, 1973). Some have applied this reasoning to one-word utterances as well (Greenfield & Smith, 1978). Braine (1974) opposed such a "rich" interpretation of children's early word combinations, denying that there is evidence of a constraint on length. Instead, he attributed the pseudo-ellipitical form of early sentences to "holophrastic lexical insertion", the child's pragmatic tendency to label a single salient feature of the action, and also to the low probability of the child's using more than one rule. It has also been argued (Todd, 1982) that more specific failures to apply rules, such as negation in tag questions and inversion in *wh* questions, should not be attributed to processing limitations but rather to context-specific knowledge.

The proposed relationship between memory and language is supported, however, by findings that language-delayed children have a more limited memory span than nondelayed children. Menyuk and Looney (1976) found that only language-disordered children had difficulty repeating sentences longer than three words. Kushnir (1986) found that preschool language-delayed children had significantly lower memory spans on both an auditory memory (word span) task and a "name-the-missing-object" task compared to normal children matched on age, sex, and nonverbal IQ. Language-delayed children of elementary school age had a selective deficit in auditory memory (word span) that exceeded their vocabulary and reading impairment and was poorer than the auditory memory of younger non-delayed children of matched verbal skills (Gathercole & Baddeley, 1990). Thus, it did not appear that the memory deficit of the language-delayed children could be attributed to poor language skills.

Direct tests of the proposal that language complexity is constrained by memory span in typical children are rare, however. Brownell (1988) found a relationship in toddlers between the number of actions that could be imitated (essentially a memory task) and the number of words in their spontaneous utterances, but this relationship may not have been independent of age. Case and Kurland (1980) gave kindergarten children a word span test and a sentence imitation task and found that the children were not able to repeat correctly those sentences containing a number of phrases exceeding their word span. Daneman and Case (1981) taught children between the ages of 2 and 6 years nonsense words that varied in syntactic complexity and that labelled actions differing in numbers of semantic features. Production and comprehension of these nonsense terms was better predicted by word span than by age. Furthermore, on both the production and comprehension tests, mastery of each additional level of complexity seemed to require an additional unit in terms of the mean word span for the group.

Apart from Brownell's (1988) study, there has been no research investigating the relationship between memory span and spontaneous language production in children at the early stages of language acquisition. The purpose of the current study was to test the proposed relationship between memory span and the complexity of both imitative and spontaneous language production in children at early and later stages of language acquisition to elucidate its time course. The notion that memory may constrain language is theoretically based in models which define working memory as the pool of operational resources that perform symbolic computations (Just & Carpenter, 1992). Such resources are conceived of as varying across individuals, resulting in capacity differences that may be reflected in varying degrees of constraints on task performance. Capacity constraints refer to limits on the total amount of activation that the system has available for maintaining elements in working memory, whether in processing or in storage (Just & Carpenter, 1992; see also Pascual-Leone, 1987). The basic question of this research was whether or not individual differences in memory span would be reflected in differences in performance on two different language tasks, one involving language comprehension and imitation and one involving spontaneously generated language. It was expected that memory span would predict both spontaneous and imitative language complexity beyond the variation attributable to age, but that the greater linguistic knowledge of older preschool children would alter the operation of a memory constraint.

EXPERIMENT 1

Method

Subjects.   The subjects were 31 children, 16 males and 15 females, ranging in age from 32 to 59 months. They were divided for statistical anlaysis into a younger and older group, using $3\frac{1}{2}$ years as the dividing age. This age was chosen as a critical age which can be viewed as separating early stages of language development in which rudimentary syntax is still being mastered (e.g. inflections, auxiliary verbs, conjoining) from later stages in which more sophisticated forms (e.g. embedded relative clauses) are being acquired. The younger group ranged in age from 32 to 41 months (mean of 36.6 months) and contained 14 children, 7 males and 7 females. The older group ranged in age from 44 months to 59 months (mean of 49.1 months) and contained 17 children, 9 males and 8 females. They attended one of three daycare centres in Toronto. The sample was heterogeneous with respect to ethnicity, but only those children whose families spoke English only were included.

Tasks and Procedure.   The children were seen individually in a separate room in their daycare centres by two experimenters who visited with them in the centres before testing them. One experimenter administered a sentence imitation task, and the other recorded a sample of their spontaneous speech and administered a word span task, all tasks being given in that order on different days. The tasks are described below.

Speech Sample.   This was recorded while the child played with a set of small toys provided by the experimenter and conversed with her. The conversation was taped on an audiocassette recorder with a separate microphone.

Word Span.   In this task, the names of 19 common animals with one or two syllables were used. The names used were bear, mouse, horse, tiger, fish, duck, sheep, cat, turtle, bird, frog, chicken, rabbit, cow, lion, dog, pig, fox, and monkey. The child was told to listen and to say exactly what the experimenter said. An ascending order was used in which the number of animal names was increased from 2 to 6, and a series of 3 trials was given for each number. A correct trial was one in which the child repeated the correct names in the correct order, and testing was discontinued when all three trials of a series were incorrect. The animal names were presented in a random order but were not repeated on a trial and occurred with approximately equal frequency across all trials. The score for this task was the largest number of names for which at least two of the three trials were correct.

Sentence Imitation Task.   This task consisted of two lists of 22 sentences that varied in length, in semantic complexity, and in syntactic complexity. The two lists were matched on all variables except for the actual lexical items. One list used a farm vocabulary, whereas the other used a circus vocabulary. The purpose of using two lists was to try to ensure that any effects would be general and not due to a particular list (see Clark, 1973). Each child was given only one of the lists to imitate, and approximately half of the children were given each list. *t*-tests showed no effect of lists on imitation scores, so that the list factor was dropped from subsequent analyses. With regard to the sentential variables of the lists, length was defined in terms of number of words and ranged from 4 to 10 words per sentence. Semantic complexity was defined in terms of number of propositions and varied from 1 to 4 propositions per sentence. Propositions were defined as the simplest ideas underlying the sentence, i.e. as the predicates (verbs or modifiers) with their associated arguments (nouns). Syntactic complexity was defined in two ways: in terms of the number of frames or phrases, and in terms of type of syntactic structure. The number of frames varied from 2 to 5 across sentences. Three basic types of syntactic structures were included: simple active affirmative declarative sentences (SAAD), co-ordinate sentences, and relative clause sentences. Examples of each of these types of sentences are given in Table 1. Sentences included under each type varied in number of words, frames, and propositions, and these variables were varied orthogonally as much as possible.

The sentences were presented as if they were said by a Snoopy puppet, who hugged the child after each repetition. The child listened to the sentence twice before repeating it, and the repetitions were taperecorded for subsequent scoring.

TABLE 1
Types of Sentences in Imitation Task

Simple Active Affirmative Declarative (SAAD)
a. The bear sits down.
    (4 words, 1 proposition, 2 frames)
b. The clown takes his brother for a drive by train.
    (10 words, 4 propositions, 5 frames)

Co-ordinate
 Forward reduction (predicate co-ordination)
a. The huge lion licks the elephant and walks away.
    (9 words, 3 propositions, 4 frames)
 Backward reduction (subject co-ordination)
b. The giraffe and the tiger find some lovely food.
    (9 words, 3 propositions, 4 frames)

Relative Clause
 Relative pronoun the subject of the embedded clause
a. The little zebra that is nibbling the monkey sneezes.
    (9 words, 3 propositions, 4 frames)
 Relative pronoun the object of the embedded clause
b. The man that the warm baby hugs strokes friendly animals.
    (10 words, 4 propositions, 5 frames)

Each sentence repetition was scored for each sentential variable separately: words, propositions, frames, and syntactic structure. Each score was based on the proportion of the variable retained in the imitation in order to equate the measures of the different variables, e.g. number of words versus syntactic structure. Thus, a child could receive a score of 0.5 for retaining half of the words in a sentence and 0.5 for retaining half of the syntactic structure. Correlational analyses were first computed between the scores on each of these separate variables and the other measures (Age, Mean Length of Utterance, Word Span). Because the pattern of correlations was the same across variables, only the total sentence imitation scores, summed across the four variables, were used in the final analyses. These total scores are a sum of proportion correct across the 22 sentences for each of the four variables, giving a maximum score of 88.

Analysis of Speech Sample.   The total number of usable utterances for each child ranged from 78 to 179, with a mean of 129. A usable utterance was an utterance containing not more than one doubtful word and no unintelligible words. To segment utterances, the cues used were long pauses, intonation, intervening turns by the experimenter, and the presence or absence of connectives.

Three estimates of language complexity were calculated originally for each speech sample: mean length of utterance (MLU), syntactic complexity, and semantic complexity. Detailed information about these estimates is available in Blake and Quartaro (1990), and the relationship between two of these measures and another commonly used measure of grammatical complexity, LARSP, is analysed in Blake, Quartaro, and Onorati (1993). Because our measure of MLU was highly correlated with both syntactic and semantic complexity ($r = 0.89$, $P < 0.001$ and $r = 0.81$, $P < 0.001$, respectively) in this sample, only MLU was used in this study.

The rules used to calculate MLU were extended considerably beyond the suggestive outline in Brown (1973, p. 54). In general, our rules were based on the principle of contrast, such that each child was credited with a particular inflection or morpheme if the necessary contrast was present in his/her speech sample. Thus, for example, the past tense of an irregular verb was credited if the present tense of that verb occurred in the sample. Also, children who used the uncontracted form of the copula were also credited with the contracted form. The extension of Brown's rules resulted in the crediting of more irregular forms, thus making our measure more appropriate for children at later stages of syntax (cf. Klee & Paul, 1981). However, we followed Brown's suggestion of counting as one morpheme compound expressions that appeared to be an unanalysed unit for the child (e.g. frying pan), i.e. when the probability of using each part of the expression independently was low.

Reliability for calculation of MLU was determined by having a second judge listen to half of the samples, revise the transcriptions, and recalculate MLU. For these samples, agreement on MLU was 91%.

Results

The means and standard deviations for MLU, Sentence Imitation, and Word Span are presented in Table 2 for the whole group and for the subgroups of younger and older children. The correlations between Age, MLU, Sentence Imitation, and Word Span scores are presented in Table 3 for the whole group and the subgroups.

The mean MLU for the older group (4-year-olds) is 1.4 morphemes higher than that of the younger group (3-year-olds) and is significantly different, $t(29) = 4.96$, $P < 0.001$. The 4-year-olds' mean total Sentence Imitation score is 15.2 points higher than the 3-year-olds' mean total Sentence Imitation score, and also significantly different, $t(29) = 3.41$, $P < 0.002$. Their mean Word Span is only 0.33 higher, however, and not significantly different.

The correlations indicate that Age was significantly related to both language measures and to Word Span, and that Sentence Imitation is significantly related to both MLU and Word Span. For the whole group, MLU and Word Span were not significantly correlated. The separate correlations for the younger and older children show that this is true only for the older group. For the younger group, MLU and Word Span were significantly correlated. In fact, for the older group, MLU was not significantly correlated with any of the other variables, including Age.

TABLE 2
Means and Standard Deviations for Language and Memory Measures for Whole Group and Subgroups: Experiment 1

	MLU	Sentence Imitation[a]	Word Span
Whole Group			
Means	4.15	45.21	3.32
s.d.	(1.04)	(19.12)	(0.70)
Younger Group			
Means	3.38	36.87	3.14
s.d.	(0.84)	(15.33)	(0.66)
Older Group			
Means	4.78	52.09	3.47
s.d.	(0.73)	(19.58)	(0.72)

[a]Out of a possible score of 88.000.

TABLE 3

Pearson Product-Moment Correlations between Age, Language Measures, and Memory Span for Whole Group and Subgroups: Experiment 1

	MLU	Sentence Imitation	Word Span
Whole Group			
Age	0.68****	0.67****	0.51**
MLU	–	0.56***	0.28
Sentence Imitation		–	0.67****
Younger Group			
Age	0.64**	0.70**	0.59*
MLU	–	0.65**	0.66**
Sentence Imitation		–	0.68**
Older Group			
Age	0.10	0.63**	0.56*
MLU	–	0.26	0.30
Sentence Imitation		–	0.63**

*$P < 0.05$; **$P < 0.01$; ***$P < 0.001$; ****$P < 0.0001$.

To determine if Word Span was a significant predictor of the variance in the language measures in addition to that accounted for by Age, hierarchical regression analyses were conducted separately on MLU and on Sentence Imitation scores. These are reported in Table 4.

For the group as a whole, not surprisingly given the correlational results, only Age was a significant predictor of MLU. When the regressions were conducted on the two age groups separately, however, Age and Word Span showed substantial shared variance for the younger group, only. For this group, Age, by itself, accounted for 41% of the variance in MLU, whereas Word Span accounted for 44% of the variance. (This can be seen by squaring the correlations on Table 3.) When Age and Word Span were entered together (see Table 4), they accounted for 54% of the variance, although neither was a significant independent predictor. Thus, adding Age to the regression equation with Word Span resulted in an additional 10% of the variance being accounted for (54% − 44%), whereas adding Word Span to the regression equation with Age resulted in an additional 13% of the variance being accounted for (54% − 41%). For the older group, Age and Word Span, when entered together, accounted for 16% of the variance in MLU; the model was not significant.

With respect to Sentence Imitation scores for the whole group, both Age and Word Span, when entered alone, accounted for 45% of the variance, as is clear from squaring the correlations on Table 3. When entered together, an additional 15% of the variance was accounted for (see Table

TABLE 4
Results of Regression Analyses: Experiment 1

Independent Variable	R^2 for Model	F-value	Prob. > F	t-value for variable	Prob. > t
MLU					
Whole Group					
Age	0.46	12.04	0.0002	4.48	0.0001
Word Span				−0.55	0.59
Younger Group					
Age	0.54	6.33	0.02	1.53	0.16
Word Span				1.70	0.12
Older Group					
Age	0.16	1.29	0.31	1.19	0.26
Word Span				−1.56	0.14
Sentence Imitation					
Whole Group					
Age	0.60	20.79	0.0001	3.19	0.004
Word Span				3.20	0.003

4), and both variables were significant predictors. Thus, both Word Span and Age were important predictors of Sentence Imitation scores for the whole group and of MLU for the 3-year-olds only.

Discussion

These results replicated the findings of Case and Kurland (1980) that word span predicts the complexity of sentence imitation and, furthermore, extended this finding to younger preschool children. The relationship between memory span and sentence imitation cannot simply be attributable to age, but both word span and age are significant predictors and account for unique variance in sentence imitation scores. They also have a great deal of shared variance. Although one can then interpret this as meaning that the relationship between memory span and sentence imitation is, in part, due to age, it can also be argued that the reverse is also true, i.e. that much of the age effect in imitation scores is attributable to memory span. This interpretation is appealing because memory span is a much more specific variable than the global factor of age.

Sentence imitation is often used in studies of language acquisition as a measure of the child's mastery of grammatical structure on the grounds that sentence imitation can tap comprehension of structure (e.g. Menyuk,

1971). Thus, we have viewed our sentence imitation task as a measure of language complexity. In contrast, the word span task has no linguistic structure. Only the two very simplest SAAD sentences in the sentence imitation task overlapped with the word span task in terms of number of words, and the number of words retained was only a part of the scoring for the sentence imitation task. The two tasks are undeniably similar, however, in that both involve a repetition component. However, correct repetition in the sentence imitation task implies an understanding of the relation between the words, whereas in the word span task it does not.

The relationship between memory span and language was not limited to measures that share repetition requirements, however. Word span was as good a predictor as age of the complexity of spontaneous language production in the younger group of children and increased the amount of variance accounted for when combined with age as a predictor. The measure of spontaneous language chosen was MLU, calculated using rules to increase its applicability to older preschool children. Despite these modified rules, MLU has been found not to capture the increasing syntactic complexity of spontaneous language beyond a score of MLU 4.5 (Blake et al., 1993). Thus, it might be argued that memory span and MLU were not related in the older group of children because MLU is not a good measure of spontaneous language complexity in these children. However, in other analyses on older preschool children, memory span was related neither to the longest sentences found in these children's speech samples nor to a measure of syntax based on phrases or frames, as used in the sentence imitation task and also by Case and Kurland (1980). The latter syntactic measure, in contrast to MLU, *has* been found to capture the increasing syntactic complexity found in the spontaneous speech of older preschool children (Blake et al., 1993). It appears clear that memory span is related to spontaneous language complexity only in children at the early stages of language. For the younger group, there is a remarkable coincidence in the mean scores of memory span and MLU, reminiscent of Case and Kurland's (1980) findings for memory span and number of imitated phrases. This coincidence disappears for the older group, whose MLU exceeds their memory span. It is not simply that the unit of programming becomes larger, because as stated earlier, a phrasal measure is not related to word span either. It appears that for older children, increasing mastery of linguistic rules enables greater automaticity of speech programming, thereby obviating memory constraints, at least in spontaneous production. In structured and complex language tasks, such as our language imitation task, in which children's language processing is presumably stretched to its limit, memory span appears to limit performance even in older preschool children. In elementary schoolchildren, more complex span measures have been found to predict very sophisticated language abilities, such as level of metaphor interpretation and conjunction use (Johnson, Fabian, & Pascual-Leone, 1989).

To confirm the relationship between memory span and MLU at the early stages of syntax, as the sample of younger children in this experiment is small, a second experiment was conducted. Only young preschool children were included to ensure that their MLUs would be below 4.5. In addition, to examine the possibility that the relationship found between memory span and MLU might be entirely due to an underlying mental ability variable, or g-factor, a measure of intelligence was also administered.

EXPERIMENT 2

Method

Subjects. The subjects were 23 children, 8 females and 15 males, ranging in age from 23 to 38 months (mean age of 32 months). They attended one of four daycare centres in Metropolitan Toronto, and their parents spoke only English.

Tasks and Procedure. The language, memory, and mental ability measures were administered on different days by three different experimenters who visited with the children before testing them. All testing was done individually in a separate quiet room in each daycare centre. A somewhat longer speech sample was recorded from each child (30–40 minutes) than in Experiment 1.

The Word Span task was administered as in Experiment 1 except that only single syllable animal names were used, and that 4 trials instead of 3 were given at each span size. The names used were dog, snake, bee, bear, sheep, horse, fox, duck, hen, frog, worm, bird, fish, fly, pig, rat, mouse, goat, cat, and cow. Again, these names were presented in a random order but occurred only once in a trial and approximately equally often across trials.

Finally, the Merrill-Palmer Scale of Mental Tests (Stutsman, 1948) was administered. This scale consists of language measures and nonverbal measures such as formboards, picture puzzles, pegboards, block-building, and matching tests. Many of the latter are contained in colourful boxes, and the child is often permitted to choose the next test from these boxes. The scoring allows for refusals and omissions. Because of this flexibility of administration and its engaging aspects, this test is relatively easy to administer to 2-year-olds and was selected for these reasons.

Data Analysis. The total number of usable utterances in the speech samples ranged from 128 to 399, with a mean of 280. Reliability on the scoring of MLU was 0.99 based on 22% of the samples.

The score on the Word Span task was the number of the highest series for which at least half of the trials were correct. The Merrill-Palmer test was scored according to manual instructions, and mental ages corresponding to the raw scores were used in the analyses.

Results

The means and standard deviations for MLU, Word Span, and Mental Age are given in Table 5, and the correlations among these measures and Chronological Age (CA) in Table 6. These children are somewhat younger than the younger group of Experiment 1 (by 4.6 months); their mean MLU is 0.4 less, but their mean Word Span is only 0.1 less. MLU and Word Span were both significantly correlated with CA, Word Span more highly than MLU, and they were also significantly correlated with Mental Age (MA), to approximately the same extent. MLU and Word Span were also highly and significantly correlated with each other. CA and MA tended to be significantly correlated ($P < 0.07$).

Hierarchical regression analyses were conducted to compare CA, MA, and Word Span as predictors of MLU. When entered alone, as is clear from the correlations, CA accounted for 21% of the variance in MLU, MA

TABLE 5
Means and (Standard Deviations) for MLU, Word Span, and Mental Age: Experiment 2

	MLU	*Word Span*	*Mental Age*
Means	2.96	3.04	42.57
s.d.	(0.80)	(0.77)	(8.32)

TABLE 6
Pearson Product-Moment Correlations between Chronological Age (CA), Mental Age (MA), MLU, and Word Span: Experiment 2

	MA	*MLU*	*Word Span*
CA	0.38	0.46*	0.70***
MA	–	0.49*	0.42*
MLU		–	0.66***

*$P < 0.05$; **$P < 0.01$; ***$P < 0.001$.

TABLE 7
Results of Regression Analyses: Experiment 2

Independent Variables MLU	R^2 for Model	F-value	Prob. > F	t-value for variable	Prob. > t
CA	0.43	7.62	0.004	−0.02	0.98
Word Span				2.78	0.01
MA	0.49	9.56	0.001	1.48	0.15
Word Span				3.10	0.006
CA	0.49	6.08	0.004	−0.21	0.83
MA				1.46	0.16
Word Span				2.44	0.02

for 24%, and Word Span for 43%. On Table 7 are presented the results of three models: Word Span entered with CA, Word Span entered with MA, and Word Span entered with both CA and MA. In all three cases, the model is significant, but only Word Span is a significant predictor. CA entered after Word Span essentially adds nothing to the 43% accounted for by Word Span alone (see earlier), whereas Word Span entered after CA accounts for an additional 22% of the variance (43% − 21%). Thus, the original 21% of the variance accounted for by CA is entirely shared with Word Span due to the high correlation between these variables. MA entered after Word Span adds only 6% to the variance accounted for (49% − 43%). In contrast, Word Span entered after MA accounts for 25% additional variance (49% − 24%). When CA is added to the model with MA and Word Span, the additional variance accounted for is only 0.1% (49.0% − 48.9%). Thus, it is clear that among these three variables, Word Span is by far the most powerful predictor, that MA accounts for a small amount of additional variance, and that CA adds essentially nothing.

Discussion

These results replicated the findings of the first experiment and are, in fact, stronger in demonstrating that memory span is a better predictor of spontaneous language complexity than age. Furthermore, the relationship between memory span and MLU was *not* due to mental age. Only memory span was a significant predictor of MLU, with CA not contributing to the variance accounted for beyond its shared variance with word span, and MA contributing only marginally. Thus, most of the variation in MLU that is related to chronological age or mental age is mediated by memory span.

As in Experiment 1 for younger children, the means for memory span and MLU coincided in Experiment 2, this time almost exactly.

The age range for the younger children in Experiment 1 was 9 months, and in Experiment 2 it was 15 months. It might be argued, then, that memory span was a more powerful predictor because the age range was restricted. However, the range in memory span scores was only 2 to 4 for both the younger children of Experiment 1 and the children in Experiment 2. In addition, the range in mental age scores was larger than in age (28 months), and MA was not a significant predictor in the equation with memory span.

Another caution might be that the samples are small, particularly with regard to the analyses of MLU in younger children. However, the fact that Experiment 2 replicates Experiment 1 makes the findings more impressive.

We would argue that the findings of Experiments 1 and 2 support the notion of a programming constraint on productive language complexity and that such a constraint is general in that it applies to both imitative and spontaneous measures of language. However, the failure of word span to predict spontaneous language complexity in 4-year-old children seems to indicate an age limit on the operation of a memory constraint, at least with respect to MLU. When children become proficient at producing complex sentences by means of such devices as conjunctions and relative clauses, it is likely that the programming of utterances changes such that attentive processing of each morphemic unit is not required. At the early stages of syntax, when more effortful attentional processing of morphemes is required, spontaneous productive complexity appears to be limited by memory span. The relationship we have demonstrated is correlational, however. Some might argue that the reverse is true (e.g. Hulme, Thomson, Muir, & Lawrence, 1984), i.e. that higher MLUs, and concomitantly better articulatory abilities, enhance memory span. If this is true, then one would expect this relationship to hold for older children, i.e. that their more complex spontaneous language would lead to higher memory spans. We have demonstrated that this is not the case, as MLU and memory span were not related in older children and 4-year-olds did not have higher memory spans than 3-year-olds in Experiment 1.

The importance of articulatory abilities is also stressed in Baddeley's (1986) model of working memory, which includes an articulatory loop made up of a phonological store and a rehearsal buffer involving subvocal articulation. Sensitivity to word length and to phonemic similarity has been used as evidence of the activation of this articulatory loop. Baddeley (1986) hypothesises that all developmental increase in memory span can be explained in terms of the articulatory loop, without recourse to possible changes in the capacity of a central executive. Thus, according to this model, speech rate increases with age, leading to faster rehearsal and improved memory. Evidence supporting the operation of an articulatory loop, or subvocal rehearsal, in older preschool children was found by Hitch, Halliday, Schaafstal, and Heffernan (1991), but only when the stimuli were labelled at presentation. Gathercole and Adams (1992) claim further that phonological skills in working memory and their relation to language acquisition are evident as young as 3 years, in that accuracy of repetition of both words and nonwords of different lengths was related to scores on the British Picture Vocabulary Scale.

Although phonological skills are undeniably important in vocabulary acquisition from an early age, it is doubtful that rehearsal is used by preschool children (Kail, 1990). The phonological skills important in vocabulary acquisition must, therefore, pertain to phonological representation, in general, and, perhaps, to the capacity of phonological storage (see also Gathercole & Baddeley, 1990). For this reason, we prefer a more general capacity model, not tied to an articulatory loop, although our tasks and results do not allow us to make claims about constraints beyond language production. Support for a general capacity model like M-power (Pascual-Leone, 1987) would require prediction of our language measures from a nonverbal measure of memory. It is clear, however, that a purely speech-based model, which stresses articulatory rate, misses what we believe to be the essential abstract nature of the constraint on linguistic rules and structure, i.e. on underlying phonological, syntactic, and semantic representation.

Just and Carpenter's (1992) capacity model is similarly limited to language comprehension. In addition, they found that constraints were manifested primarily when processing demands exceeded capacity, i.e. on difficult object-relative sentences. Our results also indicated that span predicted imitation of sentences including such complex constructions among older preschool children. In contrast, spontaneous language production did not apparently tax the resources of these older preschool children to the same extent. Another interpretation of these task differences in constraints is that spontaneous language occurs in "facilitating" contexts, whereas sentences presented for imitation may be "misleading" in their structure, thereby requiring greater activation (Pascual-Leone, 1987).

In conclusion, we have viewed our results as supporting a model of capacity constraints on language production. However, this research is correlational. Further research is needed to strengthen the case for a causal interpretation that it is processing capacity that underlies early language acquisition. Undoubtedly, later, when language is quite fully developed in most respects, between 5 and 7 years, it can, in turn, be used effectively to enhance memory.

REFERENCES

Baddeley, A.D. (1986). *Working memory*. Oxford University Press.

Blake, J., & Quartaro, G. (1990). *Manual for analyzing the complexity of spontaneous speech samples*. Toronto: York University Reports, Department of Psychology.

Blake, J., Quartaro, G., & Onorati, S. (1993). Evaluating quantitative measures of grammatical complexity in spontaneous speech samples. *Journal of Child Language, 20*, 139–152.

Bloom, L., & Lahey, M. (1978). *Language development and language disorders*. New York: Wiley.

Braine, M.D.S. (1974). Length constraints, reduction rules, and holophrastic processes in children's word combinations. *Journal of Verbal Learning and Verbal Behavior, 13*, 448–456.

Brown, R. (1973). *A first language: The early stages*. Cambridge, MA: Harvard University Press.

Brown, R., and Bellugi, U. (1964). Three processes in the child's acquisition of syntax. In E.H. Lenneberg (Ed.), *New directions in the study of language* (pp. 131–161). Cambridge, MA: MIT Press.

Brownell, C.A. (1988). Combinatorial skills: Converging developments over the second year. *Child Development, 59*, 675–685.

Case, R., & Kurland, M. (1980). A new measure for determining children's subjective organization of speech. *Journal of Experimental Child Psychology, 30*, 206–222.

Clark, H.H. (1973). The language-as-fixed effect fallacy: A critique of language statistics in psychological research. *Journal of Verbal Learning and Verbal Behavior, 12*, 335–359.

Daneman, M., & Case, R. (1981). Syntactic form, semantic complexity, and short-term memory: Influences on children's acquisition of new linguistic structures. *Developmental Psychology, 17*, 367–378.

Gathercole, S.E., & Adams, A.-M. (1992). *Phonological working memory in very young children*. Paper presented at the Vth European Conference on Developmental Psychology, Seville, September 1992.

Gathercole, S.E., & Baddeley, A.D. (1990). Phonological memory deficits in language disordered children: Is there a causal connection? *Journal of Memory and Language, 29*, 336–360.

Greenfield, P.M., & Smith, G.H. (1976). *The structure of communication in early language development*. New York: Academic Press.

Hitch, G.J., Halliday, S., Schaafstal, A.M., & Heffernan, T.M. (1991). Speech, "inner speech," and the development of short-term memory: Effects of picture-labeling on recall. *Journal of Experimental Child Psychology, 51*, 220–234.

Hulme, C., Thomson, N., Muir, C., & Lawrence, A. (1984). Speech rate and the development of short-term memory span. *Journal of Experimental Child Psychology, 38*, 241–253.

Johnson, J., Fabian, V., & Pascual-Leone, J. (1989). Quantitative hardware-stages that constrain language development. *Human Development, 32*, 245–271.

Just, M.A., & Carpenter, P.A. (1992). A capacity theory of comprehension: Individual differences in working memory. *Psychological Review, 99*, 122–149.

Kail, R. (1990). *The development of memory in children* (3rd edn.). New York: Freeman.

Klee, T.M., & Paul, R. (1981). A comparison of six structural analysis procedures: A case study. In J.F. Miller (Ed), *Assessing language production in children: Experimental procedures* (pp. 73–110). Baltimore: University Park Press.

Kushnir, C. (1986). *Identifying cognitive abilities in language-delayed children*. Unpublished PhD dissertation, York University, Canada.

Menyuk, P. (1971). *The acquisition and development of language*. Englewood Cliffs, NJ: Prentice Hall.

Menyuk, P., & Looney, P. (1976). A problem of language disorder: Length versus structure. In D.M. Morehead & A.E. Morehead (Eds), *Normal and deficient child language* (pp. 259–279). Baltimore: University Park Press.

Pascual-Leone, J. (1987). Organismic processes for neo-Piagetian theories: A dialectical causal account of cognitive development. *International Journal of Psychology*, *22*, 531–570.

Ramer, A.L.H. (1977). The development of syntactic complexity. *Journal of Psycholinguistic Research*, *6*, 145–161.

Stutsman, R. (1948). *The Merrill-Palmer Scale of Mental Tests*. Chicago: Stoelting.

Todd, P. (1982). Tagging after red herrings: Evidence against the processing capacity explanation in child language. *Journal of Child Language*, *9*, 99–114.

INTERNATIONAL JOURNAL OF BEHAVIORAL DEVELOPMENT, 1994, *17* (1), 109–124

Working Memory and Reading: A Life-span Perspective

Linda S. Siegel

Ontario Institute for Studies in Education, Canada

The relationships among working memory, memory span, and reading skills were studied in 1266 individuals, aged 6–49. They were administered tests of word recognition, pseudoword decoding, reading comprehension, a working memory (listening span) task that required the simultaneous processing of syntax and the recall of linguistic information, and a short-term memory task that required the recall of rhyming or nonrhyming letters presented visually. The results indicated that there is a gradual growth in the development of working memory skills from ages 6 to 19 and a gradual decline after adolescence. The short-term memory task did not show a decline in performance among older individuals. On both of these memory tasks and at most of the age levels, individuals with a reading disability performed at significantly lower levels than individuals with normal reading skills. An important component of the development of reading skills appears to be memory for verbal information. Age-related declines in memory appear to be related to the processing demands of the task, which may affect the degree to which rehearsal strategies are possible within the task.

INTRODUCTION

The construct of working memory has been used to explain performance on a variety of cognitive tasks (e.g. Baddeley, 1983; Hitch, 1978). Working memory refers to a temporary storage of information while processing incoming data and retrieving information from long-term storage. Working

---

Requests for reprints should be sent to Linda S. Siegel, Department of Applied Psychology, Ontario Institute for Studies in Education, 252 Bloor Street West, Toronto, Ontario, Canada M5S 1V6.

This research was supported by a grant from the Natural Sciences and Engineering Research Council of Canada. The author wishes to thank Susan D'Souza, Jane Heintz-Grove, Maureen Heywood, Norman Himel, Sharon Smith, and George Toth for help with the data collection and analyses, the individuals who graciously participated in this study, and Letty Guirnela for secretarial assistance. This article was written while the author held a Senior Research Fellowship from the Ontario Mental Health Foundation.

---

memory can be conceptualised as a cognitive process in which certain bits of information are held in a memory store characterised by rapid decay while other bits are retrieved from long-term storage.

Working memory is composed of a central co-ordinating executive system and one or more subsidiary systems (e.g. Baddeley, 1983). The central executive is assumed to exert control functions, and the subsidiary systems are assumed to store specific information about items being processed, although there is some debate about the exact nature of the subsidiary systems (Reisberg, Rappaport, & O'Shaughnessy, 1984). Thus, working memory requires both the simultaneous processing of incoming information and the retrieval of other information. An important feature of working memory is that it has a limited capacity, so that if more demands are being made on the executive, there will be less processing space and cognitive energy available for the subsidiary systems.

Working memory is assumed to play an important role in reading (e.g. Baddeley, 1983; Baddeley, Logie, Nimmo-Smith, & Brereton, 1985; Daneman & Carpenter, 1980). During reading, the executive may be conceptualised as retrieving information about syntax, word meanings, and/or grapheme-phoneme conversion rules, while the subsidiary system retains the words, phrases, or sentences while they are being processed and for brief periods in order that longer units of text can be comprehended.

A particularly important feature of reading comprehension and one in which the concept of working memory may be critical, appears to be recall of the sentences that have been read. Daneman and Carpenter (1980) designed tasks to examine the interaction between sentence-processing skills and recall of items read. In these tasks, the individual was required to read or listen to a sentence and make a judgement about the truth of the statement and recall the last word of the sentences. As the number of words that the individual was required to remember increased, the demands on working memory were assumed to increase. The size of this sentence-based working memory span has been found to relate to reading comprehension as well as more specific aspects of text integration in adult readers (Daneman, 1987; Daneman & Carpenter, 1980, 1983). Therefore, one of the contributing factors to reading difficulties may be relatively poor working memory.

The study of individuals with difficulties in reading provides an opportunity to observe the influence of deficits in working memory on reading performance. To examine this issue, Siegel and Ryan (1989a) studied working memory in normal and disabled readers, ages 7–13, using a task based on one developed by Daneman and Carpenter (1980). The disabled readers performed significantly more poorly than the normal readers on this task, indicating significant difficulties with working memory in the disabled readers. Similar difficulties with working memory in poor readers have been noted in Chinese (So & Siegel, 1992), Hebrew (Geva & Siegel, 1991), and Portuguese (Da Fontoura & Siegel, in press).

In addition to difficulties with working memory, children with reading problems experience difficulty with the phonemic coding process in short-term memory (e.g. Byrne & Shea, 1979; Liberman, Shankweiler, Liberman, Fowler, & Fischer, 1977; Mann, Liberman, & Shankweiler, 1980; Mark, Shankweiler, Liberman, & Fowler, 1977; Shankweiler, Liberman, Mark, Fowler, & Fischer, 1979; Siegel & Linder, 1984). Short-term memory tasks, unlike working memory tasks, typically do not require simultaneous processing and transformation of incoming information. In tasks involving short-term memory, young poor readers have been found to be less sensitive to phonemic similarity than normal readers. For example, Shankweiler et al. (1979) found that young poor readers, unlike good readers of the same age, did not show any differences in the recall of rhyming (e.g. B, C, D) and nonrhyming (e.g. Q, R, S) letters. If this pattern of performance is indicative of failure to use a phonemic code, and if this failure is a pervasive characteristic of reading difficulties, then we would expect that older children with reading disabilities might display the same pattern. However, Johnston (1982) and Siegel and Linder (1984) found that 9- to 14-year-old children with reading disabilities showed a phonemic-confusability effect with an auditory presentation of stimuli, and Bisanz, Das, and Mancini (1984) have shown that Grade 4 and Grade 6 poor readers showed phonemic-confusability effects for letters under conditions of delayed recall. Olson, Davidson, Kliegl, and Davies (1984) found that older disabled readers, as opposed to younger disabled readers, showed susceptibility to phonemic-confusability in a recognition memory task involving rhyming and nonrhyming words. In addition, Hall, Ewing, Tinzmann, and Wilson (1981) have found that adult poor readers did show sensitivity to phonemic similarity and had less difficulty in recalling non-rhyming than rhyming letters when an oral, as opposed to a written, response was required. However, a problem in integrating this evidence is the variation in methods across studies. The present study was designed to examine the nature of the deficit in phonemic coding in short-term memory in reading disabled individuals through childhood, adolescence, and adulthood in a single investigation.

An additional aspect of the present study was to assess the relationship between working memory and reading during childhood, adolescence, and adulthood. A maturational increase during childhood in the size of working memory has been postulated (e.g. Case, Kurland, & Goldberg, 1982; Hitch & Halliday, 1983; Pascual-Leone, 1970). The present study was designed to study the development of working memory in relation to verbal information across a 43 year age span. We are also interested in determining whether individuals with less accurate reading skills would show difficulties with working memory.

Declines with increasing age in working memory in adulthood have been noted in a number of studies such as Babcock and Salthouse (1990), Hartley (1989), Light and Anderson (1985), Salthouse, Mitchell, Skovronek, and Babcock (1989), and Stine and Wingfield (1987), and in memory for digits in a dichotic listening task in which information is delivered to two channels simultaneously (e.g. Clark & Knowles, 1973; Craik, 1965; Inglis & Caird, 1963; Mackay & Inglis, 1963; Schonfield, Trueman, & Kline, 1972). (See Salthouse, 1990, for a detailed review.) The declines in working memory are particularly pronounced for the elderly (e.g. Gick, Craik, & Morris, 1988; Light & Anderson, 1985; Morris, Gick, & Craik, 1988; Salthouse & Babcock, 1991; Stine, Wingfield, & Poon, 1986; Wingfield, Stine, Lahar, & Aberdeen, 1988; Wright, 1981). Less complex short-term memory tasks that merely involve a recall of digits and do simultaneous processing and transformation of information do not show marked decline with age (e.g. Caird, 1966; Craik, 1977).

Thus, an additional purpose of the present study was to examine the development of memory skills in children, adolescents, and adults in a complex working memory task and a simpler short-term memory-span task that involved immediate memory span without concurrent processing demands. It was expected that the working memory task would show greater declines in adulthood with increasing age than the short-term memory task, which had minimal concurrent demands and allowed the possibility of rehearsal. Although it was expected that there would be differences between normal readers and reading disabled individuals in childhood, little is known about the developmental course of these differences in adolescence and adulthood. Study of the course development of these memory processes is facilitated by the use of the same tasks through a 43 year age span from childhood to adulthood; apparently the present study is unique in this respect.

METHOD

Subjects

There were 1266 subjects in this sample, 843 individuals with normal reading skills and 423 individuals with a reading disability. Some of these individuals had participated in one of a series of published and unpublished studies (e.g. Shafrir & Siegel, 1992; Siegel, 1988, 1992, Siegel & Ryan, 1988, 1989b). They came from schools, colleges, universities, community agencies or were volunteers from the community. The sample was predominantly middle class, although there were some individuals from the lower socioeconomic class. All were educated in English, and had English as their major language. The subjects were defined as reading disabled if they had scores ≤ 25 percentile on the Wide Range Achievement Test (J.R. Jastak & S.R. Jastak, 1978; Jastak & Wilkinson, 1984) and an IQ ≥ 80 on an abbreviated version of the WISC-R (Sattler, 1982; Wechsler, 1974) or WAIS-R (Silverstein, 1982; Wechsler, 1981) that included the Vocabulary and Block Design subtests. A rationale for this definition is provided in Siegel (1989) and Siegel and Heaven (1986). Individuals with neurological problems, emotional difficulties, inadequate educational opportunities, English as a second language, severe behavioural deficits, and sensory deficits were excluded.

This sample was arbitrarily divided into 13 age groups. These age groups and the numbers of subjects in the reading disabled (first number) and normal reader (second number) groups are as follows: 6 years (20, 58), 7 years (37, 93), 8 years (53, 93), 9 years (35, 106), 10 years (38, 73), 11 years (16, 61), 12 years (25, 30), 13–14 years (31, 48), 15–16 years (14, 43), 17–19 years (18, 43), 20–29 years (81, 106), 30–39 years (43, 57), and 40–49 years (12, 32). A smaller sample ($N = 962$) was administered the letter span task, with proportionally smaller numbers in each age group.

Reading Tests

The reading subtest *Wide Range Achievement Test* (WRAT—J.R. Jastak & S.R. Jastak, 1978; WRAT-R Jastak & Wilkinson, 1984) requires the individual to read isolated words.

The *Stanford Reading Comprehension Test* (Gardner, Rudman, Karlsen, & Merwin, 1982) involves the silent reading of a series of graded paragraphs and answering multiple choice questions. For individuals 18 years and older, the Nelson–Denny Reading Comprehension Test (Brown, Bennett, & Hanna, 1981) was used. The format of the Nelson–Denny Test is similar to the Stanford Reading Test.

Tasks

Working Memory (Listening Span). The working memory task was modelled on the procedure developed by Daneman and Carpenter (1980). The subject sentences were presented aurally with the final word missing. The task was to supply the missing word and to repeat all the missing words from the set. There were three trials at each set size or level (2, 3, 4, and 5). Examples of sentences were: "In summer it is very _____"; "People go to see monkeys in a _____"; "With dinner we sometimes eat bread and

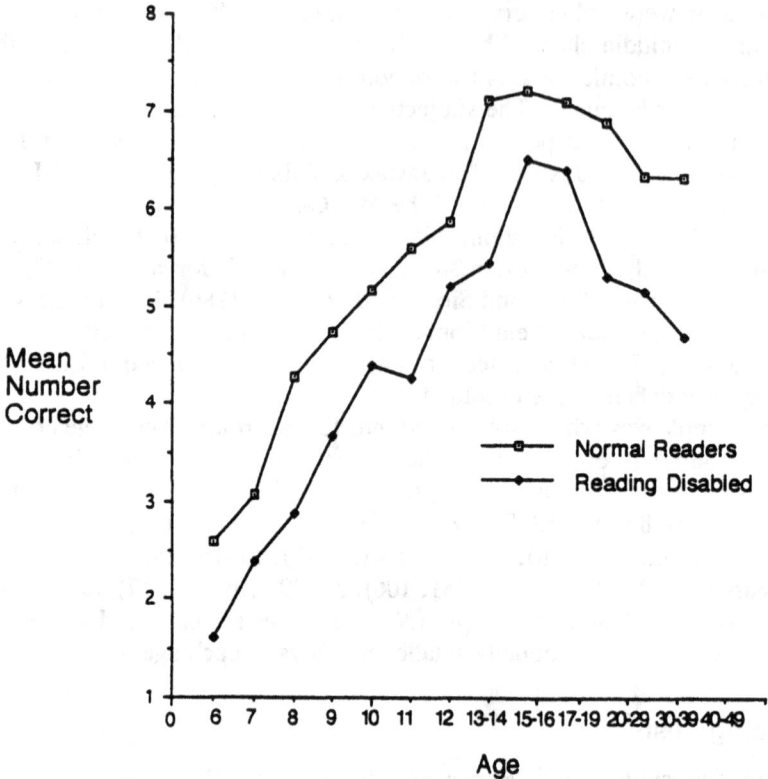

FIG. 1.   Mean number correct on the working memory task for the reading disabled and normal readers.

_____". The child was then required to repeat the three words that he or she selected, in this case *hot, zoo, butter*, in the same order that the sentences had been presented. Task administration was stopped when the individual failed all the items at one level. To calculate the total score, one point was awarded for each set in which all the words were given in the correct order. To minimise word-finding problems, the sentences were chosen so that the word was virtually predetermined. None of the individuals experienced any difficulty in supplying the missing word.

Short-term Memory.   The short-term memory task was similar to those used by Shankweiler et al. (1979) but with some minor procedural differences. For this task the individuals were shown cards with five letters on them. Half of the sets had rhyming letters, B, C, D, G, P, T, V (the Z had to be eliminated from the rhyming sets because it is pronounced "zed" in the Canadian dialect), and half of the sets were composed of nonrhyming

TABLE 1
Mean Number Correct (Maximum = 12) on the Working
Memory Task

Age	Reading Disabled		Normally Achieving	
	Mean	s.d.	Mean	s.d.
6	1.6	1.5	2.6	1.7
7	2.4	1.5	3.1	1.6
8	2.9	2.1	4.3	1.9
9	3.7	2.1	4.7	1.9
10	4.4	2.0	5.2	2.1
11	4.3	3.0	5.6	2.3
12	5.2	1.8	5.9	1.7
13–14	5.5	3.2	7.1	2.7
15–16	6.5	2.1	7.2	1.9
17–19	6.3	1.8	7.8	2.0
20–29	5.2	1.8	7.0	2.6
30–39	5.2	1.6	6.5	2.2
40–49	4.4	2.4	6.3	2.6

letters, e.g. H, K, L, Q, R, S, W. (Y was included in the Shankweiler et al. (1979) study but eliminated from the nonrhyming sets in this study.) There were seven trials of each type of stimuli, and the order was intermixed and determined randomly. The stimuli were presented for 3 seconds, and then the cards were removed. The individual was required to write down the letters that had been on the card. The maximum scores were 35 for the rhyming and nonrhyming sets. Only letters recalled in the correct serial position of each trial were scored as correct.

Some subjects were given only one of the tasks; some were administered two tasks. Of the individuals who had both tasks, approximately half of each age group had the working memory task first, the other had the short-term memory task first. The subjects were administered the WRAT Reading subtest, parts of the WAIS or WISC-R, the working memory (or short-term memory) task, a number of reading and spelling tasks that lasted 30 minutes, and then the memory task that they had not been administered previously.

RESULTS

The mean scores on the working memory task for the normal readers and the reading disabled group at each age are shown in Fig. 1 and Table 1. An ANOVA on age level and group indicated significant effects of age $F(12,1240) = 88.68$, $P < 0.0001$, effects of group $F(1,1240) = 50.95$, $P < 0.0001$ and no significant interaction. As can be seen from the data presented in Fig. 1, there was an increase in working memory capacity for the normal readers until age 20 at which point, scores on this task start to decline. A similar pattern is evident for the reading disabled group although the rate of decline appears to be steeper in this group. Individual comparisons (t-tests) indicated that the normal reader group had higher scores than the reading disabled group at each age except at 12, 15–16, and 17–19. At 10 years, the difference between the two groups did not reach conventional levels of statistical significance ($P < 0.06$). In general, there were not significant differences between adjacent age groups but there were significant differences among groups separated by 2–5 age levels. For example, there were significant increases until age 20 and the 30–39 and 40–49 year old groups had significantly lower scores than the 17–19 year olds.

TABLE 2
Mean Number Correct (Maximum = 35) on the Short-Term Memory Task[a]

Age	Reading Disabled		Normally Achieving	
	Rhyming	Nonrhyming	Rhyming	Nonrhyming
6	9.0	11.2	11.0	14.4
	(4.7)	(6.3)	(4.4)	(7.5)
7	10.34	12.2	15.8	21.2
	(3.6)	(5.3)	(4.7)	(6.7)
8	13.2	17.0	18.4	24.2
	(5.0)	(6.4)	(6.6)	(7.1)
9	15.6	21.5	22.1	27.8
	(5.9)	(7.0)	(5.3)	(5.9)
10	17.8	21.4	21.9	27.2
	(5.6)	(6.8)	(5.5)	(6.0)
11	17.6	23.2	26.0	30.2
	(3.2)	(5.3)	(6.4)	(4.7)
12	21.4	26.5	25.7	29.7
	(3.5)	(4.9)	(4.7)	(4.2)
13–14	23.2	26.4	27.5	31.3
	(5.2)	(5.6)	(4.5)	(3.3)
15–16	25.8	30.1	28.6	32.0
	(5.8)	(4.5)	(3.3)	(2.9)
17–19	26.6	28.9	29.0	31.9
	(7.0)	(6.5)	(3.9)	(3.2)
20–29	25.0	28.4	29.7	32.6
	(5.3)	(4.3)	(4.2)	(3.0)
30–39	24.6	29.3	28.7	31.9
	(5.1)	(5.7)	(4.2)	(4.3)
40–49	23.8	25.7	28.2	32.2
	(6.4)	(6.0)	(4.7)	(3.2)

[a]Standard deviations are in parentheses.

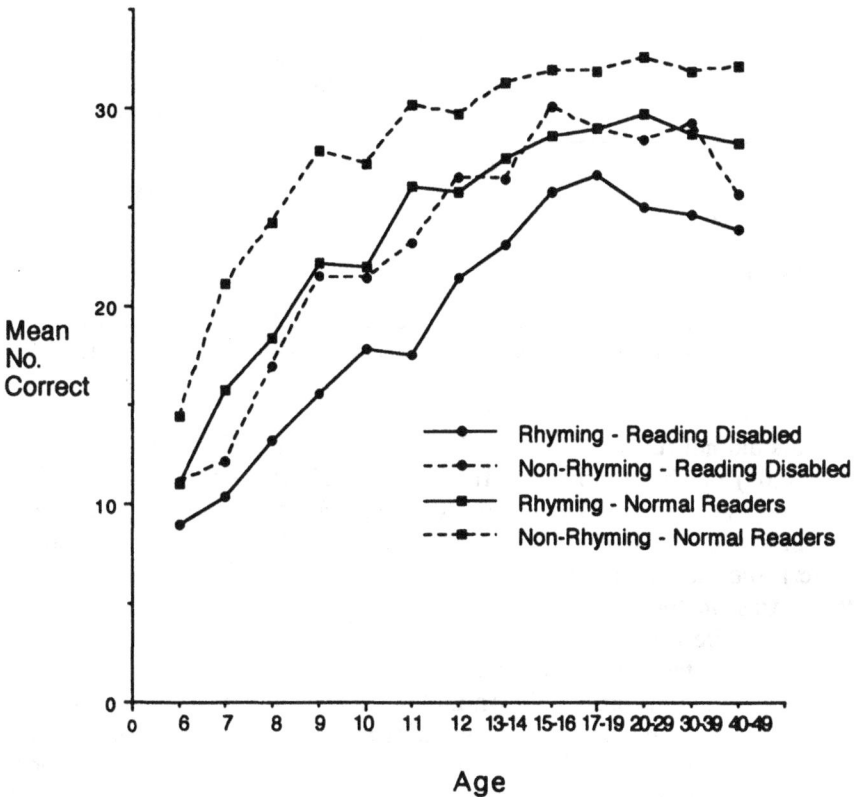

FIG. 2.   Mean number correct on the letter span task for the reading disabled and normal readers.

The results for the short-term memory (letter span) task are shown in Table 2 and Fig. 2. A three-way ANOVA was performed with two between-subjects variables of group (reading disabled vs. normal readers) and age (13 levels) and one within-subjects variable stimulus (rhyming vs. nonrhyming trials). There were significant effects of group, $F(1,936) = 207.24$, $P < 0.0001$, age, $F(12,936) = 105.51$, $P < 0.0001$, stimulus, $F(1,936) = 507.98$, $P < 0.0001$, a significant Group × Age interaction, $F(12,936) = 2.18$, $P < 0.02$, Age × Stimulus interaction, $F(12,936) = 2.61$, $P < 0.002$, and a significant Group × Age × Stimulus interaction, $F(12,936) = 1.96$, $P < 0.03$. As can be seen in Fig. 2, there were significant differences between the normal and disabled readers on both the rhyming and nonrhyming trials at every age except 6 years, which was probably due to a floor effect. Differences between the reading disabled and normal

TABLE 3
Correlations Among the Tasks[a,b]

	Short-term Memory	WRAT Reading	Reading Comprehension
Working Memory	0.44 (939)	0.23 (1266)	0.29 (535)
Short-term Memory		0.42 (962)	0.31 (533)
WRAT Reading			0.45 (535)

[a]Ns are indicated in parentheses. [b]All correlations were significant, $P < 0.0001$.

readers did not reach conventional levels of statistical significance ($0.10 > P > 0.05$) on the nonrhyming trials for the 15–16-year-olds and on the rhyming trials for the 17–19-year-old group. For each group at each age, except the 6-year-old reading disabled children (again, possibly a floor effect), the scores on the nonrhyming trials were significantly higher than the scores on the rhyming trials. In general, there were not significant differences between adjacent age levels but there were differences among groups separated by 1–4 age levels.

The correlations among the variables are shown in Table 3. As can be seen in Table 3, the scores on the working memory task and the short-term memory task were significantly but moderately correlated with the word recognition and reading comprehension and with each other.

DISCUSSION

There were differences between the reading disabled and the normal readers on the working memory task at most of the ages included in the study. Thus, the difficulties in working memory for individuals with reading problems extend beyond the period of childhood (as has been documented previously) to adolescence and adulthood. Although working memory is clearly not the only process that is important in reading (see Siegel, 1993a, 1993b, and Stanovich, 1988, for extended discussions of this issue), it is clearly one of the important ones. The correlations between the reading tasks and the memory tasks were statistically significant but moderate. For example, the present study found a correlation of 0.29 between reading comprehension and working memory. Daneman and Carpenter (1980) reported significant correlations ranging from 0.59 to 0.90 between a working memory test and various reading comprehension tests; however, the working memory task differed from the one used in the present study in that the task involved reading sentences. The working memory task in the present study involved listening to, not reading sentences, so that the reading and memory tasks are not as directly related. However, in the Daneman and Carpenter (1983) study, these correlations were between two reading tasks. However, Daneman and Carpenter did find that a listening span task was highly correlated with reading comprehension (rs ranged from 0.53 to 0.72). Light and Anderson (1985) found a correlation between a listening span measure (similar to Daneman & Carpenter, 1983) and a paragraph memory test of 0.3. This correlation is similar in magnitude to the one found in the present study. Unlike Daneman and Carpenter who used a university-based sample, the present study and Light and Anderson used a community-based sample. In addition, the relationship may not be a linear one in that very poor readers and very good readers may show, respectively, deficits or strengths in working memory and in the middle range of reading skill (the level of most of the individuals in this study), the relationship may not be as strong. Dividing the sample into poor readers and normally achieving readers did result in significant differences at most ages, indicating a relationship between reading ability and working memory. In addition, it should be noted that Cohen and Heath (1990) and Henry (this issue) provide evidence that individual differences in working memory are not related to articulation speed and proficiency, therefore differences in articulation speed probably are not the cause of the differences between the disabled and normal readers.

There were also significant differences at almost every age level, except late adolescence, between the reading disabled and normal readers on the short-term memory task. As this task involved phonological encoding and as disabled readers have difficulties in phonological processing (e.g. Bruck, 1990; Stanovich, 1988), it is not surprising that they had lower scores; however, this is the initial demonstration of this phenomenon in adults with reading disabilities. The absence of a different between the normally achieving and reading disabled on the memory tasks in late adolescence probably indicates that both groups were performing in an optimal manner at this age level. In addition, the results did not suggest, as had some previous studies, that disabled readers fail to make use of phonological coding because the disabled readers did have lower scores on the rhyming trials, indicating a phonemic similarity effect. Failures to find this effect in previous studies may have been a result of lack of statistical power. In any case, the disabled readers did appear to use some phonological coding in short-term memory but their short-term memory skills are significantly less adequate than normally achieving readers.

Both tasks showed increases in performance with increasing age up to age 15 and the working memory task showed a decline after age 20 whereas the short-term memory task did not. Some caution must be used in interpreting these differences as we do not know that the tasks measure the same components over the life span. The working memory task is a more complex one than the short-term memory because the working memory task requires the simultaneous processing and storage of information. Craik (1977, p. 391) has suggested: "There is much evidence that older subjects are especially penalised in situations where they must divide their attention: perhaps their capacity is largely taken up in 'programming' the division of attention leaving relatively little capacity to process the stimuli." Although this statement was qualified in a later publication (Morris et al., p. 366) where it was noted that "it seems possible that divided attention is too broad a category to treat as a unitary factor". Tasks that require greater processing demands show more decline with age (e.g. Gick et al., 1988; Morris et al., 1988; Salthouse, Rogan, & Prill, 1984; Spilich, 1983; Wright, 1981). The working memory task used in the present study requires a division of attention between the incoming stimulus and the previous trials; the short-term memory task does not, as only incoming information on a particular trial is relevant. These differences in task complexity may account for the differences between the tasks. In addition, the working memory task involved auditorily presented stimuli and the short-term memory task visually presented stimuli. These differences mean that caution must be used in interpreting the differences in the age trends in performance on the two tasks.

It is not possible to understand the mechanisms for the age-related decline in working memory on the basis of the data obtained in this study. However, Salthouse and Babcock (1991) have suggested that there may be declines with age at the rate at which information is activated (encoded) but not the rate at which it is lost. It may be that rehearsal helps the encoding process thus minimising age-related declines. In the working memory task, rehearsal of previous items may interfere with processing incoming information and therefore, there may be declines with age. However, the short-term memory task allows rehearsal so that there are no declines with age for normally achieving readers. The reading disabled individuals did show declines with age on the nonrhyming stimuli for which rehearsal is important so they may have a deficit in rehearsal.

Salthouse (1990) has proposed an hypothesis to account for task-related differences in the degree of memory decline with increasing age in adulthood. Specifically, he noted (1990, p. 109): "One hypothesis proposed to account for this pattern of results is that, because of smaller working-memory capacities, older adults are more likely than younger adults to lose the early information (from the initial frames) during the encoding and integration of later information (from subsequent frames)." Because of this loss of information in the initial frames, rehearsal becomes more difficult. The results of Salthouse, Babcock, and Shaw (1991) suggest that age-related decrements may be related to stimulus encoding which suggests rehearsal deficits.

In summary, deficits in working memory and in serial order recall are characteristic of disabled readers in childhood, adolescence, and adulthood. Working memory and short-term memory skills develop through adolescence but working memory skills show declines in adulthood whereas short-term memory skills do not, at least until age 50. Where rehearsal processes are possible and do not interfere with stimulus encoding, then age-related declines in adulthood in memory processes are not apparent, at least until age 50.

REFERENCES

Babcock, R.L., & Salthouse, T.A. (1990). Effects of increased demands on age differences in working memory. *Psychology and Aging, 5*, 421–428.

Baddeley, A.D. (1983). Working memory. *Philosophical Transactions of the Royal Society of London, B302*, 311–324.

Baddeley, A., Logie, R., Nimmo-Smith, I., & Brereton, N. (1985). Components of fluent reading. *Journal of Memory and Language, 24*, 119–131.

Bisanz, G.L., Das, J.P., & Mancini, G. (1984). Children's memory for phonologically confusable and non-confusable letters: Changes with age and reading ability. *Child Development, 55*, 1845–1854.

Brown, J.I., Bennett, J.M., & Hanna, G. (1981). *The Nelson–Denny Reading Test.* Lombard, IL: The Riverside Publishing Co.

Bruck, M. (1990). Word-recognition skills of adults with childhood diagnosis of dyslexia. *Developmental Psychology, 26*, 439–454.

Byrne, B., & Shea, P. (1979). Semantic and phonemic memory in beginning readers. *Memory and Cognition, 7*, 333–341.

Caird, W.K. (1966). Aging and short-term memory. *Journal of Gerontology, 21*, 295–299.

Case, R., Kurland, D.M., & Goldberg, J. (1982). Operational efficiency of short-term memory span. *Journal of Experimental Psychology, 33*, 386–404.

Clark, L.E., & Knowles, J.B. (1973). Age differences in dichotic listening performance. *Journal of Gerontology, 28*, 173–178.

Cohen, R.L., & Heath, M. (1990). The development of serial short-term memory and the articulatory loop hypotheses. *Intelligence, 14*, 151–171.

Craik, F.I.M. (1965). The nature of the age decrement in performance on dichotic listening task. *Quarterly Journal of Experimental Psychology, 17*, 227–240.

Craik, F.I.M. (1977). Age differences in human memory. In J.E. Birren & K.W. Schaie (Eds.), *Handbook of the psychology of aging* (pp. 384–420). New York: Van Nostrand Reinhold.

Da Fontoura, H.A., & Siegel, L.S. (in press). Reading, syntactic, and working memory skills of bilingual Portuguese-Canadian children. *Reading and Writing: An Interdisciplinary Journal.*

Daneman, M. (1987). Reading and working memory. In J.R. Beech & A.M. Colley (Eds.), *Cognitive approaches to reading* (pp. 57–86). New York: Wiley.

Daneman, M., & Carpenter, P.A. (1980). Individual differences in working memory and reading. *Journal of Verbal Learning and Verbal Behavior, 19,* 450–466.

Daneman, M., & Carpenter, P.A. (1983). Individual differences in integrating information between and within sentences. *Journal of Experimental Psychology: Learning, Memory, and Cognition, 9,* 561–584.

Gardner, E.F., Rudman, H.C., Karlsen, B., & Merwin, J.C. (1982). *Stanford Achievement Test.* New York: Harcourt Brace Jovanovich.

Geva, E., & Siegel, L.S. (1991). *The role of orthography and cognitive factors in the concurrent development of basic reading skills in bilingual children.* Unpublished manuscript.

Gick, M.L., Craik, F.I.M., & Morris, R.G. (1988). Task complexity and age differences in working memory. *Memory and Cognition, 16,* 353–361.

Hall, J.W., Ewing, A., Tinzmann, M.B., & Wilson, K.P. (1981). Phonetic coding in dyslexic and normal readers. *Bulletin of the Psychonomic Society, 17,* 177–178.

Hartley, J.T. (1989). Reader and text variables as determinants of discourse memory in adulthood. *Psychology and Aging, 1,* 150–158.

Henry, L.A. (this issue). The relationship between speech rate and memory span in children. *International Journal of Behavioral Development.*

Hitch, G.J. (1978). The role of short-term working memory in mental arithmetic. *Cognitive Psychology, 10,* 302–323.

Hitch, G.J., & Halliday, M.S. (1983). Working memory in children. *Philosophical Transactions of the Royal Society of London, B302,* 325–340.

Inglis, J., & Caird, W.K. (1963). Age differences in successive responses to simultaneous stimulation. *Canadian Journal of Psychology, 17,* 98–105.

Jastak, J.R., & Jastak, S.R. (1978). *Wide Range Achievement Test.* Wilmington, DE: Jastak Associates.

Jastak, S., & Wilkinson, G.S. (1984). *The Wide Range Achievement Test—Revised.* Wilmington, DE: Jastak Associates.

Johnston, R. (1982). Phonological coding in dyslexic readers. *British Journal of Psychology, 73,* 455–460.

Liberman, I.Y., Shankweiler, D., Liberman, A.M., Fowler, C., & Fischer, F.W. (1977). Phonetic segmentation and recoding in the beginning reader. In A.S. Reber & D. Scarborough (Eds.), *Toward a psychology of reading: The proceedings of the CUNY conference* (pp. 207–225). Hillsdale, NJ: Lawrence Erlbaum Associates Inc.

Light, L.L., & Anderson, P.A. (1985). Working-memory capacity, age, and memory for discourse. *Journal of Gerontology, 40,* 737–747.

Mackay, H.A., & Inglis, J. (1963). The effect of age on a short-term auditory storage process. *Gerontologia, 8,* 193–200.

Mann, V.A., Liberman, I.Y., & Shankweiler, D. (1980). Children's memory for sentences and word strings in relation to reading ability. *Memory and Cognition, 8,* 329–335.

Mark, L.S., Shankweiler, D., Liberman, I.Y., & Fowler, C.A. (1977). Phonetic recoding and reading difficulty in beginning readers. *Memory and Cognition, 5,* 623–629.

Morris, R.G., Gick, M.L., & Craik, F.I.M. (1988). Processing resources and age differences in working memory. *Memory and Cognition, 16,* 362–366.

Olson, R.K., Davidson, B.J., Kliegl, R., & Davies, S. (1984). Development of phonetic memory in disabled and normal readers. *Journal of Experimental Child Psychology, 37,* 187–206.

Pascual-Leone, J. (1970). A mathematical model for the transition rule in Piaget's developmental stages. *Acta Psychologica, 32,* 301–345.

Reisberg, D., Rappaport, I., & O'Shaughnessy, M. (1984). Limits of working memory: The digit digit-span. *Journal of Experimental Psychology: Learning, Memory, and Cognition, 10,* 203–221.

Salthouse, T.A. (1990). Working memory as a processing resource in cognitive aging. *Developmental Review, 10*, 101–124.

Salthouse, T.A., & Babcock, R.L. (1991). Decomposing age differences in working memory. *Developmental Psychology, 27*, 763–776.

Salthouse, T.A., Babcock, R.L., & Shaw, R.J. (1991). Effects of adult age on structural and operational capacities in working memory. *Psychology and Aging, 6*, 118–127.

Salthouse, T.A., Mitchell, D.R.D., Skovronek, E., & Babcock, R.L. (1989). Effects of adult age and working memory on reasoning and spatial abilities. *Journal of Experimental Psychology: Learning, Memory, and Cognition, 15*, 507–516.

Salthouse, T.A., Rogan, J.D., & Prill, K.A. (1984). Division of attention: Age differences on a visually presented memory task. *Memory and Cognition, 12*, 613–620.

Sattler, J.M. (1982). *Assessment of children's intelligence and special abilities* (3rd ed.). Boston, MA: Allyn & Bacon.

Schonfield, D., Trueman, V., & Kline, D. (1972). Recognition tests of dichotic listening and the age variable. *Journal of Gerontology, 27*, 487–493.

Shafrir, U., & Siegel, L.S. (1992). *Subtypes of learning disabilities in adolescents and adults.* Unpublished manuscript, Ontario Institute for Studies in Education, Toronto, Canada.

Shankweiler, D., Liberman, I.Y., Mark, L.S., Fowler, C.A., & Fischer, F.W. (1979). The speech code and learning to read. *Journal of Experimental Psychology: Human Learning and Memory, 5*, 531–545.

Siegel, L.S. (1988). Evidence that IQ scores are irrelevant to the definition and analysis of reading disability. *Canadian Journal of Psyhology, 42*, 201–215.

Siegel, L.S. (1989). IQ is irrelevant to the definition of learning disabilities. *Journal of Learning Disabilities, 22*, 469–478, 486.

Siegel, L.S. (1992). An evaluation of the discrepancy definition of dyslexia. *Journal of Learning Disabilities, 25*, 618–629.

Siegel, L.S. (1993a). The cognitive basis of dyslexia. In R. Pasnak & M.L. Howe (Eds.), *Emerging themes in cognitive development, Vol. II: Competencies* (pp. 33–52). New York: Springer Verlag.

Siegel, L.S. (1993b). Phonolocial processing deficits as the basis of a reading disability. *Developmental Review, 13*, 246–257.

Siegel, L.S., & Heaven, R. (1986). Defining and categorizing learning disabilities. In S.J. Ceci (Ed.), *Handbook of cognitive, social, and neuropsychological aspects of learning disabilities* (Vol. 1, pp. 95–121). Hillsdale, NJ: Lawrence Erlbaum Associates Inc.

Siegel, L.S., & Linder, B.A. (1984). Short-term memory processes in children with reading and arithmetic learning disabilities. *Developmental Psychology, 20*, 200–207.

Siegel, L.S., & Ryan, E.B. (1988). Development of grammatical-sensitivity, phonological, and short-term memory skills in normally achieving and learning disabled children. *Developmental Psychology, 24*, 28–37.

Siegel, L.S., & Ryan, E.B. (1989a). The development of working memory in normally achieving and subtypes of learning disabled children. *Child Development, 60*, 973–980.

Siegel, L.S., & Ryan, E.B. (1989b). Subtypes of developmental dyslexia: The influence of definitional variables. *Reading and Writing: An Interdisciplinary Journal, 1*, 257–287.

Silverstein, A.B. (1982). Two- and four-subset short forms of the Wechsler Adult Intelligence Scale—Revised. *Journal of Counselling and Clinical Psychology, 50*, 415–418.

So, D., & Siegel, L.S. (1992). *Learning to read Chinese: Semantic, syntactic, phonological and short-term memory skills in normally achieving and poor Chinese readers.* Unpublished manuscript.

Spilich, G.J. (1983). Life-span components of text processing: Structural and procedural differences. *Journal of Verbal Learning and Verbal Behavior, 22*, 231–244.

Stanovich, K.E. (1988). Explaining the differences between the dyslexic and garden variety poor reader: The phonological-core variance-difference model. *Journal of Learning Disabilities, 21,* 590–604, 612.

Stine, E.A., & Wingfield, A. (1987). Process and strategy in memory for speech among younger and older adults. *Psychology and Aging, 2,* 272–279.

Stine, E.H., Wingfield, A., & Poon, L.W. (1986). How much and how fast: Rapid processing of spoken language in later adulthood. *Psychology and Aging, 1,* 303–311.

Wechsler, D. (1974). *Manual for the Wechsler Intelligence Scale for Children—Revised.* New York: Psychological Corp.

Wechsler, D. (1981). *Manual for the Wechsler Adult Intelligence Scale—Revised.* San Antonio, TX: Psychological Corp.

Wingfield, A., Stine, E., Lahar, C.J., & Aberdeen, J.S. (1988). Does the capacity of working memory change with age? *Experimental Aging Research, 14,* 103–107.

Wright, R.E. (1981). Aging, divided attention, and processing capacity. *Journal of Gerontology, 36,* 605–614.

INTERNATIONAL JOURNAL OF BEHAVIORAL DEVELOPMENT, 1994, *17* (1), 125–141

Measuring the Size of Working Memory in Very Young Children: The Imitation Sorting Task

I. Ercan Alp

Department of Psychology, Boğaziçi University, Istanbul, Turkey

Development of working memory in the transitional period from infancy to preschool years was investigated from a neo-Piagetian perspective. A new task, the Imitation Sorting Task, was specifically designed for this purpose. The task involves a game of imitation. An increasing number of disparate objects are sorted into two containers and the child is asked to reproduce each demonstrated sorting. The number of objects in the largest set that the child can successfully sort in imitation determines the child's score on the task. The task was administered three times to children from 12 to 36 months of age. Scores increased in a linear fashion with age in all three administrations. Upon retesting within a few weeks after the original administration, children's score and rank remained very similar. Their score increased at the follow-up after 6 months, but their rank still remained similar to their original rank. The age-related increase in the scores appears to be about one unit every six months in this age range.

INTRODUCTION

The postulate that (a) there are inherent limits to the information-processing capacity of children, and (b) changes in these limits with age underlie cognitive development is shared by a number of neo-Piagetian theories, such as the theory of constructive operators (TCO) by Pascual-

---

Requests for reprints should be sent to I. Ercan Alp, Department of Psychology, Boğaziçi University, Bebek, Istanbul, Turkey 80815.

This study is based on a dissertation submitted in partial fulfilment of the PhD degree in the Department of Psychology, York University, Toronto, Canada.

An earlier version of this article was presented at the International Conference on Memory held at Lancaster University, England, in July 1991.

I gratefully acknowledge Juan Pascual-Leone's contributions to the design of the Imitation Sorting Task. Special thanks are due to Susan Gathercole, Graham Hitch, Anik de Ribaupierre, and Peter Willatts for their valuable comments on earlier drafts of this paper. Also, many thanks are due to the children who participated in this study as well as their parents and staff, and administrators of the daycare centres.

Leone (1970, 1987; Pascual-Leone & Goodman, 1979; Pascual-Leone, Goodman, Ammon, & Subelman, 1978; Pascual-Leone & Ijaz, 1989; Pascual-Leone & Johnson, 1991) and Case's theory (Case, 1985). The attractiveness of such theories lies in their efforts to combine the strengths of Piaget's theory with those of the information-processing approach to cognition. Thus, they provide guidelines for a fine-grained analysis of experimental tasks with respect to the demands such tasks place on the individual's information-processing system, while at the same time allowing for derivation of specific hypotheses across virtually all types of cognitive tasks. The TCO seems to be unique among them because it provides a framework within which the respective contributions of maturational variables and task-specific learning effects can be specified when modelling the individual's performance on cognitive tasks.

The present study was conceived within the theoretical framework provided by the TCO. The TCO puts forward that observed performance of the individual on a task is determined by a complex cognitive process that involves *schemes* (i.e. units of situation-specific information) in the individual's repertoire as well as *silent operators* (i.e. content-free organismic resources) that provide activation energy for the schemes. Among the various silent operators, M (mental energy or mental capacity) is the critical developmental construct. Age-related increase in M from birth until about 15 years explains developmental changes in performance on cognitive tasks. The amount of M available for an individual at any given age, M power, is defined as the maximum number of independent schemes that can be simultaneously brought to hyperactivation without any contribution from other silent operators.

The amount of M that builds up during the first two years of life, the sensorimotor period of Piaget, is designated as the e component of M. It is argued that e component of M is employed by the organism to boost executive schemes (i.e. schemes that carry the task's general instructions) in later years. The amount that is acquired beyond the second year is designated as the k component. Empirical evidence from a number of studies is consistent with the assumption that the k component increases by one unit every two years (e.g. Pascual-Leone, 1970). The growth of the e component is assumed to follow Piaget's sensorimotor stages (see Pascual-Leone & Johnson, 1991).

Because the organism can employ its M operator to bring schemes into hyperactivation, the amount of information it can simultaneously store and actively manipulate, while engaged in goal directed activity, depends to a large extent on its current M power. In fact, working memory has been equated with M power (e.g. Burtis, 1982; Pascual-Leone, 1987). Other determinants of the contents of working memory are discussed by de

Ribaupierre and Bailleux (this issue). It may be added that, depending on the nature of a cognitive task, working memory may also include schemes that are activated by silent operators other than M, such as the learning operators, L and C, and a field operator, F. Therefore, the total amount of information simultaneously stored and processed may exceed the M power.

The present study is a first attempt at investigating changes in M power in the transitional period from infancy to preschool years. A cognitive task was devised to measure the maximum amount of information children can simultaneously store and process. The Imitation Sorting Task (IST) is, as its name implies, a game of imitation. A number of disparate objects are first sorted into two containers. The objects are then taken out of the containers and placed before the child who is asked to reproduce the demonstrated sorting. The size of the sets of objects to be sorted increases from one object at the beginning of the administration of the task to a maximum of eight objects at the end. The number of objects in the largest set a child can correctly sort is that child's score on the task.

It is assumed in this study that IST scores represent a quantitative measure of the maximum amount of information very young children can store and actively manipulate in working memory. The *size of working memory* is used here to refer to this amount. Age-related increases in the scores, then, can be argued to reflect corresponding increases in the size of working memory in this age range. In the TCO, such increases may be explained by increases in M power with age.

The primary objectives of the study were (1) to chart the growth in the size of working memory in the transitional period from infancy to preschool years, and (2) to assess the usefulness of the IST as an experimental tool in the study of cognitive development in this age range.

METHOD

Design

The age range chosen for the study was divided into four age groups: 12–17 months, 18–23 months, 24–29 months, and 30–36 months. Three separate sessions were scheduled for individual children. The first two sessions were a maximum of 3 weeks apart. Children were still within their original age groups at retest. When they were retested again 6 months later, all had moved to the next older age group. Children were administered the Imitation Sorting Task (IST) in all three sessions.

Subjects

A total of 52 children were employed in the study. The first and the third age groups each comprised 12 children. There were 14 children in the second and fourth age groups. Half of the children in each age group were girls and half were boys. Five additional children were excluded from the sample. Three 12-month-old girls and two boys, a 13-month-old and a 26-month-old, were too shy to co-operate. With the exception of 34 months, there was at least one child at every age from 12 months to 36 months. The average ages for the age groups were 13.8, 20.0, 27.3, and 33.0 months, respectively. Three daycare centres agreed to participate in the study and the majority of parents were contacted through the centres. Parents who themselves attended the sessions were mostly college graduates and parents whose children were tested in the presence of daycare staff were faculty, students or staff of York University.

Second Session.   Four out of 52 children of the original sample could not be scheduled for a retest session within 3 weeks after the first testing. Also, the data from three children in the oldest age group were discarded. They were the first three children to be retested in that group and a modified procedure had been employed with them to speed-up testing. The remaining children in that age group were tested under the standard conditions (albeit with some slight alterations) because the modified procedure appeared to be confusing to the children. In sum, 45 children had data available for the analyses (see Table 1). Of those children for whom no data were available for the second session, five were girls and two were boys.

The average interval between the two sessions was 9.1 days (range: 2 to 22). A total of 12 children were 1 month older by the time they were retested. Nevertheless, their ages remained within the limits of their original age group. Half of those children were girls and half were boys. The average age of the retest sample was 22.5 months.

Follow-up Session.   The number of children who were available for the follow-up testing was 37 (see Table 1). There were 18 boys and 19 girls in the follow-up sample and the number of girls and boys remained similar across the age groups. The follow-up session was scheduled an average of 5.8 months (range: 5.5 to 8) after the first session. There was some overlap of age between the third and fourth age groups. One child in the third age group had already become 36 months old by the time a follow-up session could be scheduled for her. On the other hand, three children in the fourth age group were 36 months old at the follow-up testing. There were no other instances of age overlap between the age groups. The average age for the follow-up sample was 28.4 months.

The Longitudinal Sample.   Three children for whom a follow-up session was scheduled had not been available for the second session. Therefore, the number of children who were tested three times was 34. Those children comprised the longitudinal sample of the study. There was an equal number of boys and girls in the longitudinal sample and the sex distribution remained similar across the age groups.

The Task

The only experimental task employed in the study was the Imitation Sorting Task (IST). The IST is hierarchically organised into eight *levels* of increasing difficulty. Each level is designated with the number of toys to be sorted at that level.

There are five *sets* of toys prepared for each of the eight levels. With each set, the experimenter first demonstrates the task to the child by sorting the toys into canisters. The toys are then taken out of the canisters and handed to the child, with the request that he or she sort the toys in the same way. At Level 1 the sets consist of only one toy each and there is only one canister into which the toy can be placed. Therefore, what is tested here is whether the child can imitate dropping an object into a container. At Level 2, a second canister is introduced. The sets now comprise two toys each. With each set, one of the toys is placed into one canister and the remaining toy in the other. A successful trial is the one in which the child can imitate separating the toys by placing one toy in each of the canisters. This is the first level at which imitation of sorting actually begins.

The sets at Level 3 are sorted by placing one of the toys into one canister and the remaining two toys in the other. As long as the child places *those* two toys together in any of the canisters and the remaining toy in the other canister, the child's sorting is considered correct. That is to say, the child is *not* required to follow the same order in which the experimenter placed the toys in a set during demonstration. Similarly, those two toys do *not* have to be placed in the same canister into which the experimenter placed them. In short, the criterion for correct imitation is that the child puts the same two toys together as in the demonstration, putting the third toy into a separate container; that is, the set is divided into *exactly* the same subsets as in the demonstration. The same criterion applies at the higher levels as well. With each set, two subsets are formed by the experimenter by sorting the toys in that set into two canisters and the child is required to form *exactly* the same subsets in imitation of the experimenter. The two subsets are always of equal size at even numbered levels. At odd numbered levels, however, one of the canisters receives a toy less than the other.

The opportunity given to the child to sort in imitation constitutes a *trial*. If the child fails to imitate the sorting at the first trial, a second demonstration and a subsequent trial follows. That is to say, the child is given, at the most, two opportunities to observe and imitate the correct sorting of a set of toys. A *pass* is recorded for a particular set of toys if correct imitation takes place on either the first or the second trial with that set. Once the child passes the first set of toys at a level, the second set of toys at that level is introduced. Testing at that level continues until the child passes three sets of toys. If the child has already passed any two of the first three sets, testing continues with the first set of the next higher level.

To sum up, the criterion to *pass* a *set* of toys at any level is one correct imitation of the demonstrated sorting within a maximum of two trials. The criterion to *pass* a *level* is that the child pass three out of five sets or, alternatively, two of the first three sets of toys at that level. Testing continues until the child fails two consecutive levels. The highest level the child has passed is the score of that child for that administration of the task.

Apparatus

The 180 toys employed in the study included small toys in the shape of animals, eating utensils, fruits, carpenter tools, vehicles, etc. Other objects, such as small picture frames, puzzle pieces, and pen caps, were also employed. The size of the toys varied from 2cm to 16cm and they were of various colours. The five sets of toys prepared at all levels beyond Level 2 were carefully chosen to avoid facilitation of correct sorting on the basis of perceptual and/or conceptual similarity. Also, the order in which the sets of toys were administered was checked to avoid repetition of the same colour/size/shape/category toys being placed consistently in the right or the left canister.

The two clear plastic canisters employed in the study measured 15cm in diameter and 24cm in height. They were designated each with a different two-colour tape glued inside the canister 2cm below the top circumference. An 80cm × 30cm wooden tray was installed on an ordinary wooden highchair. One well, into which a canister can be placed, was built on each side of the tray approximately 15cm from the seat and 40cm apart from each other. When placed in the wells, the canister stood 11cm tall.

Procedure[1]

A session started when the accompanying adult brought the child into the testing room and sat in the chair with the child on her lap. The experimenter brought out a warm-up toy and started a conversation with the adult paying casual attention to the child at the beginning. This interval was used for communicating the instructions to the adult, if it was the first time that she was attending a session. When the child was judged to be ready for testing, the experimenter took the toy away from the child. He lightly hit the toy on the tray three times on the way to the canister and uttered "hop!" each time it hit the tray. Next, he retrieved the toy and handed it back to the child saying: "Now, you do it!" or "Now, (*child's name*) does it!" The child's imitation of dropping the toy in the canister was rewarded with cheers and clapping by both the experimenter and the adult. This sequence was repeated with the first level toys until the game was established. The game was judged to be established when the child began to imitate promptly and with apparent enthusiasm. At that point, the child was transferred to the highchair, the second canister was placed in the left well and the first set of toys at Level 2 was introduced. Administration of the task continued until the child failed two consecutive levels. At all trials, correct imitation was rewarded as described above. In the case of failure, however, the experimenter maintained a positive facial expression and proceeded with the second demonstration saying: "Let's do it again". The subsequent set of toys was always introduced with: "I've got more toys for you". The adult was discouraged from interfering with the testing beginning at Level 2 and, with the exception of joining in to reward correct imitations, remained silent throughout testing.

The procedure was closely followed in all three sessions with a few minor modifications. First, the warm-up part was curtailed for those children who seemed to have enjoyed an earlier session(s) and who appeared to be ready to start. Second, testing with older children who had advanced to higher levels of the task in the first session, started at Level 2. Third, children who had passed Level 5 or higher levels in the first session were administered only one set of toys at the second and third levels in the second session. Fourth, again in the second session only, the order in which the sets were administered was reversed at every level in an attempt to minimise potential carryover effects.

---

[1]More detailed information about the administration of the task can be obtained from the author.

Beginning at Level 2, the experimenter recorded the imitation of the child at the end of each trial as *pass* or *fail*.[2] At the end of the session, the highest level passed by the child was recorded as his or her score for the session.

The duration of sessions varied depending on the highest level a child passed. Also, the frustration tolerance of individual children affected the length of sessions. Whereas some children tolerated the experimenter's requests to continue despite their awareness that they could not imitate correctly anymore, others quickly gave up trying. Although sessions lasted up to 60 minutes, in some cases in the older age groups, the duration generally was much shorter.

Interobserver Reliability

During the first 42 sessions of the study an unobtrusive observer took extensive notes of the child's responses, such as the order in which individual toys were manipulated by the child and dropped into respective canisters. Immediately following the child's departure from the testing room, the experimenter went over her notes with her. Even though the experimenter had not independently recorded the outcome of each trial in those sessions, it was he who decided, on the basis of his own judgement of the outcome of a trial, whether to administer a second demonstration and a subsequent trial, or to move on to the next set of toys, or to move to the next higher level. Therefore, any disagreement between him and the observer ought to have led to anomalies in the observer's record of the session. No anomalies were detected in any of the 42 cases. In this sense, the interobserver reliability of the measure of this study was 100%.

RESULTS

Children were assigned a score for every session they attended. A score indicated the highest level of the IST the child had passed at that session. In the first set of analyses, the data from each session were analysed

---

[2]It was only at Level 1 that the experimenter began for the first time to interact directly with the child and an initial shyness observed in some children required prompting from the accompanying adult as well as the experimenter at this level. In fact, Level 1 was included in the task partly as an extension of the warm-up period because the skill of dropping objects into a container is typically acquired by the time children are 1 year old. Once the child started imitating dropping the toys at Level 1 into the canister and showed apparent enthusiasm in this activity, the experiment proper began by introducing sets at Level 2. It was also then that formal recording of responses began.

separately. Next, the data from the longitudinal sample ($n = 34$) were analysed.

Cross-sectional Data

Individual scores in the first session ranged from 0 to 7. The lowest score belonged to a 12-month-old who could not imitate dropping objects into a canister. A 34-month-old, on the other hand, successfully sorted sets of seven objects in imitation of the experimenter and received the highest score. In terms of the age groups, the average scores steadily increased from the youngest to the oldest age group (see Table 1).

This apparently linear increase in children's score with age was explored in a regression analysis. Age was treated as a quantitative independent variable with linear effects and a dummy variable was constructed for the sex of the child. A further term constructed for Age × Sex interaction became the third independent variable in the analysis. The results indicate that children's age reliably predicts their score, $F(1,48) = 55.90$, $P < 0.001$.[3] Children's sex, alone or in interaction with age, did not contribute to the prediction of the scores. Boys and girls appeared to have obtained similar scores across the age range covered. Furthermore, the association

TABLE 1
Summary of the Experimental Design and the Cross-sectional Data

	Age Group			
	1	*2*	*3*	*4*
Score 1	1.2 (0–3)	2.4 (1–5)	3.3 (1–6)	4.2 (2–7)
Age 1	13.8	20.0	27.3	33.1
n	12	14	12	14
Score 2	1.2 (1–2)	2.1 (1–4)	3.1 (1–5)	4.4 (2–6)
Age 2	14.0	20.4	27.3	32.5
n	12	14	11	8
Score 3	2.0 (1–3)	3.4 (2–7)	5.8 (3–8)	5.9 (3–8)
Age 3	20.0	25.4	33.9	38.3
n	11	10	8	8

Note. Range of the scores is presented in parentheses next to the mean score for each age group. Age is expressed in months.

---

[3]F values were calculated using the appropriate sum of squares obtained in the regression analysis.

between age and scores was a fairly strong one in that more than 50% of the variance was accounted for by age, $r^2 = 0.55$.

An inspection of the scatter plot of the residuals from the analysis suggested that the variability of the scores shows an increase after 19 months and remains essentially the same for the rest of the age range (see Fig. 1). To explore further the relation between age and scores, a second regression analysis was carried out on the residuals. For this analysis, a new dummy variable, *group*, was constructed to compare children who were 19 months or younger with those who were older than 19 months. An additional term for the Age × Group interaction was also constructed. Next, the absolute residuals from the original analysis were regressed on children's age, group, and Age × Group interaction.

The group term reached statistical significance indicating that the size of the absolute residuals of the original analysis was larger in children who were older than 19 months, $F(1,48) = 5.10$, $P < 0.05$. There was, however, no evidence that the size increased with age in either group as indicated by the negligible Age and Age × Group interaction terms. This indicated that the variability of the scores remained the same across the age range except for a stepwise increase between 19 and 20 months.

The Second Session. The retest data had been collected from 45 children who were available for the second session. Again, the average scores increased from the youngest to the oldest age group (see Table 1). Despite a somewhat reduced range of scores for each age group, individual children mostly retained their original rank, $r = 0.80$. The association between the two sets of scores for individual children remained substantial even after controlling for the age group variable, $r = 0.66$. Furthermore, the actual scores of the children did not change from the first to the second testing, $t(44) = 0$, $P = 1$.

When the children's retest score was regressed on their age, sex, and Age × Sex interaction, the results showed that scores reliably increased with age, $F(1,41) = 72.33$, $P < 0.001$, and that there were no sex differences. As was the case with the first session scores, there was again a strong association between age and scores, $r^2 = 0.64$. A scatter plot of the residuals from this analysis is presented in Fig. 1. The size of the absolute residuals from the analysis were also regressed on age, group, and Age × Group interaction. The group term again reached statistical significance, $F(1,41) = 4.56$, $P < 0.05$, indicating that the value of the absolute residuals was larger for children older than 19 months. Age and Age × Group interaction terms were again negligible.

In summary, the results of analyses of the retest data fully replicated earlier results. Analyses performed on both sets of data have yielded results that indicated a strong linear relation between children's age and

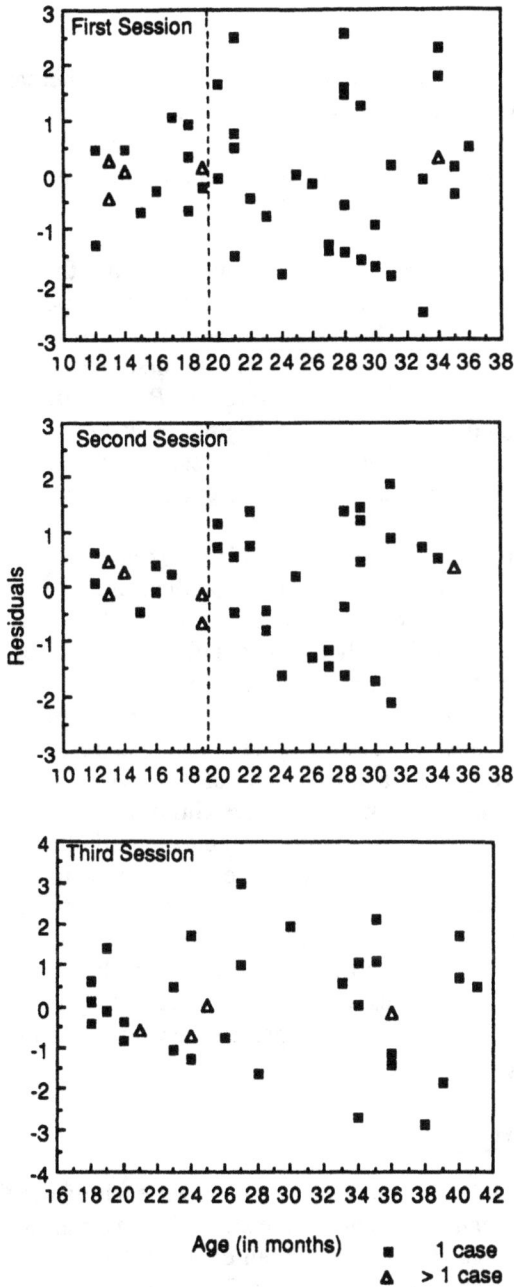

FIG. 1. Residuals from the regression of the first session (top), the second session (middle), and the third session scores (bottom) on age, sex, and Age × Sex interaction.

their score on the IST. The scores increase with increasing age. The variability of the scores, however, remains constant across the entire age range with the single exception of a stepwise increase around 19 months. These results are consistent with the inference that there is a transition around 19 months.

The Follow-up Session. At the follow-up testing, the lower boundary for the age range had shifted to 18 months and the upper boundary to 41 months. The scores of 37 children, who were followed up about 6 months later, increased from an average of 2.5 at the first session to an average of 4.0 at the follow-up session, $t(36) = 6.43$, $P = < 0.001$. Their rank, however, remained similar to their original rank as indicated by a high correlation between the two sets of scores, $r = 0.75$. The association between the scores remained fairly strong even after controlling for the age group variable, $r = 0.55$.

The average follow-up scores and their range are presented in Table 1. When the children's score was regressed on their age, sex, and Age $\times$ Sex interaction, no sex differences emerged. The results of this analysis indicate that children's age reliably predicts their score, $F(1,33) = 59.89$, $P < 0.001$. The association between age and scores was again very strong, $r^2 = 0.65$. A scatter plot of the residuals from this analysis is presented in Fig. 1. When the size of absolute residuals were again regressed on age, group, and Age $\times$ Group interaction, none of the terms reached statistical significance. Because there were only five children who were 19 months or younger at the follow-up, the failure to replicate earlier results concerning a transition around 19 months may not be worthy of serious consideration.

On the whole, these results complement those from the analyses on the first and second session data. Children's score on the IST steadily increases with age. This seems to hold true also when the same children are repeatedly tested. Retesting yields higher scores only if the children are tested again at an older age. A more conservative test of the effects of repeated testing is presented next.

Longitudinal Data

The data of 34 children who had a score from each of the three sessions constituted the longitudinal data of the study. The average and the range of scores for each age group are presented in Table 2. The scores were analysed with a 4 $\times$ 3 (Age group $\times$ Session) mixed model analysis of variance with session serving as a repeated measure. In this analysis, the linear, quadratic, and cubic components of age group were treated separately. In addition, session was further decomposed into two contrasts. The scores from the first session were compared with those from the second

TABLE 2
Mean IST Scores of the Age Groups of the Longitudinal Sample

Session	Age Group			
	1 (n = 11)	2 (n = 10)	3 (n = 7)	4 (n = 6)
1	1.2 (0–3)	2.3 (1–5)	3.7 (1–6)	3.5 (2–5)
2	1.2 (1–2)	2.1 (2–4)	3.4 (1–5)	4.0 (2–5)
3	2.0 (2–3)	3.4 (2–7)	5.6 (3–8)	5.7 (3–8)

Note. The age groups had moved to the next higher age at the third session. The range of scores is shown in parentheses.

session in one of the contrasts (1 vs. 2). The other contrast involved a comparison of the scores from the third session with the average of the first two sessions (1 and 2 vs. 3).

A significant main effect of the linear component of age group, $F(1,30) = 35.00$, $P = < 0.001$, showed that across the sessions, scores increased steadily from the first to the fourth age group. Also, the main effect of the "1 and 2 vs. 3" contrast was highly significant, $F(1,30) = 43.14$, $P < 0.001$. This result explains the significant main effect of session, $F(2,60) = 32.82$, $P < 0.001$, as being due to an increase in the scores in the third session.

Furthermore, the Age group (linear) × "1 and 2 vs. 3" interaction approached significance, $F(1,30) = 4.01$, $P = 0.054$. The linear increase in the scores appeared to be sharper in the third session than the first two sessions. The major contribution to this difference seemed to come from the third and fourth age groups that showed greater improvement relative to the other age groups when tested for the third time (see Table 2).

To summarise, across the age groups, the scores did not change from the first to the second session, but they increased in the third session. Children attain similar scores when they are retested at about the same age, but show marked improvement when retested again six months later. Furthermore, in all three sessions, the increase in the scores from the youngest to the oldest age group is linear. There is, however, some evidence suggesting that the rate of this linear increase may be somewhat greater when they are tested for the third time.

In fact, when considered in terms of the *age groups*, cross-sectional data from the follow-up session also failed to replicate a sequence of regular increments from the second to the fourth age group observed in the first two sessions (see Table 1). Because the two older age groups were represented by about half the original number of children at the follow-up, selective attrition may explain this interaction effect. Another factor that might be considered is the actual ages of the children at the follow-up. As mentioned in the Method section, three children in the oldest age group were only 36 months at the follow-up and the average age for this age group was only 4.4 months older than that of the third age group. A more pronounced difference between their average scores might have been observed if the age at follow-up could have been better controlled. Given the modest sample size, further analyses on the data to explore this effect in depth do not seem to be called for. Until the study is independently replicated, therefore, the interpretation of the interaction will remain ambiguous.

In general, the results of the analysis of the longitudinal data replicated earlier results. Both sets of analyses indicated (1) a strong linear relation between age and scores on the IST, and (2) no effect of repeated administrations on the scores, provided that the children's age does not increase appreciably in the interim.

DISCUSSION

The results of this study show that the IST may qualify as a sound psychometric instrument. The IST seems to have a very high retest reliability. Thus, even after an interval of six months, the correlation between scores remained high ($r = 0.75$) in a period of relatively fast development.

The results also seem to suggest that the IST has a good construct validity. First, the finding that children's scores do not change upon retesting within a few weeks implies that the scores are relatively immune to learning effects. The scores seem to reflect an underlying capacity rather than specific learned responses. In the theory of constructive operators, this capacity is identified as the amount of M at the child's disposal at a given age. Upon retesting at a later age, however, children's score increases. Age differentiation is, in fact, a major criterion against which several traditional IQ tests have been validated (Anastasi, 1990).

Secondly, in the present study, almost all children in the first age group (12–17 months) failed to imitate sorting objects into two canisters. At levels beyond Level 1, they placed all the objects in a set into one canister. With a few exceptions, older children were able to use *both* canisters. The evidence for a transition in the data around 19 months, in fact, reflects this change in performance with age. This finding closely replicates findings from investigations of classification in infancy. The age at which infants first begin sorting out objects into two groups in a free play situation has been reported to be 17.2 months (range: 15.5–20.9) by Gopnik and Meltzoff (1987) and 18 months by Riccuiti (1965) and Sugarman (1982).

In an unpublished study, Myers, Perlmutter, and Cohen (cited in Myers & Perlmutter, 1978) employed a task somewhat similar to the IST. They presented 3-year-olds with eight small objects that were arranged in a 2 × 4 spatial array. Later, the objects were taken out, placed before the child and the child was asked to reproduce the same arrangement. Three-year-olds correctly relocated an average of 6.5 objects. In the present study, the age of the fourth age group at follow-up testing was close to the age of their subjects. As presented in Table 1, those children obtained an average score of 5.9; that is, they were able to sort about six disparate objects in imitation of the experimenter. The similarity between the observed values is striking. It may be argued that even the oldest children in the present study tried to keep track of each object's location separately despite the fact that there were only two containers into which those objects were sorted. Thus, their results not only seem to provide some evidence for construct validity of the IST, but also have implications for the strategies children have employed.

In the present study, children's responses were only coded as pass or fail on each trial. That is why hardly any statement can be made about the children's strategies except for reporting informal observations made during testing. It was originally presumed that, because they are too young to construct proper executive schemes, children in the age range chosen for the study would attempt to encode each object's location separately. Myers et al.'s results seem to lend some support for this presumption. If, for example, children had tried to remember only the toys that go to one of the canisters and then put all the remaining ones by default to the other canister, one would have expected, at least in the oldest age group, much higher scores than the ones actually observed. In fact, only two children ever passed Level 8. Informal observations made during testing also seem to suggest that children were unlikely to be employing complex strategies. For example, when the set size increased beyond the child's competence, usually a breakdown in performance was seen; the child began to put all of the objects into one canister irrespective of the highest level passed until then.

The results also show that the size of working memory, as measured by the IST, increases in a linear fashion in the transitional period from infancy to preschool years. The increase seems to be approximately one unit every six months interval from 12 to 36 months of age. Within the theoretical framework of the TCO, this finding may be interpreted as reflecting corresponding increases in M power in this age range. To be convincing, however, this interpretation must be supported by a theory-guided task analysis, such as the one presented by Alp (1992), as well as further empirical data on the IST.

The evidence for a linear increase in the size of working memory may be challenged on methodological grounds. It may be argued that, because a variable pass criterion was employed in this study, the same score may not reflect the same level of competence in different children. At the extreme,

TABLE 3
Mean Success Rates on the Highest Level Achieved by the Age Groups across Sessions

Session	Age Group			
	1	2	3	4
1	45.0 (2)	82.8 (12)	70.9 (11)	65.1 (14)
2	75.0 (2)	61.5 (10)	73.8 (10)	60.9 (8)
3	77.5 (9)	73.3 (10)	57.6 (8)	54.7 (8)

Note. The values represent mean percentages of success rate on the highest level obtained by the children in each age group across the three sessions. The number of children represented in each mean value is shown in parentheses.

the procedure allowed for passing a level by being successful in only three out of ten trials (i.e. passing only three of the five sets administered at a level and always at the second trial with each set). Across the three administrations of the task, the lowest success rate on the highest level passed was 33.3%. A total of six such instances were observed: Three in the first, one in the second, and two in the third session. Average success rates on the highest level passed by the age groups are presented in Table 3. With the exception of the youngest age group on first testing and the two older age groups on follow-up testing, the success rates were greater than 60%.

The average score for the youngest age group on first testing was 1.2 and only two children in this age group obtained a score greater than 1. The fact that they obtained those scores at a low success rate does not seem to present a challenge to the interpretation offered here. The low success rates of the two older age groups at the follow-up may, in fact, suggest that their scores might have been inflated beyond their true competence because of the variable success criterion adopted in this study. If indeed this were true, the disproportionately greater increase observed in their scores would have been interpreted as an artefact of the procedure. Thus, the evidence for a steady increase in the scores with age would have been further enhanced.

The reason for adopting in this study a somewhat flexible criterion was a desire to observe the best performance of the child. At the same time, passing a level by chance was reduced to a minimum by preparing five sets of toys at each level. Moreover, testing continued until children failed two consecutive levels. It may be argued that if children could not, under these conditions, succeed beyond a certain level, it is because they had reached their processing limits. The results of this study with respect to the comparison of the first session scores with those of the second session indirectly supports this argument. Children's rank and actual scores remained very similar upon retesting.

In conclusion, the IST appears to be an experimental task that can effectively be used to assess the size of working memory in the transitional period from infancy to preschool years. Comparisons of children's performance on IST with their performance on different tasks, coupled with a theory-guided task analysis for each of the tasks, may lead to a better understanding of working memory in this age range.

REFERENCES

Alp, I.E. (1992, September). *A task analysis of the Imitation Sorting Task.* Paper presented at the Vth European Conference on Developmental Psychology, Seville, 6–9 September.

Anastasi, A. (1990). *Psychological testing* (6th ed.). New York: Macmillan.

Burtis, P.J. (1982). Capacity increase and chunking in the development of short-term memory. *Journal of Experimental Child Psychology, 34,* 387–413.

Case, R. (1985). *Intellectual development: Birth to adulthood.* Orlando, FL: Academic Press.

Gopnik, A., & Meltzoff, A. (1987). The development of categorization in the second year and its relation to other cognitive and linguistic developments. *Child Development, 58,* 1523–1531.

Myers, N.A., & Perlmutter, M. (1978). Memory in the years from two to five. In P.A. Ornstein (Ed.), *Memory development in children* (pp. 191–218). Hillsdale, NJ: Lawrence Erlbaum Associates Inc.

Pascual-Leone, J. (1970). A mathematical model for the transition rule in Piaget's developmental stages. *Acta Psychologica, 32,* 301–345.

Pascual-Leone, J. (1987). Organismic processes for neo-Piagetian theories: A dialectical causal account of cognitive development. *International Journal of Psychology, 22,* 531–570.

Pascual-Leone, J., & Goodman, D. (1979). Intelligence and experience: A neo-Piagetian approach. *Instructional Science, 8,* 301–367.

Pascual-Leone, J., Goodman, D., Ammon, P., & Subelman, I. (1978). Piagetian theory and neo-Piagetian analysis as psychological guides in education. In J.M. Callagher & J.A. Easley (Eds.), *Knowledge and development* (Vol. 2). New York: Plenum.

Pascual-Leone, J., & Ijaz, H. (1989). Mental capacity testing as a form of intellectual-developmental assessment. In R.J. Samuda, S.L. Kong, J. Cummins, J. Pascual-Leone, & J. Lewis (Eds.), *Assessment and placement of minority students* (pp. 143–171). Toronto: Hogrefe.

Pascual-Leone, J., & Johnson, J. (1991). Psychological unit and its role in task analysis: A reinterpretation of object permanence. In M. Chandler & M. Chapman (Eds.), *Criteria for competence: Controversies in the assessment of children's abilities.* Hillsdale, NJ: Lawrence Erlbaum Associates Inc.

Riccuiti, H. (1965). Object grouping and selective ordering behavior in infants 12 to 24 months old. *Merrill Palmer Quarterly, 11,* 129–148.

Sugarman, S. (1982). Developmental change in early representational intelligence: Evidence from spatial classification strategies and related verbal expressions. *Cognitive Psychology, 14,* 410–449.

INTERNATIONAL JOURNAL OF BEHAVIORAL DEVELOPMENT, 1994, *17* (1), 143–159

Issues in Working Memory Measurement: Testing for M Capacity

Sergio Morra

Istituto di Psicologia, Università di Cagliari, Italy

Two studies on measurement of *M* capacity are reported. Study 1, with 191 subjects aged 6–11, found factor-analytical and correlational evidence that five *M* capacity tests share a common source of variance, and that, with age, they increase at a similar rate. Study 2, with 124 subjects aged 6–10 years, replicated the previous findings. It is suggested that, in this age range, *M* capacity can be measured with a battery of tests.

INTRODUCTION

The term "working memory" generically refers to the temporary storage and processing of information. However, the existence of a single mechanism serving these functions is implausible. Rather, it has often been suggested that a set of mechanisms codetermine the capacity and properties of working memory.

The major theories in this field posit different mechanisms or components of working memory, and different developmental processes. For instance, Baddeley (1986) argues for the existence of a central executive and a set of slave storage systems, such as an articulatory loop and a visuo-spatial sketch pad. In contrast, other authors (e.g. Cowan, 1988; Shiffrin, 1976) discard the concept of short-term stores and regard working memory as the activated subset of long-term memory.

One supporter of the latter view is Pascual-Leone (1970, 1987; Pascual-Leone & Goodman, 1979), whose theory includes two levels of cognitive

Requests for reprints should be sent to Sergio Morra, Università di Cagliari, Facoltà di Magistero, Istituto di Psicologia, Sa Duchessa 09100, Cagliari, Italy.

The author is very grateful to Alda Scopesi and Chiara Stoffel for their valuable collaboration in organising and conducting this research. Many thanks are also due to Ivana Bacci, Carla Moizo, and Ludovica Tognoni for their assistance in Study I, and to Robbie Case, Graham Hitch, Charles Hulme, Daniel Keating, Bob Logie, Juan Pascual-Leone, and Anik de Ribaupierre for useful suggestions, comments, and unpublished material.

operators. At the first level there are cognitive units, called *schemes* in the Piagetian tradition. They are classified as figurative or operative (for a similar distinction between declarative and procedural knowledge, see Anderson, 1983). Executive schemes, that stipulate goals, plans, and well-practised procedures, are a subclass of operative schemes. A scheme has a specific informational content, and a subject's long-term memory is called his/her repertoire of schemes.

At the second level there are general purpose mechanisms or "silent operators". For instance, the M operator is conceived as a mechanism, controlled by the executive schemes and endowed with limited attentional resources, having the function of activating a limited number of task-relevant schemes. The I operator is a mechanism complementary to M in that it inhibits task-irrelevant schemes. The L operator represents the learning of new schemes or scheme hierarchies, the F operator field effects, and so on (for detailed accounts, see Pascual-Leone, 1969, 1976, 1987; Pascual-Leone & Goodman, 1979). In general, the "silent operators" have the function of increasing or decreasing the activation of schemes.

Pascual-Leone (1969, 1970) proposed his theory as an account of development in Piagetian tasks. In particular, he suggested that M capacity (i.e. the capacity of the M operator) increases with age, thus allowing more complex cognitive performance. It was also suggested that the M operator has a more important function in "misleading" than "facilitating" tasks (e.g. Pascual-Leone, 1969, 1989; Pascual-Leone & Morra, 1991). In line with Piaget's distinction between sensorimotor and representational schemes it was proposed that, on the average, a 3-year-old child has the capacity of activating one representational scheme via the M operator. This capacity would increase to two schemes at the age of 5, and continue increasing by one unit every second year until a capacity of simultaneously activating seven representational schemes is reached at about the age of 15.

Pascual-Leone (1989) also suggested that the M operator corresponds, in neuropsychological terms, to Luria's excitatory attentional system, located in the prefrontal lobe, and to the connections that allow this lobe to monitor the excitatory impulses sent to the cortex by subcortical structures. One can assume that, as an attentional energy resource, M capacity increases with age in a continuous way. However, the function of the M operator boosts the activation of a discrete number of cognitive units (i.e. schemes). Thus, continuous increase in the underlying physiological variable would be psychologically manifest as a discrete increase in the number of schemes that the M operator can activate.

Unfortunately, *there is no one-to-one correspondence between the constructs included in different theories*. For instance, the functions that in Baddeley's theory are served by one component, the central executive, in Pascual-Leone's theory functions are shared among three (the M operator, the *I* operator, and the executive schemes). Another component of Baddeley's theory, the articulatory loop, has no matching construct in Pascual-Leone's theory. If one intended to account, within the framework of Pascual-Leone's theory, for subvocal rehearsal in STM span tasks, then a complex model should be spelled out (e.g. Morra & Stoffel, submitted).

This state of affairs may be one of the reasons why it has not only proved difficult to integrate different theories or approaches to working memory, but also to make a direct comparison between them. Perhaps one reasonable way out of this *impasse* is attempting an indirect comparison, by testing different predictions derived from different theories, so as to identify their strong and weak points.

A preliminary issue is that of measurement. Let us assume that human behaviour is overdetermined, so that a given component of the mind is involved in many tasks and perhaps no single task is accomplished in using that component alone. In everyday language, for instance, we would say that every cognitive task involves some kind of perception, retrieval of information from memory, and so on. In the terms of Pascual-Leone's theory, no task is performed by means of one single operator. The various operators are assumed to be taxed to a different extent in different tasks, but cognitive performance will be the result of their interaction. If so, measuring a component of the mind seems problematic, because no simple measure based on a single task will do. However, a construct that cannot be measured (eventually with a complex procedure involving more tasks) lacks supporting evidence. If we discard the naïve operationist view that constructs are defined by measurement procedures, and we take the alternative view that they are defined within the system of a theoretical language, then *measurement is essential to show the very existence of a theoretically posited construct.*

The studies reported in this article were aimed at dealing with the issue of construct measurement that is preliminary to any exhaustive comparison or integration of theories. Two constructs were considered: the *M* Operator (from Pascual-Leone's theory); and the Articulatory Loop (from Baddeley's theory). They were selected because each of them is the most extensively studied within the corresponding theory, and estimates of their capacity have often been proposed. It seemed necessary to consider whether each of them can be measured meaningfully. If this was not possible, then co-ordinating the two theories would be a rather problematic enterprise. Thus, in the studies reported below, the reader will find variables usually related to *either* of these constructs. However, for reasons of space, *only the results relevant to the* M *Operator* will be reported and discussed here.

A number of measures of *M* capacity have been proposed, such as the Compound Stimuli Visual Information Task (Pascual-Leone, 1970), the

Figural Intersections Test (henceforth FIT: Pascual-Leone & Ijaz, 1989), the Backwrad Digit Span (Case & Globerson, 1974), the Counting Span Test (Case, Kurland, & Goldberg, 1982), the Mr Cucumber Test (De Avila, Havassy, & Pascual-Leone, 1976), and a number ordering task (Case, 1972).

Let us consider how some of these tasks, used in this research and described in detail below, are related to M capacity. In a broad sense, if we accept the assumption that performance is overdetermined, all cognitive tasks involve the M operator to some extent. Thus, a measure of M capacity must first satisfy the requirements that the M operator is heavily taxed, and secondly, that other sources of variance are minimised.

The counting span and the backward digit span demand that digits are stored while operations are performed on them (either counting or reversing their order). These tests had previously been used as M capacity tests (e.g. Case, 1977, 1985; Chapman & Lindenberger, 1989; Globerson, 1983; Morra, 1984; Scardamalia, 1977). Also, the Mr Cucumber test demands that information is transformed (i.e. abstract spatial encoding of a colourful picture, and motor responding to such abstract codes), as well as stored. It has been used as a test of M capacity (e.g. Case, 1985; Dennis, 1992; de Ribaupierre & Bailleux, this issue; de Ribaupierre, Keizer, Sancho, Spira, & Thomas, 1990). Finally, the FIT places an information load, because it requires simultaneously considering a number of shapes, which often are rotated or enlarged and always overlapping (so that transforming information enters the picture). It has been used as an M capacity test (e.g. Burtis, 1982; Chapman & Lindenberger, 1989; Johnson & Pascual-Leone, 1989; Scardamalia, 1977).

Of course, traditional short-term memory tasks, such as forward digit or word span, also place high demands on subjects in terms of information load. As such, they can be expected to be related to M capacity, and actually, it has been shown that they are (e.g. Burtis, 1982; Morra & Stoffel, submitted). However, they demand very little in the way of transforming information. As a consequence, the efficiency of a rote rehearsal strategy turns out to be a major source of variance, also in terms of individual differences (e.g. Baddeley, Thomson, & Buchanan, 1975; Hulme & Tordoff, 1989). Thus, the requirement that other sources of variance are minimised is not satisfied, and they are not tests of M capacity.

By contrast, some other tasks used in this research require transforming information but do not place a high information load. In addition, others are likely to have a large proportion of variance accounted for by other operators, including domain-specific knowledge, either figurative or operative (i.e. strategic). As a consequence, they are clearly not measures of M capacity.

It is conceivable, by analogy with the backward digit span, that also backward word span or the backward condition of Corsi's test (described later) can be used as *M* capacity tests. Relevant data are lacking, however: Semantic or motor encoding strategies, respectively, may bring into these tasks an excessive amount of variance not accounted for by *M* capacity. Exploring this empirical question is one of the goals of this research.

When the *M* capacity required by performing a task is studied, methodological problems arise in identifying *which* pieces of information are to be counted as separate schemes (e.g. see Case, 1974; de Ribaupierre & Pascual-Leone, 1979). However, when one's goal is only to measure subjects' *M* capacity, these difficulties may be circumvented by using tasks in which: (a) all stimuli are distinguishable, unrelated units; (b) all items have the same content and are likely to be performed with the same strategy; and (c) the only difference among items is the number of stimuli (i.e. figurative schemes) that they involve. Although these test construction criteria might run into a risk of oversimplifying issues, they have already been used successfully (e.g. Case, 1985). They also allow one to compare performance across tests, because all test scores are based on the assumption that simple, distinguishable, unrelated stimuli can be counted as separate units.

One more issue must be discussed here, i.e. why the *number of stimuli in each item* is directly taken as the measure of *M* capacity demanded by that item. Here, Pascual-Leone's and Case's views are somewhat different. According to Case (1985), the answer is straightforward, because he defines STSS (short-term storage space) as the number of outputs of cognitive operations that one can retain while performing another transforming operation. Pascual-Leone and Ijaz (1989) pointed out that the most common strategy in the FIT consists in taking one of the shapes as a background, and intersecting all other shapes on it. Thus, one unit of *M* capacity would be used in activating the intersection operative scheme, and the other k-1 units in activating the shapes mentally operated upon (and in addition, background shape is directly activated by input). On this, Pascual-Leone and Case would probably agree. However, Pascual-Leone's account of other tasks would be more complex. One should first specify, according to a hypothesised strategy, how many operative schemes are involved at a time; then, one should make assumptions on the role of other operators and on the probability of retrieving other stimuli, in addition to those currently activated by the *M* operator. Such detailed task analyses are beyond the scope of this paper (see Burtis, 1982; Morra & Stoffel, submitted, for similar models).[1]

---

[1] It is only suggested here that one or two units of *M* capacity are generally used for operative schemes. Broadly speaking and with a few differences among tests, and provided that an item does not include too many stimuli, this amount can be compensated by retrieving one or two partially decaying schemes. This issue will be considered further in the General Discussion.

In spite of extensive research on the M operator, only a few studies (e.g. Case, 1985; Case & Globerson, 1974) have set out to explore the relationships among a number of potential measures. This article is focused on the relationships among different measures proposed for the same construct.

Possibly, there are both developmental and individual differences in M capacity. If this is the case, then two consequences follow, which are tested in the studies reported later.

1. One can find positive correlations among performance measures in tasks which heavily tax the M operator (although the correlations may not be high, because each task may involve a number of different processes).
2. There should be a reasonable consistency among different measures or estimates of M capacity, and among their developmental trends.

STUDY 1

The first study, using a sample of primary schoolchildren, aimed at finding evidence of consistency among different measures that have been suggested for the same construct. Tasks that are supposed to tap either the M operator or the articulatory loop were administered, along with a number of other tests (generally, those that are well known and widely used for research or applied cognitive testing). The M capacity tests were the Figural Intersections Test, the Mr Cucumber Test, the Counting Span Test, the Backward Digit Span, and the Backward Word Span. We emphasise that backward, but not forward span is considered among the M capacity measures. Empirical evidence that forward and backward memory span tap different abilities was reported by Schofield and Ashman (1986), and Case (1972) had suggested that this is the case because forward memory span tests merely demand reproducing a sequence of stimuli, whereas backward span tests require reorganising a sequence.

The main questions were:

1. Different tests of M capacity have different contents and presumably involve different strategies. Do they show, nevertheless, significant correlations?
2. In factor analyses of mental abilities a verbal and a spatial factor are usually found. Can one find a factor that *specifically* loads M capacity tests, although they have different contents?
3. M capacity tests were devised with a common (hypothetical) unit of measurement; thus, they should show a similar rate of increase with age. Do they?

Method

Subjects

The subjects were 191 children (100 boys, 91 girls) attending elementary schools that serve a heterogeneous SES population in a large town in northern Italy. The age range was 6;0–10;11 (mean age 8;10). There were 10 six-year-olds, 39 seven-year-olds, 50 eight-year-olds, 49 nine-year-olds, and 43 ten-year-olds.

Materials and Procedure

Each subject received 17 tests in a fixed order. Three of the tests were group administered. Two group sessions were followed by two individual sessions.

The first group session included:
Raven's Matrixes PM47. The score was the number of correct responses.
Goodenough's Draw-A-Man. The score was given according to the manual.
The second group session included the *Figural Intersections Test* (FIT). Each item requires finding the area of overlap of a number of shapes (one of which is irrelevant in some items). The level of each item is given by the number of such shapes. A subject's score is the highest level at which at least 75% responses are correct, provided that this criterion is also fulfilled at all the lower levels.

The first individual session included:
An adaptation (Keating & Bobbitt, 1978; Morra, 1984) of *Posner's speeded letter classification task*. After practice, there were three timed trials for both Physical Identity and Name Identity conditions; each trial required sorting 20 cards, 10 of which carried "same" and 10 "different" letter pairs. No more than one error was allowed in each trial. The NI-PI score was the difference between the second best time in the Name Identity (NI) and the second best time in the Physical Identity (PI) conditions.
Forward Digit Span (from the WISC). The score was the highest number of digits correctly repeated in order.
Backward Digit Span (from the WISC). The score was the highest number of digits correctly repeated in reverse order.
Corsi's Block-Tapping Test: Forward (e.g. see Cornoldi & Soresi, 1980). Nine identical cubes are glued on a board in apparently random order (i.e. not as a matrix). The tester touches sets of cubes of increasing number, like in a memory span procedure, and the subject has to imitate the tester after

each set. The score is the highest number of positions reproduced in the correct order.

Corsi's Block-Tapping Test: Backward. The score is the highest number of positions reproduced in reverse order. One can ask, by analogy with the backward digit span, if this test can also be used as a measure of *M* capacity.

Speeded Articulation of Digits. The subject was required to count aloud repeatedly the numbers from 1 to 10, as fast as possible, without stopping. After five consecutive countings, the subject was timed using a stopwatch. The best time out of two trials was used.

Verbal Fluency. This is a subtest of Thurstone's PMA. We adapted it for schoolchildren by oral response, with a time limit of 3 minutes.

Figure Reconstruction (from the WISC). The raw score given according to the manual's instructions was used.

The second individual session included:

Counting Span Test. Subjects rapidly count aloud the several sets of coloured dots and then must recall the number in each set. The level of an item is given by how many sets it comprises. There are three items at each level from 1 to 8, but the third is skipped when a subject correctly responds to the first two; the test is discontinued when a subject fails all three of them. The score is the highest level when the subject gets at least two of the three items correct.

Mr Cucumber Test. The outline of an extraterrestrial figure, to which coloured stickers had been attached, is displayed. There are three items at each level from 1 to 8 (i.e. with stickers in 1 to 8 positions). The exposure time is 5 seconds, except for items at levels higher than 5; these are exposed for as many seconds as there are stickers attached. The subject must then show, on an outline without coloured stickers, the positions of the stickers. The test is discontinued when a subject fails all three items at one level. One point is given for each consecutive level when a subject gets at least two items correct, and one-third of a point for each correct item above that level. Scores are rounded up or down to the nearest unit.

Block Design (from the WISC). It was intended to use the raw scores, but their distribution turned out to be highly asymmetric. Thus, they were converted into a weighed score, i.e. a normal distribution in *T* scores.

Forward Word Span. We constructed this test in a similar way to the forward digit span test, using high frequency concrete words of two or three syllables. The score used was the highest number of words correctly repeated in order.

Backward Word Span. As above, with the words to be repeated in reverse order.

Vocabulary (from the WISC). The raw score was assigned according to the manual.

Results and Discussion

A factor analysis (principal components model; orthogonal rotation, retaining the components with an eigenvalue greater than 1) yielded three factors, which account for 44% of the total variance (see Table 1).

The tests that show the highest loadings on the first factor are: Raven's PM47, Figure Reconstruction, Block Design, Draw-A-Man, FIT, and Corsi's Test: Backward. The tests with highest loadings have a spatial content and have been shown to involve field-restructuring ability (e.g. Case & Globerson, 1974; Witkin, Dyk, Faterson, Goodenough, & Karp, 1962). Therefore, this factor will be called Spatial Ability and Field Independence.

The second factor clearly identifies Verbal Ability. It brings together Forward Digit Span, Vocabulary, Forward Word Span, Speeded Articulation of Digits, Verbal Fluency, Counting Span, and Backward Word Span.

The tests with highest loadings on the third factor were: Mr Cucumber, Counting Span, Backward Digit Span, FIT, and Backward Word Span; no

TABLE 1
Factor Loadings of the Tests used in Study 1

Tests	F1	F2	F3
Mr Cucumber Test	*38*	08	*53*
Counting Span Test	28	*42*	*48*
Backward Digit Span	*38*	28	*40*
Figural Intersections Test	*56*	16	*38*
Backward Word Span	30	*39*	*35*
Forward Digit Span	11	*57*	28
Vocabulary	*49*	*56*	17
Forward Word Span	27	*54*	19
Speeded Articulation of Digits	33	*49*	13
Verbal Fluency	19	*43*	18
Raven's Matrixes PM47	*78*	20	19
Figure Reconstruction	*71*	*37*	−5
Block Design	*67*	27	23
Goodenough's Draw-A-Man	*57*	34	24
Corsi's Test: Backward	*51*	24	30
Corsi's Test: Forward	32	25	34
Posner's NI-PI	−1	18	34
% of total variance	20.6	13.7	9.4
Eigenvalue	3.5	2.3	1.6

Note: $N = 183$ in this analysis, because of missing values. Decimal points omitted; sign of time measures loadings inverted; loadings of 0.35 or higher are in italics.

TABLE 2
Correlations (With Age Partialled Out) Among Measures of *M* Capacity

	MCT	*CST*	*BDS*	*FIT*	*BWS*
MCT (Mr Cucumber Test)		25*	23**	31*	21**
CST (Counting Span Test)			29*	21**	33*
BDS (Backward Digit Span)				25*	28*
FIT (Figural Intersections Test)					24*
BWS (Backward Word Span)					

Note: $N = 191$, $df = 188$ for all correlations. Decimal points omitted.
*$P < 0.001$; **$P < 0.01$.

other test had loadings greater than 0.35 in this factor, so it can be concluded that it represents *M* capacity. All measures of *M* capacity loaded on the third factor (and usually also on another according to their specific content).

Incidentally, it can be noted that Corsi's Test: Backward loaded on the first, but not the third factor. Informal observation of subjects' performance suggested that at least some subjects used a strategy of spatial patterning, rather than rearranging separate units, in solving this task. The hypothesis that this test could be used as a measure of *M* capacity thus seems to be ruled out. One can also note that, consistent with previous findings (Keating, List, & Merriman, 1985; Morra, 1984), Posner's NI-PI variable proved of little interest for the measurement of abilities.

Interpreting factor analysis, however, involves well-known problems, so that close inspection of correlations, with age partialled out, is advisable before drawing firm conclusions.

Table 2 reports the correlations, with age partialled out, among the measures of *M* capacity.

All partial correlations among *M* capacity measures were significant at $P < 0.001$, except three that were only significant at $P < 0.01$. However, the correlations were not very high (median = 0.25). This, and the fact that each of these tests had a bi-factorial composition, suggested that none of them can be regarded as a "pure" measure of the *M* operator. Therefore it would seem advisable to use *a battery* of tests for measuring its capacity.

The subjects' scores in the *M* capacity tests were submitted to analyses of variance, with age and tests as factors. The results are reported in Table 3.

As one could expect, the means of the various age groups were significantly different, $F(4,186) = 29.06$, $P < 0.001$; *post hoc* *t*-tests showed significant improvements ($P < 0.02$ or better) from each age group to the next. The mean scores in the single tests were also different, $F(4,744) = 16.71$, $P < 0.001$; *post hoc* *t*-tests showed that the Backward Digit Span was

TABLE 3
Mean Scores of the Tests of *M* Capacity by Age and Test in Study 1

Age Group	Test					Mean
	MCT	CST	BDS	FIT	BWS	
6 years	2.20	2.40	2.80	2.10	2.50	2.40
7 years	2.79	2.44	3.18	2.79	3.08	2.86
8 years	2.86	2.92	3.58	3.04	3.34	3.15
9 years	3.29	3.12	3.86	3.51	3.47	3.45
10 years	3.93	3.84	4.12	4.14	3.86	3.98
Mean	3.16	3.05	3.65	3.31	3.39	

easier than any other test, the Backward Word Span was easier than the Counting Span and the Mr Cucumber tests, and the FIT was easier than the Counting Span. The *t*-test was used in *post hoc* comparisons because it is most powerful in detecting (unwanted) differences among tests, thus testing our measurement assumptions under most severe conditions. Differences in scoring criteria, task demands, and possibly other factors may be responsible for differences (not large in absolute value, but highly significant) among these five tests.

Finally, the interaction was not significant, $F(16,744) = 1.34$, $P > 0.16$, suggesting that scores in these tests increase at the same rate in this age range. This is in agreement with the assumption that the figurative schemes involved in these tests are equivalent in terms of *M* capacity demand.

For each subject the variance of *M* capacity tests was computed. For instance, a hypothetical child whose scores were 2, 3, 4, 5, 6 would have a within-subject variance of 2.5, whereas another one who scored 3, 3, 4, 4, 5 would have a variance of 0.56; it seems intuitively clear that the mean score of the whole battery is far more reliable in the latter case than in the former. In this sample, 71% of the subjects had a variance less than or equal to 0.56, a further indication that these tests may be used as a battery with a same unit of measurement, namely schemes. Only 10% of the subjects had a variance greater than 1. This also strengthens the point of using them as a battery. In fact, this use was successfully made in studies on the relationship between *M* capacity and other cognitive tasks (e.g. Morra, Moizo, & Scopesi, 1988).

In sum, this study found a factor that loads five tests of *M* capacity, all of which significantly correlate with one another. There were significant differences among the mean scores of these tests, but their rate of increase with age was the same, and most subjects had a small variance among the scores in this battery of tests.

STUDY 2

Regarding M capacity, the aim of this study was to replicate the findings of Study 1, which supported the hypothesis that it can be measured by a battery of tests, sampling our subjects from a socially different environment. In addition, this study also addressed a number of questions on the articulatory loop, but the results are not reported here.

Method

Subjects

The subjects were 124 children (27, 28, 32, and 37 of them, respectively, attending grades 1 to 4), from small towns and villages in an alpine valley. The age range was 5;10–9;9 (mean age 8;0). In particular, the mean ages were 6;3, 7;5, 8;5, and 9;4 in grades 1 to 4, respectively.

Materials and Procedure

All subjects received in a fixed order five tests in two sessions. The Figural Intersections Test (FIT) was group administered in the first session.

In the second session, the Forward and Backward Digit Span, the Mr Cucumber Test, and the Counting Span Test were individually administered. (The Backward Word Span was not administered in this study, in order to avoid strategy carryover effects.)

In a third session, STM span, rate of articulation, vocabulary, and verbal fluency were individually tested in selected subjects. However, only the results of the first two sessions, that concern M capacity, are reported in this article.

Results and Discussion

The main point considered is whether the results regarding M capacity were replicated. The correlations, with age partialled out, are reported in Table 4. All the results except one, were significant at $P < 0.01$ or $P < 0.001$; the median was 0.25, as in Study 1.

The mean scores by grade and test are reported in Table 5. Significant effects were found for grade, $F(3,120) = 42.55$, $P < 0.001$ and test, $F(3,360) = 28.71$, $P < 0.001$, but not for the interaction, $F(9,360) = 1.33$, $P > 0.22$. This was the same pattern found in Study 1.

Post hoc t-tests showed that the Backward Digit Span and the FIT were easier than the Counting Span and the Mr Cucumber tests. This pattern was similar, although not identical, to that found in Study 1.

TABLE 4
Correlations (With Age Partialled Out) Among Measures of *M* Capacity in Study 2

	MCT	CST	BDS	FIT
MCT (Mr Cucumber Test)		39*	25**	20**
CST (Counting Span Test)			42*	24**
BDS (Backward Digit Span)				03
FIT (Figural Intersections Test)				

Note: $N = 124$, $df = 121$ for all correlations. Decimal points omitted.
*$P < 0.001$; **$P < 0.01$.

TABLE 5
Mean Scores of the Tests of *M* Capacity by Grade and Test in Study 2

Grade	Test				Mean
	MCT	CST	BDS	FIT	
1	1.82	1.74	2.19	2.52	2.07
2	2.32	2.50	3.00	2.86	2.67
3	2.50	2.41	3.00	3.03	2.73
4	3.11	3.16	3.57	4.13	3.49
Mean	2.49	2.51	2.99	3.21	

It can thus be concluded that (with the exception of the partial correlation between Backward Digit Span and FIT, and with minor differences in mean score differences) the results of Study 1 were replicated in a sample from a socially different environment.

GENERAL DISCUSSION

This article explored construct measurement problems of the *M* operator. Such problems were conceived, at the beginning, as preliminary issues to comparing and eventually integrating Baddeley's and Pascual-Leone's theories. However, recent unpublished studies from our laboratory tend to suggest that it is debatable whether the articulatory loop is actually a separate store with a time-limited capacity. Until this issue is solved successfully, it may be premature to even attempt to integrate constructs from the two theories. Thus, in this discussion only *M* capacity measurement issues were considered, and eventual integration across theories is postponed for future research.

Both Studies 1 and 2 suggested that a battery of tests (i.e. FIT, Mr Cucumber, Counting Span, Backward Digit Span, and Backward Word

Span) can be used to assess M capacity in children aged from 6 to 11 years. Correlational and factor-analytical evidence supported this view. In addition, these tests had been constructed with the assumption of a common measurement unit (Case, 1985); the ANOVAs showed that differences among scores in these tests, although significant, were not very large, and that scores in these tests increase at about the same rate during childhood. This developmental trend is consistent with Pascual-Leone's and Case's models, which predict the same rate of increase of M capacity during this age range, although they differ in other respects.

Some minor discrepancies between Studies 1 and 2 were also found (see Tables 3 and 5 and related text). We believe, however, that they are relatively unimportant. The children in Study 2 came from a different environment, and were slightly younger than in Study 1 because they were tested at the beginning of the school year (see Subjects section in Study 2); these points may account for slightly lower mean scores in Study 2. In addition, Backward Digit Span was easier than the FIT in Study 1, but not in Study 2. There are informal reports that there is lower verbal ability in the inhabitants of the alpine region where Study 2 was conducted, although it is also possible that the lifestyle in that area fosters children's spatial ability, which is one source of variance in FIT scores. Thus, one may consider that differences between Studies 1 and 2 are of little theoretical relevance, and rather, it is important to note that, despite being conducted in a quite different environment, Study 2 has replicated most findings of Study 1.

The use of a battery of four or five tests in order to assess M capacity is advised following these studies. In general, this is not difficult, because the FIT can be group administered in 1 hour or less, and the individual tests used here do not take very long. Let us mention, however, that sometimes only two tests were used and averaged, with satisfactory results. For instance, both Chapman and Lindenberger (1989) and Scardamalia (1977) used the Backward Digit Span and the FIT, whereas Johnson and Pascual-Leone (1989) used the FIT and the Serial Stimuli Visual Information task (not used in this research). In general, both the Serial and the Compound Stimuli Visual Information tasks are considered good M capacity measures (e.g. see Pascual-Leone, 1978), but they have the disadvantage of a complex and time-consuming administration procedure. Some tests could also be less appropriate for use with young subjects. For instance, Morra and Perchinenna (1993) also had a sample of pre-schoolers in their research, and thus preferred to avoid using the FIT and the Counting Span, which may cause instructions comprehension problems or lack of motivation in young children. Therefore, only the Mr Cucumber and the Backward Digit Span were used, but care was taken to equate the scoring rules of Backward Digit Span to those of the Mr Cucumber test.

As mentioned in the Study 1 discussion, scoring rules could be problematical. They have been set according to reasonable pass/fall criteria for each task; e.g. a rather strict criterion of at least 75% items per level correct is used in the FIT, in which more or less sophisticated strategies may lead subjects to pass a few items beyond their M capacity. In the Counting Span we used the habitual criterion of 2 out of 3 correct, whereas in the Backward Digit Span (and the Backward Word Span, parallel to it), a criterion of 1 out of 2 is prescribed by the manual of the Italian version of WISC, perhaps with no good reason for this difference. In addition, as the instructions of these tests allow to skip items after passing a level, we could not modify the scoring criteria. However, in the Mr Cucumber test we slightly modified the usual scoring criteria in order to capture more variance. We suggest that in future studies the scoring criteria are equated at least across those tests that require subjects to respond by recalling information. In particular, it is likely that slightly higher scores in the Backward Digit Span are partially accounted for by less strict scoring criteria.

The reader may remember that differences among mean scores of different tests, although significant, were not very great. I am inclined to think, however, that different scoring criteria do not fully account for differences in mean scores. It was mentioned in the Introduction that, according to Pascual-Leone's theory, one should specify the operative schemes involved and the role of different operators in each task. Although such detailed modelling is beyond the scope of this paper, it can be noted that the I operator is likely to be taxed very heavily in the Counting Span and in the Mr Cucumber test. In the former, subjects are required to count aloud quickly, that tends to cause interference with memory storage of digits. In the Mr Cucumber test, motor responding is likely to interfere with activation of abstract spatial codes (e.g. see Quinn, 1991). The other tests used in this research do not place such demands of resisting to interference on the subjects, and this may well be an additional source of variance across tests.

Finally, it must be stressed that the studies reported here only considered an age range between the years of 6 and 11. There are different views on the development of the M capacity beyond this age (e.g. compare Case, 1985 and Pascual-Leone, 1970, 1987). Deciding among such different views requires not only testing older subjects, but also that more tests are used,[2] and detailed task analyses are fully specified. There is little available research on this issue, and in our laboratory we are still at a preliminary stage; the theoretical controversy, therefore, must remain

---

[2]It should also be mentioned that some tests (e.g. the FIT and the Compound Stimuli Visual Information) were designed for use in a wide age range, whereas others (e.g. the Mr Cucumber and the Counting Span) were specifically designed for children.

unsettled. We have found significant correlations and a specific factor in adult subjects, but evidence is not sufficiently strong enough for us to identify a set of tests that can validly be used for measuring *M* capacity after the age of 11. We can thus conclude that, although a battery of tests can yield a reasonably valid measure of *M* capacity in individual subjects between the ages of 6 and 11, more research is needed with older subjects.

REFERENCES

Anderson, J.R. (1983). *The architecture of cognition.* Cambridge, MA: Harvard University Press.

Baddeley, A.D. (1986). *Working memory.* Oxford University Press.

Baddeley, A.D., Thomson, N., & Buchanan, M. (1974). Word length and the structure of short term memory. *Journal of Verbal Learning and Verbal Behavior, 14,* 575–589.

Burtis, P.J. (1982). Capacity increase and chunking in the development of short-term memory. *Journal of Experimental Child Psychology, 34,* 387–413.

Case, R. (1972). Validation of a neo-Piagetian capacity construct. *Journal of Experimental Child Psychology, 14,* 287–302.

Case, R. (1974). Structures and strictures: Some functional limitations on the course of cognitive growth. *Cognitive Psychology, 6,* 544–573.

Case, R. (1977). Responsiveness to conservation training as a function of induced subjective uncertainty, M-space, and cognitive style. *Canadian Journal of Behavioural Science, 9,* 12–25.

Case, R. (1985). *Intellectual development: Birth to adulthood.* New York: Academic Press.

Case, R., & Globerson, T. (1974). Field independence and central computing space. *Child Development, 45,* 772–778.

Case, R., Kurland, D.M., and Goldberg, J. (1982). Operational efficiency and the growth of short-term memory span. *Journal of Experimental Child Psychology, 33,* 386–404.

Chapman, M., & Lindenberger, U. (1989). Concrete operations and attentional capacity. *Journal of Experimental Child Psychology, 47,* 236–258.

Cornoldi, C., & Soresi, S. (1980). *La diagnosi psicologica nelle difficoltà di apprendimento.* Pordenone: ERIP.

Cowan, N. (1988). Evolving conceptions of memory storage, selective attention, and their mutual constraints within the human information-processing system. *Psychological Bulletin, 104,* 163–191.

De Avila, E., Havassy, B., and Pascual-Leone, J. (1976). *Mexican-American school children: A neo-Piagetian analysis.* Washington, DC: George Washington University Press.

Dennis, S. (1992). Stage and structure in the development of children's spatial representations. In R. Case (Ed.), *The mind's staircase* (pp. 229–245). Hillsdale, NJ: Lawrence Erlbaum Associates Inc.

Globerson, T. (1983). Mental capacity, mental effort, and cognitive style. *Developmental Review, 3,* 292–302.

Hulme, C., & Tordoff, V. (1989). Working memory development: The effects of speech rate, word length, and acoustic similarity on serial recall. *Journal of Experimental Child Psychology, 47,* 72–87.

Johnson, J., & Pascual-Leone, J. (1989). Developmental levels of processing in metaphor interpretation. *Journal of Experimental Child Psychology, 48,* 1–31.

Keating, D.P., & Bobbitt, B.L. (1978). Individual and developmental differences in cognitive-processing components of mental ability. *Child Development, 49,* 155–167.

Keating, D.P., List, J.A., & Merriman, W.E. (1985). Cognitive processing and cognitive ability: a multivariate validity investigation. *Intelligence, 9,* 149–170.

Morra, S. (1984). Classification in children: Two developmental information-processing models. *International Journal of Behavioral Development, 7,* 1–20.

Morra, S., Moizo, C., & Scopesi, A. (1988). Working memory (or the M operator) and the planning of children's drawings. *Journal of Experimental Child Psychology, 46,* 41–73.

Morra, S., & Perchinenna, R. (1993). *Thinkable images: Cognitive accounts of change in drawings.* Paper given at the VIth European Conference on Developmental Psychology, Bonn, 28 August–1 September.

Morra, S., & Stoffel, C. (submitted). *Toward a new model of verbal short-term memory development.*

Pascual-Leone, J. (1969). *Cognitive development and cognitive style: A general psychological integration.* Unpublished Ph.D. thesis, Université de Genève.

Pascual-Leone, J. (1970). A mathematical model for the transition rule in Piaget's developmental stages. *Acta Psychologica, 63,* 301–345.

Pascual-Leone, J. (1976). On learning and development, Piagetian style. *Canadian Psychological Review, 17,* 270–297.

Pascual-Leone, J. (1978). Compounds, confounds, and models in developmental information processing: A reply to Trabasso and Foellinger. *Journal of Experimental Child Psychology, 26,* 18–40.

Pascual-Leone, J. (1987). Organismic processes for neo-Piagetian theories: A dialectical causal account of cognitive development. *International Journal of Psychology, 22,* 531–570.

Pascual-Leone, J. (1989). An organismic process model of Witkin's field dependence-independence. In T. Globerson & T. Zelniker (Eds.), *Cognitive style and cognitive development* (pp. 36–70). Norwood, NJ: Ablex.

Pascual-Leone, J., & Goodman, D. (1979). Intelligence and experience: a neo-Piagetian approach. *Instructional Science, 8,* 301–367.

Pascual-Leone, J., & Ijaz, H. (1989). Mental capacity testing as a form of intellectual-developmental assessment. In R. Samuda, S. Kong, J. Cummins, J. Pascual-Leone, & J. Lewis (Eds.), *Assessment and placement of minority students* (pp. 143–171). Toronto: Hogrefe.

Pascual-Leone, J., & Morra, S. (1991). Horizontality of water level: A neo-Piagetian developmental review. In H.W. Reese (Ed.), *Advances in child development and behavior* (Vol. 23, pp. 231–276). Orlando, FL: Academic Press.

Quinn, G. (1991). *Encoding and maintenance of information in visual working memory.* In R. Logie & M. Denis (Eds.), Mental images in human cognition (pp. 95–104). Amsterdam: North Holland.

de Ribaupierre, A., Keizer, I., Sancho, A., Spira, A., & Thomas, L. (1990). *Etude longitudinale de la capacité d'attention mentale chez l'enfant de 5 à 12 ans.* FNRS Research Report, Université de Genève.

de Ribaupierre, A., & Pascual-Leone, J. (1979). Formal operations and M Power: a neo-Piagetian investigation. *New Directions in Child Development, 5,* 1–43.

Scardamalia, M. (1977). Information processing capacity and the problem of horizontal décalage: A demonstration using combinatorial reasoning tasks. *Child Development, 48,* 28–37.

Schofield, N.J., & Ashman, A.F. (1986). The relationship between digit span and cognitive processing across ability groups. *Intelligence, 10,* 59–73.

Shiffrin, R.H. (1976). Capacity limitations in information processing, attention, and memory. In W.K. Estes (Ed.), *Handbook of learning and cognitive processes* (pp. 177–236). Hillsdale, NJ: Lawrence Erlbaum Associates Inc.

Witkin, H.A., Dyk, R.B., Faterson, H.F., Goodenough, D.R., & Karp, S.A. (1962). *Psychological differentiation.* New York: Wiley.

INTERNATIONAL JOURNAL OF BEHAVIORAL DEVELOPMENT, 1994, *17* (1), 161–200

Developmental Measurement of Mental Attention

Juan Pascual-Leone and Raymond Baillargeon
York University, Ontario, Canada

A dialectical constructivist model of mental attention ("effort") and of working memory is briefly presented, and used to explicate subjects' processing in misleading test items. We illustrate with task analyses of the Figural Intersections Test (FIT). We semantically derive a set of 10 Theoretical Structural Predictions (TSP) that stipulate relations between mental attentional resources (mental-power: Mp) and the systematically varied mental demand of items (mental-demand: Md), as they jointly codetermine probable performance (conditional probabilities of passing and failing). These predictions are evaluated on first approximation using a known family of ordered Latent Class models, all probabilistic versions of Guttman's unidimensional scale. Parameters of these models were estimated using the Categorical Data Analysis System of Eliason (1990). Main results are: (1) Data fit Lazarsfeld's latent-distance model, providing initial support for our 10 predictions; (2) The M-power of children (latent Mp-classes) when assessed behaviourally may increase with age in a discrete manner, and have the potential to generate interval scales of measurement; (3) In the light of our results what statisticians often consider "error of measurement" appears (in part) to be signal, not noise: The organismic signal of misleading (Y-) processes that in their dialectical (trade-off) interaction with success-producing (X-) processes generate performance.

Requests for reprints should be sent to J. Pascual-Leone, Psychology Department, York University, 4700 Keele Street, North York, Ontario, Canada, M3J 1P3.

Preparation of the paper and research work was supported by research grant No. 551019 from the Social Sciences and Humanities Research Council of Canada to the first author and by a postgraduate scholarship from the Fonds de Recherche et de Formation des Chercheurs to the second author. We are indebted to J. Johnson for her thoughtful comments on an earlier version of the paper, to R. England for his computer-graphics preparation of the testing instruments, to John Fox, Ross Traub, and Scott Eliason for their statistical advice in latent class analysis. We are grateful to A. von Eye, the editors, and two other anonymous referees, for their very constructive criticisms. We also thank G.W. Ho, C. Lee, E. Peretz, N. DeFrancesco, and M. Artuso for their help in collecting and scoring the data. Thanks are due to the York Region Roman Catholic Separate School Board and York Region Public School Board, and participating schools, for their co-operation.

INTRODUCTION

The idea that mental attentional "energy" or capacity (nowadays often thought of as "working memory") is essential in cognitive development might go back to Binet (1911), James (1966), and Spearman (1927). For "tough-minded" (James, 1955/1907) psychologists, however, the notion of a *mental attentional energy* raises fear of theoretical ghosts, possibly because tough-minded psychologists prefer extensive constructs to intensive ones.[1] Thus when Pascual-Leone (1970, Pascual-Leone & Smith, 1969) re-introduced the intensive construct of mental attentional energy (the "M-operator") and offered a quantitative measure, the work was largely ignored by the establishment. To this day only Kahneman (1973), whose book reviewed experimental but not developmental evidence and did not offer a measure of mental attention, is generally credited with re-introducing intensive attention (James, 1966, "mental effort") in psychology. Experimentalists refer to this construct in terms such as *"mental effort"* (Hasher & Zacks, 1979; Kahneman, 1973), "undifferentiated" or "generic" *resources*, and *resource-limited processes* (e.g. Bjorklund & Harnishfeger, 1990; Wickens, 1984) or as a *"supervisory attentional system"* or *central executive* that is free to apply across the different extensive content domains or modular memories (Baddeley, 1992a,b; Moscovitch, 1992; Norman & Shallice, 1980). However, serious criticisms have been raised against these intensive constructs (e.g. Allport, 1980; de Ribaupierre & Pascual-Leone, 1984). Because this attentional "effort", or "resource-limited process", is not measured independently from the memory data which it is meant to explain, there is danger of a vicious circle: Is mental attention just a theoretical ghost?

Organismic developmental theory and the developmental method can help in resolving this problem. They make possible concurrent experimental variations of subjects' mental-attentional capacity levels (which we call *M-power* levels) and of tasks' mental demand (*M-demand* levels). This leads to measurement structures that assess directly the subjects' mental-attentional capacities. To take advantage of this opportunity, however, one must give up monolithic constructs and think of the organism as

---

[1]Constructs are extensive or extensional if their meaning can be properly represented by way of extensive measurement—quantities that can be added, subtracted, etc., as physical measures can; they are intensive if their meaning cannot be so grasped but must be reached by way of qualitative models which analogically capture the meaning in question. For instance, "working memory", with its reference to a "mental space" that could be measured, is extensional; but "mental energy" as a general-purpose, limited-resource of the mind is an intensional construct. One might however argue that hidden behind extensive constructs are intensive ones that serve as scaffolding.

constituted by a "republic" (a dialectical organisation) of separate functional and often modular systems or "operators" (Johnson, Fabian, & Pascual-Leone, 1989; Pascual-Leone, 1980, 1987, 1990; Pascual-Leone & Goodman, 1979), which *in their dynamic interaction* constitute different modular memories as well as the open, general-purpose mechanics of *mental attention*.

The purpose of this paper is to investigate, with one of our mental capacity (*M-measurement*) tasks, some quantitative-structural conditions for the measurement of mental attention. Measurement as such will not be discussed. In the process we shall address the following points. (1) The intensive aspect of attention can be explicated as a dynamic system of modular "operators" that in their interaction create mental attention and working memory. (2) One dynamic "operator" that models the intensive aspect of attention, mental attentional energy (also called *M-capacity* or *M-operator*), can be quantified in terms of the number of separate schemes that a subject can simultaneously boost into activation, and which are not being boosted by the situation as such (this set-theoretical quantification we call *M-power*). (3) This construct, when suitably quantified, appears as *latent variable* of a measure which increases with age in normal children, and might produce an interval scale of measurement (e.g. Johnson, Fabian, & Pascual-Leone, 1989; Pascual-Leone, 1970, 1987). (4) This growth is endogenous, a function of maturation, and is indexed by chronological age in normal subjects. This "hidden" measure, a child's M-power, is a numerical characteristic of Piaget's and neo-Piagetian qualitative stages of cognitive development, and a major innate component of developmental *and* general intelligence (e.g. Case, 1992; Johnson et al., 1989; Pascual-Leone, 1970, 1980; Pascual-Leone & Goodman, 1979). (5) Mental capacity is one of two endogenous attentional resources (both "operators" modelling the intensive aspect of attention) that function in tandem and are developmentally interlocked; the second one is a mental/willful inhibition mechanism or *interrupt*. The application of these two mechanisms causes the so-called "mental effort". (6) The extensional aspect of attention can be explicated in terms of three different but interrelated constructs: first, *M-space*, i.e. the set of schemes currently boosted by the M-operator (M-power is the maximum size of M-space that a subject can muster); secondly, *working memory*, i.e. the set of schemes currently hyperactivated or highly activated, whether because they are in M-space or because they are being boosted by other "operators" (such as affects, or automatised complex schemes that we call "L-structures"—see later); thirdly, *field of activation*, i.e. the total set of schemes currently activated (whether hyperactivated or not) in the repertoire (i.e. in long-term memory). Notice that these three extensive constructs are nested: The latter include the former as a part. Some authors broaden the notion of working memory making it, in practice, synonymous with mental attention. To expand working memory to include intensive aspects of mental attention, as Baddeley (1992a,b) does, is an error—it conflates the intensive and extensive aspects of attention and makes harder causal analysis and M-measurement.

In what follows, we first present a selective summary of our theory. We then summarise some principles of M-measurement and illustrate them with the Figural Intersections Task (FIT). Finally, we present new results on the FIT that support claims made above, and show that M-capacity is a dynamic *hidden variable* of the organism, perhaps measurable with the power of an interval scale.

A BRIEF NOTE ON THE THEORY OF CONSTRUCTIVE OPERATORS

We can summarise this theory by distinguishing three sorts of constructs: subjective operators of the psychological organism, which we call *schemes*; silent/hidden operators of the brain's hardware, which we call *capacities* (or *operators*, when the intended meaning is not ambiguous); and organismic *principles* of the brain's hardware stipulating how schemes and operators interact to produce actual performances.

Organismic Schemes

Schemes are information-bearing, elementary, modular units of both human mental processing and long-term memory; the content of subjective and objective experience, and its structure, is embodied in them. They can be conceptualised as functional systems released by conditions, which produce processing or behavioural effects when applying. Elsewhere, we have given a neuropsychological interpretation of schemes (e.g. Pascual-Leone, 1989; Pascual-Leone & Johnson, 1991) and discussed their modalities and modes of processing (Johnson, 1991; Pascual-Leone, 1984, 1980, 1989; Pascual-Leone & Irwin, 1992).

Hidden "Hardware" Operators, and Principles

The hidden "hardware" operators stand for independent, dynamically interacting sources of organismic constraints that, together with organismic principles, model the organismic "wet" hardware; and they model it as a dialectical organisation (trade-off principles, overdetermination, nonlinear dynamics) that influences mental processing, schemes, and performance. We mention here only hidden operators relevant to our task, and discuss them as we explicate two complex organismic functions: learning and mental attention.

We define *Learning* as essentially resulting from the interaction of two mechanisms: *C-operator* and *L-operator* (for details see Pascual-Leone, 1980, 1984, 1989; Pascual-Leone & Goodman, 1979; Pascual-Leone & Ijaz, 1989; Pascual-Leone & Irwin, 1992). The *C-operator* is content (C) learning, which is indigenous to perceptual and motor modalities: Subrepertoires of basic schemes for our input/output memory modules, and main cause of the priming effect (cf. Schacter & Tulving, 1992). The *L-operator* is logical (L), i.e. structural learning—the learning of patterns and relations holding within sets of schemes. The organism achieves this L-learning in three alternative ways: LC-learning, LA-learning, and LM-learning.

LC-learning is overlearning of C-schemes, which leads to co-ordination and "chunking" of C-schemes whenever they are co-functional and often co-activated within the same context (or sort of situation). These LC-schemes become *L-structures* when they are properly automatised and can be used without mental effort. LC-learning is a slow cumulative learning, rich in contextual detail, the sort of "low-road" learning (Pascual-Leone & Irwin, 1992; Salomon & Perkins, 1989) that is so useful in *facilitating situations* (i.e. situations where all schemes activated by the context are relevant, or at least compatible, with the task at hand—Pascual-Leone, 1980, 1984, 1989).

LA-learning is L-learning made possible by high activation of cognitive schemes brought about by potent affects—affective schemes that boost contextually salient cognitive schemes relevant for the affects in question.

LM-learning is L-learning brought about by mental effort: The boosting of a set of task-relevant schemes by means of the M-operator (see later), often after the I-operator (the Interrupt mechanism) has, under executive control, "willfully" inhibited the contextually activated irrelevant schemes. LM-learning is fast and selective (few contextual details are retained); it is capable of abstracting relational pattern structures that are mobile and suffer little interference from the context. The "operational" mental structures that Piaget attributed to high developmental intelligence are of this type, as is the result of "high-road" learning (Pascual-Leone & Irwin, 1992; Salomon & Perkins, 1989). Notice that in *misleading situations* (Pascual-Leone, 1980, 1984, 1989), i.e. when the context activates schemes that can induce subjects to error *vis-à-vis* the intended task, LM-learning and LM-structures are the only processes that can succeed. Notice also that mental attention is used both to learn and to use (retrieve from memory and apply) LM-structures. LM learning is a byproduct of mental attention's repeated working with schemes of memory (rather than a byproduct of "working memory").

Mental attention is a complex function of the brain; we define it as a functional system, constituted by four operators in dialectical interaction, and integrated by an organismic principle: The mechanism for Schematic

Overdetermination of Performance (SOP). We denote each of these constructs by one or more capital letters that suggest their function (Johnson et al., 1989; Pascual-Leone, 1980, 1984, 1987, 1989, 1990; Pascual-Leone & Johnson, 1991; Pascual-Leone & Morra, 1991).

The first operator of endogenous attention is E.[2] This is the dominant set of compatible executive schemes here-and-now activated and directing the mental process (executives are schemes that embody temporally structured plans for action or mental processing). We call such a set *the Executive* or *E-operator*. This Executive is activated initially by dominant *affective schemes*, or goals, of the subject; and in turn it can mobilise and allocate *M-* and *I-operators* to change the state of working memory (i.e. the set of highly activated or hyperactivated schemes in the total repertoire—what Piaget called "Centration"), in accordance with the Executive plan. It is generally accepted in neuropsychology that executive schemes—plans and planning—are located in the dorsolateral areas of the prefrontal lobes (e.g. Fuster, 1989; Goldman-Rakic, 1987).

M is the hardware operator that serves to *boost* endogenously into hyperactivation the task-relevant schemes (or in the extensive metaphor: "Place these schemes in the M-space"). This *M-capacity* is a limited resource—a kind of *mental energy*—that increases endogenously with human development up to adolescence. Its measure—the number of schemes that it can boost simultaneously—is a quantitative *stage-characteristic* of Piagetian and neo-Piagetian qualitative stages (for empirical validation of this claim see, e.g. Case, 1992; Johnson et al., 1989; Pascual-Leone, 1970, 1980, 1987; Pascual-Leone & Ijaz, 1989, Johnson & Pascual-Leone, 1989; plus references cited in these papers).

A subject's M-operator capacity (*M-capacity*) can be measured, and the measure grows in discrete fashion with each Piagetian or neo-Piagetian stage of development. This growth of M-capacity enables the structural integration of more (nonsalient but relevant) schemes in the process of solving tasks. Thus, whenever adequate experience is already provided, this growth of M-capacity constitutes the "transition rule" for passing from one qualitative developmental stage to the next (Pascual-Leone, 1970)—a quantitative-structural explication of development. The idealised (quantitative-structural) values taken by this *hidden parameter* of mental attention were predicted (Pascual-Leone, 1970) as stated in Table 1.

The third operator of endogenous attention is the capacity to actively inhibit or *interrupt* activation of task-irrelevant schemes. We call this organismic factor *interrupt* or *I-operator* (Pascual-Leone, 1989; Pascual-Leone, Goodman, Ammon, & Subelman, 1978; Pascual-Leone, Johnson,

---

[2]Strictly speaking, E is not an operator but a collection of schemes of a special kind— executive schemes—that have the power to monitor and regulate the use of hidden operators such as M and I.

TABLE 1
Predicted M-power Values as a Function of Age and their Correspondence to the
Piagetian Substage Sequence

M-power $(e + k)$	Piagetian substage	Chronological Age (Years)
$e + 1$	Low preoperations	3–4
$e + 2$	High preoperations	5–6
$e + 3$	Low concrete operations	7–8
$e + 4$	High concrete operations	9–10
$e + 5$	Transition to formal operations	11–12
$e + 6$	Low formal operations	13–14
$e + 7$	High formal operations	15–16

Note: In this model, e is the M-power that develops during the first 26–28 months of life, later used as a constant to maintain hyperactivation of the task's general executive. Variable k is the M-power emerging later, often used to activate "action" schemes.

Goodman, Hameluck, & Theodor, 1981). The importance of *central* inhibitory factors (such as our I-operator), is nowadays well recognised (e.g. Case, 1992; Dempster, 1992; Fuster, 1989; Stuss, 1992). The I-operator is important in the management of attention. It serves to eliminate or reduce activation of task-irrelevant schemes (often activated by the context), thus ensuring that schemes currently boosted by M become dominant and determine performance (see later); it also serves to produce focal and selective attention (by way of interrupting irrelevant schemes), eliminating distractions, and allowing stable dominance by the current executive (directed thinking). We think (Pascual-Leone, 1974, 1989), consistent with neuropsychology (e.g. Fuster, 1989; Goldman-Rakic, 1987; Stuss, 1992), that the M- and *I-operators* are connected with the prefrontal lobes, because these operators are general-purpose and monitored by the Executive.

The fourth constituent of mental attention is the subject's endogenous capacity to produce as performance a single integrated whole, even though often many different schemes co-determine the performance in question. This fourth capacity is what Gestalt psychologists and Piaget called internal-autochthonous "Field" processes (the "Minimum Principle" of perception, the "S-R compatibility" principle of performance, etc.). We attribute these phenomena to a performance-closure dynamic mechanism called the *F-operator*, which makes performance (perception, imagery, thinking, language, motor activity, etc.) simultaneously minimally complex and maximally adaptive (Pascual-Leone, 1989; Pascual-Leone & Johnson, 1991; Pascual-Leone & Morra, 1991).

The *F-operator* works in co-ordination with an important silent principle of the brain's hardware, which we shall not discuss here. This is the principle of Schematic Overdetermination of Performance (*SOP prin-*

ciple). This *Overdetermination principle states that performance at any time is synthesised by the dominant* (most activated) *cluster of compatible schemes available in the brain's field of activation at the time of responding; and the probability of this performance is proportional to the relative dominance of the cluster of schemes generating it* (Pascual-Leone, 1989; Pascual-Leone & Goodman, 1979; Pascual-Leone & Johnson, 1991; Pascual-Leone & Morra, 1991).

Together, the F-operator and the SOP principle constitute an *F-SOP mechanism* that, at each moment, causes a *dynamic synthesis* of performance out of the currently dominant cluster of compatible schemes (cf. Pascual-Leone, 1984, 1987, 1989; Pascual-Leone & Goodman, 1979; Pascual-Leone & Johnson, 1991). This conception of a subconscious dynamic "choice" that via overdetermination generates performance is congenial to modern psychometric theories of intelligence (Horn & Hofer, 1992) and current computational theories of induction (e.g. Holland, Holyoak, Nisbett, & Thagard, 1986); and also evokes epistemologically the "relaxation" algorithms used in connectionist/neuronal programming to resolve conflicts among competing processes (e.g. Smolensky, 1988).

CONTROL OF MENTAL ATTENTION IN MISLEADING CONTEXTS

In Fig. 1 we have symbolised the dynamic model of mental attention sketched previously, and indicate some of the brain areas that may be involved in it. The three key constituents of mental attention, i.e. the *M-operator* (mental energy M), the *I-operator* (central inhibition or interrupt I), and the currently dominant set of executive schemes (i.e. E) are symbolised by a rectangular "flashlight" located in the prefrontal lobes.

This "flashlight" of mental attention "illuminates", i.e. boosts with activation, a region (the inner ellipse in Fig. 1) of the repertoire of *action*[3] schemes; this region is the *M-space* (M-centration) or focus of endogenous mental attention. *Action schemes* are schemes other than executives that move subjects into actual, covert or overt, performance. Mental energy applies on E and on the "chosen" action schemes H to empower them to produce performance. This is symbolised in Fig. 1 by the expression $M(E, H)$. Figure 1 assumes that the task the subject is dealing with is a very *misleading* situation: Schemes that are not relevant and not inside the M-space must be interrupted to reduce interference. This interruption is

---

[3]By "action" here we mean in a broad sense any activity of the organism that in an immediate or mediated fashion determines performance, with the exception of planning (executive) steps. Mental imaginal representations and other mental processes we call action if they are beyond the level of executive processing (Pascual-Leone, 1990).

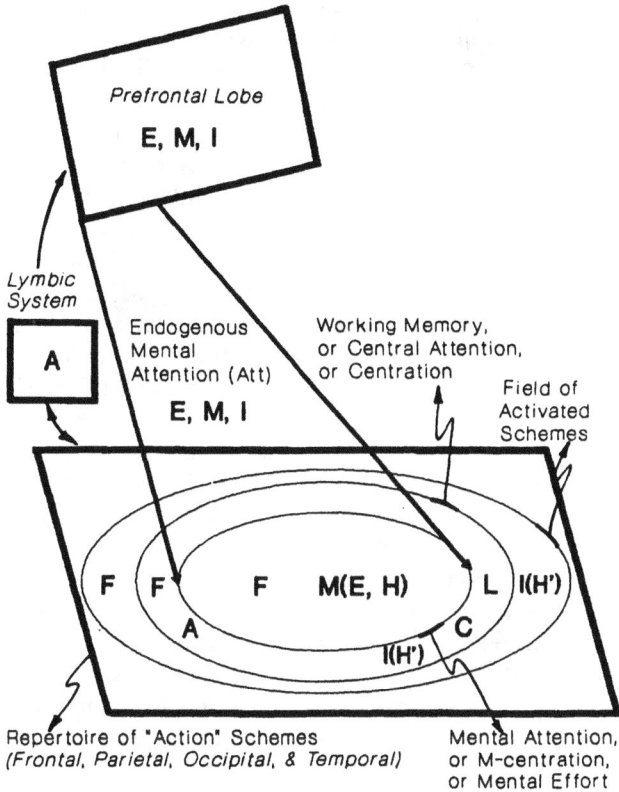

FIG. 1.   Determinants of mental attention. The Theory of Constructive Operators symbolised in terms of a flashlight metaphor. Capital letters represent "hardware" operators or scheme processes discussed in the text.

indicated in Fig. 1 by the expression $I(H')$ found in both the outer ellipse (i.e. the *field of activation*) and the middle ellipse—the working memory or central attention region which is often highly activated due to factors, such as A (affective schemes), C (content schemes), and L (logical-structural, i.e. relational, schemes). Whenever these factors of working memory are boosting misleading schemes, the executive E must block them by applying the Interrupt operator, thus effectively reducing the current working memory to the M-space. Notice that in this sort of situation the area within the "beam" of attention is only the M-space (area inside the inner ellipse); the "edge" of this "beam" (the ellipse) results from interruption caused by the I-operator; the phenomenological closure of the field of mental attention is done by the *F-SOP* mechanism.

The task discussed later is of this kind. But there are other kinds of situations (facilitating, mildly distracting, etc.) that are best handled using other Mental-Strategy or processual *MS-formulas* (Pascual-Leone, 1984, 1987, 1989; Pascual-Leone & Goodman, 1979). For instance, in a fully facilitating situation (e.g. when one is watching a well-constructed play or movie) one can best process the information by practising *dis-Interruption*, i.e. by cancelling all interruption, even the mild one that is normally automatically applied on schemes that are not being boosted by *M* in the current act of mental attention (Pascual-Leone, 1984). Observe that under these facilitating conditions the working memory of practised subjects might become nearly as large as the whole field of activation. Thus, a subject must have good *executive controls* to regulate differential use of his/her attentional resources in tune with the MS-formula of the situation at hand.

Misleading situations (test items in our case) have, as misleading factors, contextually elicited processes driven by C- and LC-schemes (automatised modular memory processes), and also perceptually based F-operator saliences (Gestaltist field effects and S-R compatibility factors); both sets of factors hinder perception of the total intersection in our FIT task (see later). These contextually driven strategies (later called *Y-strategies*) compete with and often distort the intended performance (which results from relevant executive-driven strategies—later called *X-strategies*). Context in these situations is part of the problem (the misleading context) as much as part of the solution (the relevant information to be picked up). Elsewhere (Pascual-Leone, 1989) we have characterised this state of affairs in *misleading situations* with the following processual formula:

$$\left\{ [E \text{ and } M \text{ and } I](x) \; \underline{\text{V}} \; [LC \text{ or } F](y) \right\} \text{ V} \left\{ \; \ldots \; \right\} \qquad \text{(MS1)}$$

In this *MS formula* (mental-strategies formula) at least two sets, X and Y, of strategies are in conflict; they are mutually exclusive ($\underline{\text{V}}$), and compete to produce the performance. The correct *strategies X* are indicated in (MS1) by the expression $[EMI](x)$. This expression means that the activation dominance of relevant schemes (x) is being driven by the dominant executive schemes. *E* can mobilise I-interruption to inhibit irrelevant schemes (y-schemes) that constitute the *Y-strategies*. *E* can also direct the M-operator to boost the activation of relevant schemes included in (x). Schemes included in (x) change from one step to another of the task solution. The incorrect strategies Y are indicated in (MS1) by the expression $[LCF](y)$. This expression means that the set of task-irrelevant schemes (y) is consistently boosted by *LC* (e.g. misleading automatised patterns) and by *F*. In misleading situations *F* often supports the Y-strategies initially. The expression V $\left\{ \; \ldots \; \right\}$ in (MS1) refers to other contextual strategies that are not incompatible with the X-strategies. In misleading situations, however, non-misleading contextual strategies are rare (otherwise, the situation would not be misleading).

Pascual-Leone (1989) has emphasised that the X-vs.-Y conflict of misleading situations may occur among figurative schemes (e.g. perceptual representations), as in situations measuring the cognitive style Field-Dependence-Independence; but other times the X-vs.-Y conflict occurs among operative schemes (in alternative solution strategies), as happens with Guildford's Adaptive Flexibility tasks; or perhaps the X-vs.-Y conflict is both figurative and operative, as is the case with our Figural Intersections Task (FIT). Irrespective of how the Y-strategies are constituted, X-strategies will dominate whenever the E, M, and I operators can localise and inhibit y-schemes, and simultaneously bring into hyperactivation the x-schemes. However, if LC and F operators are dominant, y-schemes and thus Y-strategies may dominate. There are usually many different Y-strategies—many different ways of performing incorrectly.

THE FIGURAL INTERSECTION TASK AND ITS PROCESS/TASK ANALYSIS

We have used the Figural Intersections Task (FIT) in a group administered paper-and-pencil test. After introductory items where practice and training is given, the testing items are introduced. Figure 2 illustrates one of these items.

Every item presents on the right-hand side of the page a number of geometric shapes separated from one another. Shapes on the right-hand side are the task's *relevant* figures. The number of these figures in each item varies randomly from 2 to 8, and this number, j, defines the *M-class* (equivalence class) of the item. On the left-hand side there is a *figural*

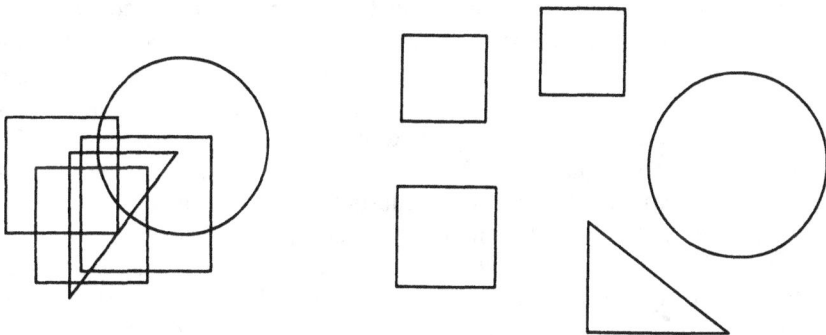

FIG. 2.   FIT-Relevant test item that includes five relevant figures to intersect (i.e. Md = 5).

compound with all relevant (i.e. right-hand side) figures overlapping in a common *total intersection*. In other versions of the task (see later) this figural compound may contain one irrelevant figure, not found in the right-hand side, which is not in the total intersection. When present, the irrelevant figure is a distractor that must be ignored.

Every item has two subtasks (Pascual-Leone & Ijaz, 1989): (1) to place a dot inside each figure found on the right-hand side of the page—this is to ensure proper exploration of all relevant figures—and (2) on the left-hand side, to place a *single dot* that is inside all relevant figures at the same time. Item difficulty differences are generally due to three factors: *first*, to the M-demand imposed by the M-class *j* of each item (i.e. the number of relevant figures to be kept in mind using M-power—this is part of the X-strategy, and causes the M-power/M-demand trade-off mentioned later); *secondly*, the dynamic Gestaltist patterning created by the compound configuration (via F, C, LC, and SOP factors), which may hinder the perceptual segregation of separate figures (attention to this Gestalt patterning is one strategy Y); *thirdly*, the number and strength of Y-strategies elicited by the item's context increases with the number *j* of figures available in it—because the more relevant figures that are contained in an item the more partial intersections exist (see later), and therefore more numerous and stronger Y-strategies as a whole become. Presence of Y-strategies forces the need for using willful mental attention (i.e. M-power and I-interruption —henceforth called M-power for brevity) within X-strategies to keep Y-strategies in abeyance. Thus, a subject's M-power, which we shall estimate as *t*, must be used for two purposes: to boost relevant schemes of the X-strategy, and to detect and interrupt irrelevant schemes of the Y-strategies. Because an item's M-demand estimated by the value *j* indicates the M-power needed to boost task-relevant schemes, the *difference t − j (or, better, the ratio t/j) gives an estimate of the free M-power, free X-strategy resources in general, available to control Y-strategies elicited by the item's context.* This hidden conflict between correct strategies X and misleading wrong strategies Y is what we call *Contextual Overdetermination Trade-off*.

In item construction we strive to maintain the same processual Mental Strategy formula for all items, so as to keep similar the Contextual Overdetermination Trade-off; but we let the contextual misleadingness factors increase in strength in a graded manner with the Md-class *j* of the item. We do so because the M-power needed by subjects capable of passing the Md-class of items in question also increases in a graded manner. As a result, performance becomes probabilistic, but the MS formula of items remains invariant over the test; and a single major determinant of item difficulty appears which is the M-power/M-demand (Mp/Md) trade-off. Contextual Overdetermination Trade-off acts then only as moderator variable.

Consider in more detail the task analysis. We have found two mental substrategies X for solving the task, which can be combined to the subject's advantage given enough executive sophistication. These are the holistic Total Intersection procedure and the analytical Partial Intersections procedure. The *Total-Intersection procedure* keeps in mind separately all the relevant figures involved, with the exception of one figure that is used as background. For instance, taking the item of Fig. 2 as an example, the subject might use the circle—a salient figure—as background within which to search for three squares and a triangle. The background figure (call it f_1) becomes easily automatised into a perceptual L-structure which does not require M-boosting; but M-boosting is needed for an operative scheme OP_i that can find the total intersection in the figural compound. Analysis of this process might be symbolised as follows:

$$M(OP_i, \{f_1\}_{LC,F}, f_2, f_3, f_4, f_5) => i_{12345}. \qquad (TA1)$$

Where f_1 stands for whichever figure the subject chooses as background; and the braces $\{\ \}$ that surround f_1 and the subscripts in the $\{f_1\}_{LC,F}$ indicate that f_1 *is not* being boosted by the M-operator, but instead is boosted by an automatised (LC) attentional L-structure that serves to hold in mind effortlessly the chosen perceptual frame, as well as by the Gestaltist Field saliency (F) of the figure f_1 when the executive uses it consistently as background. The other figures $f_2 \ldots f_5$ stand, respectively, for the three squares and the triangle, and the M-parentheses indicate that the included schemes (except a scheme placed in braces) are being boosted by M (are in the M-space). This mental operation leads to the finding of the common total intersection i_{12345}. Using this strategy the item of Fig. 2 has a mental M-demand of 5 (accessible to "ideal" children of 11 years or older, see Table 1).

Many children, however, invent more efficient strategies using the *Partial Intersections procedure*. This procedure consists in reaching partial intersections, remembering the configuration of these partial intersections, and using them instead of the figures for generating other intersections. With such a procedure children of 7 or 8 years (mental M-power = 3) could solve items with an M-demand of 6 or of 7, in particular if the test's misleadingness is not too high. But sophisticated executives and M/I controls are needed to achieve this result. The procedure might be this one:

(1) $M(OP_1, \{f_1\}_{LC,F}, f_2, f_3)$ $=> i_{123}$ (TA2)
(2) $M(OP_i, i_{123}, f_4)$ $=> i_{1234}$
(3) $M(OP_i, i_{1234}, f_5)$ $=> i_{12345}$
(4) $M(OP_i, i_{12345}, f_6)$ $=> i_{123456}.$

Such a strategy is unlikely in a young child, but 6-year-olds with sophisticated executives might achieve it if they had sufficiently strong perceptual L-structures to segregate figures f_3 to f_6 without the need of M-boosting, or if they use the partial intersections i_{123} and/or i_{1234} as *background* within which to search for the other figures (a strategy that saves M- because such background figure becomes automatised). This is unlikely, however, without practice or special mentoring, because the strategy's Executive demand is too high for 8-year-olds: four steps must be planned and carried out against misleading contextual factors. In contrast the procedure would be easier for 9- and 10-year-olds: (who have a mental M-power of 4) to invent and realise:

$$\text{(1)} \quad M(OP_i, \{f_1\}_{LC,F}, f_2, f_3, f_4) \quad => i_{1234} \quad\quad\quad \text{(TA3)}$$
$$\text{(2)} \quad M(OP_i, i_{1234}, f_5, f_6) \quad => i_{123456}.$$

These Partial Intersections strategies introduce disturbances when one wants to analyse carefully, item by item, the latent M-demand ordinal structure (i.e. the difficulty level) of the items. To minimise this difficulty, our subjects were administered an alternative form of FIT that contained in each item one irrelevant figure (the FIT-irrelevant); this was done prior to testing with the main FIT-relevant task. Because the presence of irrelevant figures in the figural compound (the left-hand side of the item) makes it harder to use a Partial Intersections strategy, children might acquire an executive habit of not using partial intersections, and this bias could then be transferred to the FIT-relevant administered later. In this manner we hoped to minimise the use of Partial Intersections strategy in the FIT-relevant task.

In the next two sections we present theoretical predictions that follow from this model of the Figural Intersections Task (FIT). Readers concerned mainly with empirical results may choose to skip these two sections and return to them after the paper has been read.

Mp/Md TRADE-OFF AND CONTEXTUAL OVERDETERMINATION TRADE-OFF

As experienced by the subject (whether consciously or not), misleading tasks often elicit two different dialectical (i.e. trade-off) processes that interact; and this dynamic interaction affects item difficulty and makes performance probabilistic. The two dialectical processes are the M-power/M-demand Trade-off and the Contextual Overdetermination Trade-off. We discuss them successively and then illustrate their dynamic interaction.

The *M-demand (Md)* of an item is the minimum M-capacity that a subject needs to solve the item using a stipulated solution strategy (the simplest of these strategies serves to define the E-demand). *M-power* (*Mp*), the measure of M-capacity, can be ideally defined by the number of separate schemes that a subject is able to M-boost simultaneously to solve tasks or items actually passed by him/her. These "separate schemes" can be inferred "a priori" via task analysis, or empirically estimated from the highest Md-class of items passed by a subject in an M-measure task such as FIT. Our postulate for the *Mp/Md Trade-Off*, which we call *Postulate 1* (P1), states that ideal[4] items in misleading contexts cannot be solved unless the subject's maximum M-capacity is equal to or greater than the item's M-demand. Thus, when $Mp \geq Md$ (cells of data where the ratio t/j is equal or larger than 1—see Fig. 1), the correct X-strategies $[EMI](x)$ dominate over the Y-strategies and the subject tends to succeed. When $Md > Mp$ (cells of data where t/j is smaller than 1—see Fig. 1), however, Y-strategies $[LCF](y)$ largely determine performance, leading to failure with a high probability, and the degree of failure (determined by the Contextual Overdetermination Trade-off—see later) depends on the strength of Mp relative to Md. The Mp/Md Trade-off occurs between the actual power of the subject's E-, M-, and I-operators, which generally increase with age due to maturation and experience, and the item's "mental difficulty"—the item's E-demand (complexity of rele-vant strategy), M-demand, and I-demand (number and/or strength of irrelevant or misleading schemes to be interrupted—see Contextual Over-determination Trade-off given later). When E-demand and I-demand are controlled by the experimenter via item construction and subject training, a parametric variation of M-demand can be created across items and used to scale the subjects' M-power. In this form of measurement (*M-measurement*) the M-power of subjects and M-demand of items are *conjointly* measured using the same hidden/latent variable *M*.

Under these conditions, performance level reflects, according to our theory, the equilibrium between the subject's M-power and the task's M-demand—for ideally perfect items and ideal subjects this trade-off can generate passing levels exhibiting the developmental trace of a "staircase", as prescribed in Table 1 and empirically demonstrated in various studies ·(e.g. Johnson et al., 1989; Pascual-Leone, 1987; Todor, 1977, 1979). In less ideal tasks this "staircase" might also be demonstrated by way of a *dynamic polarisation effect* predicted by our theory in the Mp/Md Trade-off boundary of the data matrix. We now explain this predicted effect which we use later. Recall that in misleading items salient features of the situation induce Y-strategies that compete with the correct strategy X to lower the chance of a good result. The X-strategy has no chance to apply unless an executive (E) directs mental attention to boost relevant schemes

---

[4]Ideal because they do not elicit unintended processes.

with M-energy and to inhibit (via the I-operator) misleading Y-schemes. The dynamics is one that generates a "bipolar dimension" or *dynamic polarisation*—a polarity of solution strategies that gives the task a flip-flop, all-or-none, character with regard to the M-power/M-demand trade-off: If the X-strategy is strong enough (i.e. there is enough M-power, I-power, and Executive know-how) the task will be solved with high probability; otherwise the Y-strategies will dominate, and the item will be failed with high probability, making its probability of success very low.

Consider a matrix of data such as that in Fig. 3. The rows represent items of a misleading M-measurement task like FIT, where each row contains an item of M-demand j, and all rows are ordered by these values ($j = 2, \ldots,$ 7). The columns contain types of subjects in terms of their task-estimated M-power t, ordered by these values ($t = 1, \ldots, 7$). The Mp/Md Trade-off boundary run between data cells where Mp $\geq$ Md (cells of data with high theoretical probability of success) and those where Md $>$ Mp (high theoretical probability of failure); this is a *dynamic polarisation boundary*.

In ideal cases, probability of success should be very high in cells above the main diagonal (Mp/Md Trade-off boundary), and very low below it; we denote this state of affairs symbolically in Fig. 3 by means of arrows ($<$---$<$) in two directions that criss-cross the depicted Mp/Md Trade-off

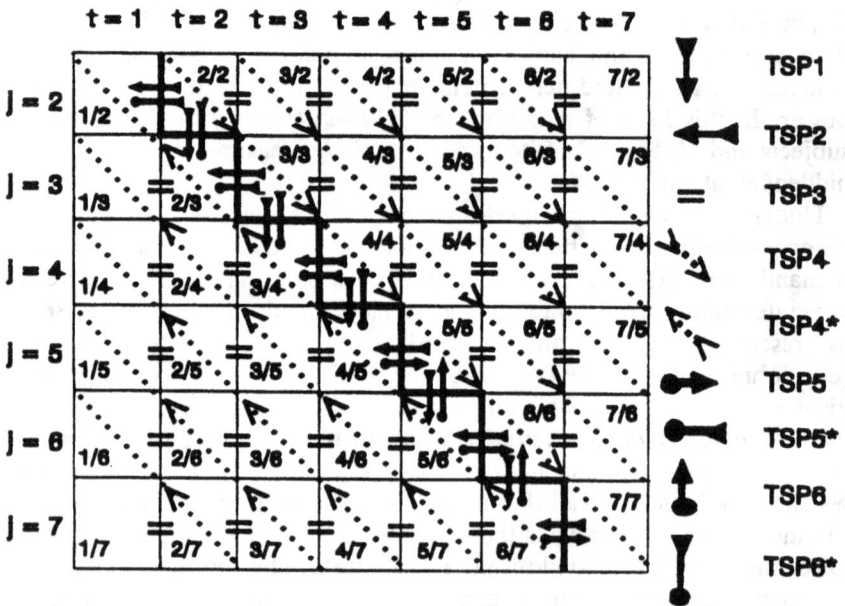

FIG. 3.   Matrix of Theoretical Structural Predictions postulated on the data of Conditional Probabilities.

boundary (main diagonal). Notice that this dynamic polarisation boundary has the shape of a staircase. The existence of this dynamic polarisation boundary constitutes our predictions TSP1 and TSP2, given later.

The *Contextual Overdetermination Trade-off*, caused by the Overdetermination (SOP) principle, is our *Postulate 2* (P2). It asserts that there is a trade-off between the relative strength (misleadingness and variety) of the Y-strategies an item elicits in a subject, and degree of success of the X-strategies afforded by this subject (here relative strength of elicited Y-strategies is assessed against the strength of X-strategies required to succeed). The strength of X-strategies is indexed by the subject's M-power index t, estimated in the task. The strength of the item's Y-strategies can in the FIT be estimated by the number j of figures to be intersected. The strength of Y-strategies relative to X-strategies we estimate by the ratio t/j when emphasis is on the *free X-strategies* available after X-strategies have been applied to control Y-strategies; it can be estimated by the ratio j/t when emphasis is just on assessment of Y-strategies. In both cases it is a ratio, because as the number j of figure grows, it multiplies, in a combinatorial fashion, the number of partial intersections, each partial intersection becoming a misleading feature in the subject's search for a total intersection. Coping with the task requires executive control of Y-strategies using mental attention. As misleadingness increases, indexed by the size of j (i.e. the Md-class of the item), more *free A-resources* (indexed by the ratio t/j) are needed to counteract the Y-strategies. If this ratio t/j is greater than 1 (see Mp/Md Trade-off principle), the greater the ratio the more likely it is that the item will be passed, up to some maximum. If the ratio t/j is less than 1, the smaller the ratio the more likely it is that the item will be failed, up to another maximum. This inference, that the ratio between t and j (above/below the critical ratio value of 1) can affect the probability of success/failure in an item, is what we call the *Mp/Md difference effect*—a key manifestation of the Contextual Overdetermination Trade-off. To facilitate evaluation of this effect we have written in the cells of our theoretical matrix in Fig. 3 the values to the corresponding ratios t/j. Notice that this effect predicts ordinal relations among probabilities of success in cells located along columns and diagonals of the matrix. Some of these ordinal relations are indicated by lines and/or "larger-than" symbols ($>$) in Fig. 3, for they constitute our predictions (TSP4) and (TSP4*) given later.

We illustrate further the close dynamic interaction between the Mp/Md Trade-off and Contextual Overdetermination Trade-off by emphasising other predictions. Because probabilities of success above the main diagonal of our theoretical data matrix are determined primarily (but not solely) by X-strategies, and probabilities of failure below the main diagonal are primarily caused by Y-strategies; and as X- and Y-strategies constitute two qualitatively different processes, we can expect that probabilities generated by these two different processes will have different maxima. Thus, *within each item* the error rate (1—probability of success) above the main diagonal should be of different magnitude than the probability of failure below the main diagonal. This is the foundation of our predictions TSP4, TSP5*, TSP6, and TSP6* mentioned later.

LATENT RELATIONAL PREDICTIONS OF THE MODEL

Let us assume that (as happens with the FIT) we have a mental-attention task constituted by classes of items (i.e. homogeneous scales), with each class incrementing by one of the M-demand relative to the previous class, so that all relevant values of M-power are assessed in the task. Further, the formula of mental strategies (MS-formula) elicited by each item is essentially the same across items and across subjects. Processes other than Mp/Md Trade-off, e.g. Contextual Overdetermination Trade-off processes, are held constant, relative to the item's M-demand, in item construction across item scales (Md-classes). Under these circumstances, and assuming our theory correct, we summarise in five postulates the essential conditions needed to measure mental capacity in misleading situations:

Postulate 1 (P1): i.e. summary postulate representing the Mp/Md Trade-off: In misleading situations an ideal item cannot be reliably solved unless the subject's maximum M-power is equal to or greater than the item's M-demand. See the previous section for details.

Postulate 2 (P2): i.e. summary postulate standing for the Contextual Overdetermination Trade-off: There is a dynamic trade-off between relative strength of an item's Y-strategies and degree of success of the X-strategies afforded by a subject. The strength of X-strategies can be estimated by t, which indexes a subject's M-power value (i.e. his/her M-capacity estimate, developmental level, or subject type) when assessed within the same FIT task. The strength of Y-strategies can be estimated by j (i.e. the number of relevant figures to be intersected in the item in question). The *relative strength of the item's Y-strategies* is given by the ratio j/t, and the still available *free X-strategies* is given by ratio t/j. Postulate 2 outlines how, in the Contextual Overdetermination principle given earlier, small variations in item misleadingness (elicited Y-strategies) can, relative to the subject's X-strategies (i.e. M-power and Executive know-how), change the rate of success of the item in question. See the previous section for details.

Postulate 3 (P3): M-capacity, and thus its hidden (ideal theoretical) measure or M-power, increases with age in normal subjects with the maturational schedule stipulated in Table 1.

Postulate 4 (P4): i.e. postulate of local independence. If an ideal M-measurement task constituted by different Md-classes of items is administered to subjects who belong to the same latent Mp-class of M-capacity, pass/fail responses to any two of these *ideal* items will be mutually independent (Lazarsfeld's axiom of *local independence* among items). This is because what creates dependency relations among responses to items is their differential M-demand relative to the subjects' M-power; if all subjects have the same M-power this dependency cannot be manifested.

Postulate 5 (P5): which derives from postulates P1 and P3: If subjects pass tasks/items of M-demand k, they should also pass with high probability any task/item of M-demand $k-1$, $k-2$, ... etc., found in lower Md-classes: k is indexed in the models by the empirical parameter j (number of figures to be intersected in the FIT item).

These five postulates (P1, P2, P3, P4, and P5) are sufficient to generate, with the aid of process/task analysis, a system of *M-measurement* (Pascual-Leone, 1980, 1987; Pascual-Leone, Baillargeon, Lee, & Ho, 1991; Pascual-Leone & Ijaz, 1989; Pascual-Leone & Johnson 1991; de Ribaupierre & Pascual-Leone, 1984). The purpose of the present study is not, however, to develop or validate this method of mental-attention measurement. Elsewhere we have investigated this measurement both developmentally (e.g. Johnson et al., 1989; Pascual-Leone, 1970; Pascual-Leone & Ijaz, 1989) and using Item Response Theory (Baillargeon, 1993; Pascual-Leone et al., 1991). Our current purpose is to evaluate empirically quantitative-structural assumptions that are central to this system of measurement, and we do not present here measurement results as such. The theoretical assumptions were summarised in our five postulates; we test these assumptions with 10 Theoretical Structural Predictions (TSP) based on the trade-off principles discussed earlier. The predictions stipulate relational constraints for a suitable matrix of data, such as that illustrated in Fig. 3, that embody our developmental theory—and do so without making reference to chronological age.[5] The reader should notice that these predictions are

---

[5]Chronological age is not used in this developmental theory as a causal variable for two reasons: (1) a growth of M-capacity is instead postulated as a necessary endogenous mechanism of developmental-stage transitions (Pascual-Leone, 1970); (2) M-capacity can be estimated independently from age. The idealised theoretical correspondence between M-capacity growth and chronological age is postulated in Table 1. A structuralist test of this correspondence will be provided in the Results section, in connection with Table 6.

assumed (by virtue of the SOP-F principle) *simultaneously* to impose their constraints on the subject's performance, which results from the dialectical balance (trade-off) among the various constraints involved. Consequently, the manifest (in contrast to the latent) structure of the empirical data may not show clearly some of these predicted patterns. For instance, predictions TSP3 or TSP3*, given later, may not be manifested clearly because predictions TSP4 or TSP4* overshadow them; or predictions TSP5 and TSP6 may not appear in simple empirical data (e.g. proportions of pass per class of items and age group) because older subjects using a Partial-Intersections strategy in the FIT can obtain a performance level higher than expected with the Total-Intersection strategy, which our main model assumes. These constraints, however, should be manifested in the latent structure (Latent Class Analysis) of the data.

The first theoretical Structural Prediction can be represented mathematically as follows:

$$\text{If} \quad t-j \geqslant 0 > t-j'$$
$$\text{Then} \quad \Pr[Md_j(1)Mp_t] \ggg \Pr[Md_{j'}(1)/Mp_t]. \tag{TSP1}$$

This formula states that: *If* t (i.e. the index of a subject's M-power estimated within the task) minus j (i.e. the item's M-demand index) is equal-to-or-greater-than ($\geqslant$) zero; and zero is greater than t minus j' (i.e. $Md_{j'} > Mp_t$) *then* the conditional probability (Pr) of giving a correct response (1) to an item of M-demand j (Md_j), given that ($|$) subjects have an M-power t (Mp_t), is much-much-greater-than ($\ggg$) another probability: The probability (Pr) of giving a correct response ($|$) to an item of M-demand j' ($Md_{j'}$), given that ($|$) subjects have an M-power t (Mp_t).

This prediction is based on postulate P1 (*dynamic polarisation boundary*), and grounds for postulating a "much-much-greater-than" ($\ggg$) relation are given in section "Mp/Md Trade-off and Contextual Overdetermination Trade-off". In Fig. 3 this prediction is symbolised by arrows (➡) *placed vertically* and directed downwards between cells contiguous to the main diagonal (i.e. the Mp/Md Trade-off or dynamic polarisation boundary). The greater-than symbol formed by the "feathers" of the arrow (i.e. >) is here meaningful, and indicates that probabilities of success in cells situated on the "greater-than" side of the symbol, >, are much greater than the probablities of cells situated on the "smaller-than" side. A similar convention is followed with other symbols in Fig. 3 regarding other predictions. TSP1 is re-written using a similar, more compact notation in Table 2.

All Predictions in Table 2 use the same compact notation. Prediction TSP2, dual of TSP1 and produced by the same mechanisms, appears in Table 2. TSP2 is symbolised in Fig. 3 by a *horizontal* arrow (⬅). Analysis of Fig. 3 in the light of the formula should clarify TSP2's signi-

TABLE 2
Theoretical Structural Predictions on the Conditional Probabilities of the Data Matrix

If $(t-j) \geq 0 > (t-j')$ then $\Pr[j(1)|t]$ $\gg$ $\Pr[j'(1)|t]$	(TSP1)
If $(t-j) \geq 0 > (t'-j)$ then $\Pr[j(1)|t]$ $\gg$ $\Pr[j(1)|t']$	(TSP2)
If $(t-j) > (t'-j) \geq 0$ and $LM(X\text{-st})$ then $\Pr[j(1)|t] = \Pr[j(1)|t']$	(TSP3)
If $0 > (t-j) > (t'-j)$ and $LM(X\text{-st})$ then $\Pr[j(1)|t] = \Pr(j(1)|t']$	(TSP3*)
If $(t-j) \geq (t'-j') \geq 0$ and $j < j'$ and $t < t'$ then $\Pr[j(1)|t] > \Pr[j'(1)|t']$	(TSP4)
If $0 > (t-j) \geq (t'-j')$ and $j > j'$ and $t > t'$ then $\Pr[j(1)|t) < \Pr[j'(1)|t']$	(TSP4*)
If $(t-j) \geq 0 > (t'-j)$ and $j \geq 5$ then $\Pr[j(1)|t] < \Pr[j(0)|t']$	(TSP5)
If $(t-j) \geq 0 > (t'-j)$ and $j < 5$ then $\Pr[j(1)|t] > \Pr[j(0)|t']$	(TSP5*)
If $(t-j) \geq 0 > (t-j')$ and $t \geq 5$ then $\Pr[j(1)|t] < \Pr[j'(0)|t]$	(TSP6)
If $(t-j) \geq 0 > (t-j')$ and $t < 5$ then $\Pr[j(1)|t] > \Pr[j'(0)|t]$	(TSP6*)

Note: The relation $\gg$ means "much-much-greater than". Grounds for predicting $\gg$ rather than simply $>$ are given in the section Mp/Md Trade-off and Contextual Overdetermination Trade-off. Condition LM(X-st) means the X-strategy is overlearned (LM-learned).

ficance. Third and fourth predictions based on the Mp/Md Trade-off principle appear in Table 2 as TSP3 (and TSP3*), and in Fig. 3 as equal signs (=) placed between cells in all rows above (and below) the main diagonal.

TSP3 states that probabilities of success in item j, for subjects with M-power t or t', should be equal or similar if both t and t' are larger than j, provided that the X-strategy (X-st) producing the effect is well learned, i.e. is LM-learned [LM(X-st)]. TSP3 is predicted on the basis of Postulate P1: When the X-strategy is dominant, i.e. $t-j \geq 0$, and overlearned, i.e. LM(X-st), dynamic polarity due to the MP/Md Trade-off should lead to equal and high passing rates irrespective of t-values. This is because a well-practised X-strategy inhibits (via an interrupt, i.e. the I-operator) y-schemes that locally (in each item) might lower the probability of success. Thus, TSP3 stipulates a *maximum* probability of success that tends to be constant across cells from the same row, although (due to TSP4) this maximum should decrease with the size of j. In other words, the state of balance between X- and Y-strategies is item-specific, and tends to be stable within each item across t-values. TSP3* makes similar predictions but applying to the matrix area below the main diagonal. These are cells where Y-strategies dominate over X-strategies. For this reason TSP3* only applies to subjects with sophisticated overlearned (LM) executives that nonetheless fail to put together a dominant X-strategy for lack of sufficient M-power (and thus produce a Y-strategy). These people should maintain executive control to actively inhibit (interrupt) y-schemes other than those relevant to the chosen Y-strategy. Because subjects were pretested with FIT-Irrelevant we believe that this prediction may be true for our subjects.

In predictions given thus far (TSP1, TSP2, TSP3, TSP3*) Mp/Md Trade-off processes play perhaps a more important role than do Contextual Overdetermination Trade-off processes. The converse is the case for predictions TSP4, TSP4*, TSP5, TSP5*, TSP6, and TSP6*. TSP4 and TSP4* (see Table 2) are based on the Mp/Md Difference Effect discussed in the previous section. Figure 3 highlights the significance of these two predictions: Contiguous cells placed along *diagonals* and in *columns* of the matrix have probabilities of success that are ordered in magnitude as indicated by the attached "greater-than" symbols (and by the ratios t/j that appear in the cells of Fig. 3).

Another way of testing the Mp/Md Trade-off and Contextual Overdetermination Trade-off principles was mentioned in the section that introduced these principles: The error rate (1 − probability of success) in cells above the main diagonal should have a different magnitude than the probability of failure below the main diagonal, within each item. This is the foundation of our predictions TSP5, TTSP5*, TSP6, and TSP6* These predictions appear in Table 2; they are symbolised in Fig. 3 by modified arrowheads or arrowtails (e.g. ●━, ●➡), which are either vertical or horizontal, and criss-cross the Mp/Md Trade-off boundary. These symbols represent ordinal relations between probability of success in cells above the main diagonal and probabilities of failure in cells below the main diagonal (the arrow modification, i.e. ●, signifies failure). The reader can observe in Fig. 3 that the predicted order changes direction from TSP5 and TSP6, to TSP5* and TSP6* This predicted change in direction is a third line of evidence in support of our Trade-off principles. The change in order is explained as follows: In TSP5 and TSP6, where t and j are large (of values 5, 6, or 7) the ratio t/j will have a value close to 1 and thus the *free* X-strategies available to control Y-strategies will be weak; but the Y-strategies, because j is large, will be augmented in their strength. Consequently, the likelihood of passing item j in a cell above the main diagonal (i.e. $\Pr[j(1)t]$) should be smaller than the likelihood of failing item j (i.e. $\Pr[j(0)t']$) in a contiguous cell situated below this diagonal (or dynamic polarisation boundary). A more detailed derivation of this prediction as it bears on latent-structure conditional probabilities is given in the Appendix.

Consider now predictions TSP5* and TSP6* (see Table 2) where both t and j are of small magnitude ($t = 2, 3, 4$, and $j = 2, 3, 4$; i.e. $t < 5$ and $j < 5$). Because both t and j are small, the ratio t/j will have a value close to 1 and the free X-strategy will be weak; but as j is small the Y-strategies themselves will be weak, making them controllable by the X-strategies. Thus probability of passing (i.e. $\Pr[j(1)t]$) in boundary cells situated above the main diagonal will be high, potentiated by the I-interruption of Y-strategies (this is prediction TSP2). In contrast probability of failing (i.e. $\Pr[j(0)t']$) in contiguous cells below this Mp/Md Trade-off boundary will be low: j is low, and this causes weak Y-strategies.

In what follows, we test these predictions as a set of simultaneous constraints in Latent Class models.

LATENT STRUCTURE MODELS

The methods of latent structure analysis (Lazarsfeld & Henry, 1968) and more particularly the response-error models with ordered latent classes (Clogg & Sawyer, 1981; McCutcheon, 1987) can serve to test simultaneously the 10 predictions. To do this, we begin with six dichotomously scored items, each from a different class of items. No larger number is allowed by the Categorical Data Analysis program available to us (CDA System, PROG MLLSA module of Eliason, 1990). If the item responses were fully independent, i.e. free from constraints caused by the Mp/Md Trade-off which affects their performance, we should find no latent structure: All 64 possible (i.e. 2^6) distinct response patterns of data might occur irrespective of any other pattern. Each of these patterns is constituted by an ordered set (vector) of 6 item-slots each containing either 1 (item passed) or 0 (item failed). Our theory, however, predicts (TSP1, TSP2) a strong latent structure: It predicts probabilistically and relative to the type (Mp-class) of subjects, that the frequency in the data of all but 76 response patterns (postulates P1, P2, P3, and P5) will be minimal. Ours is a latent (probabilistic) version of Guttman's scale (Lazarsfeld & Henry, 1968; Clogg & Sawyer, 1981). We equate M-power (our *Mp-classes*) with the *cumulative M-class* of items that can be passed using at least t amount of M-power. Thus, if (a, b, c, d, e, f) symbolise items belonging respectively to ordered M-demand classes (*M-classes*) a, b, c, d, e, f (where a is the class with least M-demand), the expected response patterns (*cumulative M-classes*) in question are: (0,0,0,0,0,0), all items failed, and (1,0,0,0,0,0), (1,1,0,0,0,0), (1,1,1,0,0,0), (1,1,1,1,0,0), (1,1,1,1,1,0), (1,1,1,1,1,1).

Further, if chronological ages for attaining these latent Mp-classes (or developmental levels) should approximate prescriptions of Table 1 (Postulate P3), the models may indirectly test a controversial developmental assumption: that M-power grows in spurts of *discrete* values. We test (on first approximation) our predictions using three response-error models along with a total independence model that serves as baseline. The test is only approximative because the models are not fully constrained by the predictions.

The *Total Independence Model* assumes that there is no latent Guttman structure and that items are totally independent in their behaviour; therefore, all 64 possible 1/0 (pass-fail) patterns of responding have frequencies independent from each other (a "one class" model—Clogg, 1988). In this case all our predictions are violated.

In the *Proctor Model* the latent probabilistic variable has the same (pass or fail) error rate for all items, if the population is homogeneous. The model is specified by an equality restriction:

$$\pi_{2(0)|1} = \pi_{2(1)|2} = \pi_{2(1)|3} = \pi_{2(1)|4} = \pi_{2(1)|5} = \pi_{2(1)|6} = \pi_{2(1)|7} =$$
$$\pi_{3(0)|1} = \pi_{3(0)|2} = \pi_{3(1)|3} = \pi_{3(1)|4} = \pi_{3(1)|5} = \pi_{3(1)|6} = \pi_{3(1)|7} =$$
$$\pi_{4(0)|1} = \pi_{4(0)|2} = \pi_{4(0)|3} = \pi_{4(1)|4} = \pi_{4(1)|5} = \pi_{4(1)|6} = \pi_{4(1)|7} =$$
$$\pi_{5(0)|1} = \pi_{5(0)|2} = \pi_{5(0)|3} = \pi_{5(0)|4} = \pi_{5(1)|5} = \pi_{5(1)|6} = \pi_{5(1)|7} =$$
$$\pi_{6(0)|1} = \pi_{6(0)|2} = \pi_{6(0)|3} = \pi_{6(0)|4} = \pi_{6(0)|5} = \pi_{6(1)|6} = \pi_{6(1)|7} =$$
$$\pi_{7(0)|1} = \pi_{7(0)|2} = \pi_{7(0)|3} = \pi_{7(0)|4} = \pi_{7(0)|5} = \pi_{7(0)|6} = \pi_{7(1)|7}.$$

Elements of this matrix are the conditional probabilities $\Pr[Md_j(k)Mp_t]$ that govern success (1) or failure (0) in the sketched theoretical matrix of Fig. 3. Parameters j, k, and t stand, respectively, for items, response values (pass/1 or fail/0) and latent Mp-classes (i.e. cumulative M-classes). Analysis of this model in terms of our predictions (Table 2 and Fig. 3) shows the following. (1) Predictions TSP1 and TSP2 are upheld, because passed and failed items in this model are ordered into a simple structure. (2) Predictions TSP3 and TSP3* are upheld because of the prescribed equality (=) of passed/failed probabilities. (3) Predictions TSP4, TSP4*, TSP5, TSP5*, TSP6, and TSP6* are violated, because in this model all probabilities are equal.

The *Item-Specific Error Rate Model* assumes one item-specific error rate (only one conditional-probability value) associated with each of the six items. A relaxation of Proctor's model, the relation among conditional probabilities is now undefined between items, but still constant within items. These structural restrictions describe the model:

$$\pi_{2(0)|1} = \pi_{2(1)|2} = \pi_{2(1)|3} = \pi_{2(1)|4} = \pi_{2(1)|5} = \pi_{2(1)|6} = \pi_{2(1)|7}$$
$$\pi_{3(0)|1} = \pi_{3(0)|2} = \pi_{3(1)|3} = \pi_{3(1)|4} = \pi_{3(1)|5} = \pi_{3(1)|6} = \pi_{3(1)|7}$$
$$\pi_{4(0)|1} = \pi_{4(0)|2} = \pi_{4(0)|3} = \pi_{4(1)|4} = \pi_{4(1)|5} = \pi_{4(1)|6} = \pi_{4(1)|7}$$
$$\pi_{5(0)|1} = \pi_{5(0)|2} = \pi_{5(0)|3} = \pi_{5(0)|4} = \pi_{5(1)|5} = \pi_{5(1)|6} = \pi_{5(1)|7}$$
$$\pi_{6(0)|1} = \pi_{6(0)|2} = \pi_{6(0)|3} = \pi_{6(0)|4} = \pi_{6(0)|5} = \pi_{6(1)|6} = \pi_{6(1)|7}$$
$$\pi_{7(0)|1} = \pi_{7(0)|2} = \pi_{7(0)|3} = \pi_{7(0)|4} = \pi_{7(0)|5} = \pi_{7(0)|6} = \pi_{7(1)|7}.$$

Comparison with Table 2 and Fig. 3 shows the following. (1) Predictions TSP2, TSP3, and TSP3* are upheld (pass/fail probabilities well ordered, and equal within an item j). (2) Predictions TSP1, TSP4, TSP4*, TSP6, and TSP6* are undefined and thus not violated (relations among probabilities across Mp-classes rest undefined). (3) Predictions TSP5 and TSP5* are violated (no "greater-than" relations allowed within items).

Although less important for us, we also present results for the *Type-specific Error Rate Model* (Clogg & Sawyer, 1981; McCutcheon, 1987).

This model differs from the Item Specific Model in that it leaves relations among probabilities undefined within items, but makes them equal within each t-value (i.e. each Mp-class or type of subject). This model contradicts our postulates in predicting equal probabilities across Mp-types of subjects (and violates predictions TSP6 and TSP6*; but upholds TSP1, leaving other predictions undefined). It cannot be compared statistically to the other models because it is not hierarchically related.

The *Latent Distance Model*, first proposed by Lazarsfeld (Lazarsfeld & Henry, 1968), is similar to the Item-specific Error Rate model, but makes error rates for passing items different from error rates for failing items. This assumption is implemented for all items except the first and last one (i.e. j-values 2 and 7). As Lazarsfeld and Henry (1968, pp. 123–138) demonstrate, it is not possible to estimate more than one error rate for each extreme item. This model allows error rates to be conjointly determined by items (Md-classes) and by latent Mp-classes (i.e. cumulative M-classes) in specified ways (Clogg & Sawyer, 1981).

The following matrix embodies these constraints:

$$\pi_{2(0)|1} = \pi_{2(1)|2} = \pi_{2(1)|3} = \pi_{2(1)|4} = \pi_{2(1)|5} = \pi_{2(1)|6} = \pi_{2(1)|7}$$
$$\pi_{3(0)|1} = \pi_{3(0)|2} \quad \pi_{3(1)|3} = \pi_{3(1)|4} = \pi_{3(1)|5} = \pi_{3(1)|6} = \pi_{3(1)|7}$$
$$\pi_{4(0)|1} = \pi_{4(0)|2} = \pi_{4(0)|3} \quad \pi_{4(1)|4} = \pi_{4(1)|5} = \pi_{4(1)|6} = \pi_{4(1)|7}$$
$$\pi_{5(0)|1} = \pi_{5(0)|2} = \pi_{5(0)|3} = \pi_{5(0)|4} \quad \pi_{5(1)|5} = \pi_{5(1)|6} = \pi_{5(1)|7}$$
$$\pi_{6(0)|1} = \pi_{6(0)|2} = \pi_{6(0)|3} = \pi_{6(0)|4} = \pi_{6(0)|5} \quad \pi_{6(1)|6} = \pi_{6(1)|7}$$
$$\pi_{7(0)|1} = \pi_{7(0)|2} = \pi_{7(0)|3} = \pi_{7(0)|4} = \pi_{7(0)|5} = \pi_{7(0)|6} = \pi_{7(1)|7}.$$

Analysis of this model compared to Table 2 and Fig. 3 shows the following. (1) Predictions TSP3 and TSP3* are upheld (probabilities are equal within each item above the main diagonal, and similarity below it). (2) Predictions TSP1, TSP4, and TSP4* are undefined (not violated), because relation between probabilities is unspecified across items. (3) Predictions TSP2, TSP5, TSP5*, and TSP6* are undefined (nonviolated) because relations in the matrix between probabilities of passing versus failing are unspecified within j and across t, t'.

Conclusions from these theoretical analyses can be summarised by two main experimental predictions. First (*Experimental Prediction 1*), Lazarsfeld's Latent Distance Model does not contradict any constraint derived from our Mp/Md Trade-off and Contextual Overdetermination Trade-off principles. Secondly (*Experimental Prediction 2*), the four main models can be ordered in terms of the number of predictions they violate (V) and the number they uphold (UP)—predictions (out of a total of 10) that are neither violated nor upheld rest undefined within a model. This order, from best to worst fitness, is as follows: Lazarsfeld's Model (0V, 2UP) $\gg$ Item-specific Model (2V, 3UP) $>$ Type-specific Model

(2V, 1UP) $\gg$ Proctor's Model (6V, 4UP) $\gg$ Total Independence Model (10V, 0UP). We expect that the degree of fitness of these models to our data, as shown by goodness-of-fit Chi-squares, or Maximum Likelihood equivalents (likelihood ratio L^2), will reproduce the ordinal pattern just predicted. We use first the number of violations as a criterion for ordering models because, if predictions were correct, violations would cause a mismatch between model and data easily detected in goodness-of-fit tests; number of upheld predictions, by contrast, should affect much less goodness-of-fit tests.

METHOD

Subjects

A total of 616 children were tested, their ages ranging from 5 to 14 years. Table 3 gives relevant parameters of this sample. All children were in their normal grade in schools, one catholic and two public, that were situated in greater Toronto's York region. Subjects came from very diverse sociocultural backgrounds with Italian ancestry being dominant.

Material and Procedure

In the FIT-relevant task the number of items used for each Md-class (M-class) was 4 in classes Md=2, and Md=8 (although class 8 items were not scored) and 6 in classes Md=3, Md=4, Md=5, Md=6, and Md=7, for

TABLE 3
Distribution of Subjects Tested on the FIT by Age, Grade, and Sex

Grade	n	Sex		Age (years)									
		M	F	5	6	7	8	9	10	11	12	13	14
K[a]	49	22	27	32	17	–	–	–	–	–	–	–	–
1	72	39	33	–	41	31	–	–	–	–	–	–	–
2	78	35	43	–	–	46	32	–	–	–	–	–	–
3	77	40	37	–	–	–	44	33	–	–	–	–	–
4	98	39	59	–	–	–	–	61	35	02	–	–	–
5	113	54	59	–	–	–	–	01	71	41	–	–	–
6	83	38	45	–	–	–	–	–	03	50	28	02	–
7	46	17	29	–	–	–	–	–	–	–	33	12	01
Total	616	284	332	32	58	77	76	95	109	93	61	14	01

Note. A dash (–) indicates the no subjects of this age were tested for that particular grade.
[a]Kindergarten.

a total of 38 items. The FIT-relevant task used is, in most respects, like the older FIT task currently available, on request, from our laboratory for experimental purposes. The changes are: (1) all items have been redrawn to a larger size; (2) none contains irrelevant shapes; and (3) a few items have been redesigned. Changes (1) and (2) might have rendered this version less misleading than the original one, but this point needs to be researched.

To minimise executive deficiencies and frequent use of partial-intersections strategies in the group-administered experimental task (FIT-relevant), children were group pretrained with another version of the FIT (FIT-irrelevant). Results from this pretraining FIT task are not presented. Each test required one session of about 45–50 minutes. Testing, conducted in the classroom by two assistants, followed standard administration procedures. Elaborate training, conducted with Introductory items, teaches the following solution procedure: attend to each separate shape on the right-hand side of the page and place a single dot inside each of the shapes; then find the same relevant shapes on the left-hand side and place a single dot inside their total intersection.

An item is scored as passed (1) when the subject marks the total intersection in the figural compound, and (as instructed) the mark neither extends into another area nor there is more than one mark on the left-hand side of the response sheet; otherwise items are scored failed (0).

RESULTS AND DISCUSSION

Because the maximum-likelihood Latent Structure Analysis program of Eliason (1990) can handle only 10 dimensions—in our case six Md-class/items—we selected (using item characteristic curves) the best four items of each of the six Md-classes used in actual scoring (classes 2 to 7) and created four subsets, each with an item from every M-class. The four subsets were analysed, yielding similar results.

Relative Fitness of the Various Models

Table 4 summarises goodness-of-fit data for the latent structure models and the Total Independence model. According to the likelihood-ratio Chi-square statistics (L^2) we see that (this is *Experimental Prediction 1*) only Lazarsfeld's latent-distance model fits the FIT data, and does so very well in the first three subsets of items (first subset: $L^2 = 53.77$, $df = 47$, $P < 0.2311$).

Experimental Prediction 2 is also statistically confirmed. Ordered from best to worst fit in terms of their Likelihood Ratio Chi-square (L^2) the

TABLE 4
Goodness-of-fit and Likelihood-ratio Chi-square Statistics for Some Scaling Models in
the 4 Subsets of 6 Test Items

Model	Goodness-of-fit Chi-square (χ^2)	Likelihood-ratio Chi-square (L^2)	df	P^a
1st subset of 6 test items				
Independence model	1631.20	686.13	57	0.0000
Proctor's model	176.81	187.65	56	0.0000
Item-specific model	99.00	106.30	51	0.0000
Type-specific model[b]	146.84	159.36	51	0.0000
Latent distance model	45.19	53.77	47	0.2311
2nd subset of 6 test items				
Independence model	1465.68	576.44	57	0.0000
Proctor's model	193.24	227.36	56	0.0000
Item-specific model	104.37	99.36	51	0.0000
Type-specific model[b]	167.91	192.04	51	0.0000
Latent distance model[c]	40.45	56.80	48	0.1799
3rd subset of 6 test items				
Independence model	1662.61	546.17	57	0.0000
Proctor's model	236.95	243.83	56	0.0000
Item-specific model	115.69	110.16	51	0.0000
Type-specific model[d]	195.35	206.61	51	0.0000
Latent distance model[e]	46.46	48.00	48	0.4729
4th subset of 6 test items				
Independence model	1446.54	524.83	57	0.0000
Proctor's model	194.15	199.92	56	0.0000
Item-specific model	87.87	102.60	51	0.0000
Type-specific model	171.19	172.07	50	0.0000
Latent distance model[c]	51.89	69.81	48	0.0215

[a]Significance level associated with the likelihood-ratio Chi-square statistics.
[b]One of the conditional probabilities $(\pi_{j(1)|1})$ has been assigned a fixed value of 0.
[c]One of the conditional probabilities $(\pi_{1(1)|2,3,...,7})$ has been assigned a fixed value of 1.
[d]One of the conditional probabilities $(\pi_{j(1)|2})$ has been assigned a fixed value of 1.
[e]One of the conditional probabilities $(\pi_{5(1)|1,2,...,5})$ has been assigned a fixed value of 0.

models show, in all four subsets of items (Table 4), the following order:
Lazarsfeld's model > Item-specific Model > Type-specific Model > Proctor's model > Total Independence model. We place a bold sign >
(meaning "statistically-better-fitting-than") between most contiguous
models because likelihood-ratio Chi-square statistics permit evaluation of
the difference between their respective L^2 statistics. For instance, in the
first subset of items, Proctor's model has $L^2 = 187.65$, and the Independence model has $L^2 = 686.13$; their difference 498.48 is statistically significant ($df = 57 - 56 = 1$, $P < 0.0001$). This finding shows that Proctor's

seven-latent class "Guttman scale" model, predicted by TSP1 and TSP2, fits much better than the assumption of no structure at all, i.e. the "one class" model of Total Independence.

The Type-specific model also improves significantly over Proctor's model (first subset: $L^2 = 187.65 - 159.36 = 28.29$, $df = 56 - 51 = 5$, $P < 0.0001$); and even more so does the Item-specific model (first subset: $L^2 = 187.65 - 106.30 = 81.35$, $df = 56 - 51 = 5$, $P < 0.0001$). Using L^2 we cannot directly compare the Type-specific model to the Item-specific model because they are not hierarchical. We now notice that our data seem consistent with theoretical predictions TSP4, and TSP4*, which only Proctor's model violates.

To evaluate predictions TSP5 and TSP5*, we compared the Item-specific model (which violates them) with Lazarsfeld's latent-distance model, and found support for the predictions (first subset: $L^2 = 106.30 - 53.77 = 52.53$, $df = 51 - 47 = 4$, $P < 0.0001$). Validity of TSP6 and TSP6* (violated by the Type-specific Model) is indirectly suggested by the fact that the Type-specific model does not pass the goodness-of-fit Chi-square test, but Lazarsfeld's model does. Taken together, results suggest that developmental latent "Guttman-scale" models must, to fit these data, have two different error rates, one for the main probabilities of passing and another for the main probabilities of failing. This is predicted in our theory as due to competing and qualitatively different processes, the X-strategies and the Y-strategies (whose dialectics produce Mp/Md Trade-off and Contextual Overdetermination Trade-off).

Because in these models assignment of observations to latent classes (i.e. Mp-types) is necessarily probabilistic (Clogg, 1988; McCutcheon, 1987), we investigated whether assignment of response patterns to Lazarsfeld's model did not involve more error than it did for other models. Clogg has developed two suitable measures. These are the percentage of correctly classified observations and the Lambda (Goodman & Kruskal, 1954) of this assignment. Although we do not report these indices they are very similar for the four latent-class models. For Lazarsfeld's model in the first subset, the value of these two measures is 0.78 (Lambda) and 83.53 (percentage of correctly allocated observations).

Evaluating Absolute Fitness in Lazarsfeld's Model

One powerful way of evaluating how well data fit Lazarsfeld's model is to compute differences between observed and (Lazarsfeld's) expected frequencies for each of the 64 (2^6) possible patterns of pass/fail responses produced to the six items. These differences are divided by the corresponding standard error of the frequency estimate, to obtain standardised residuals. These data, which we do not report, show that few standardised residuals are large and that the larger residuals are associated with response patterns that have small observed frequencies. These observations speak for the *rational fitness* to our data of the Lazarsfeld model. We say rational, and not empiricist, statistical fitness, because there are predictable organismic processes, such as cognitive oscillations in a subject's available level of capacity (functional M-capacity—Pascual-Leone, 1970) or Contextual Overdetermination Trade-off, which can produce significant residuals in the empiricist fitness of statistical models. Statisticians often adopt an empiricist attitude that regards the sort of organismic processes we have just mentioned as "noise" or unreliability; they treat statistical models as the true embodiment of the theory being tested. This is not so for us; we know that *simplifying assumptions* are made in testing organismic models with statistical models (Pascual-Leone, 1978; Pascual-Leone & Sparkman, 1980). In addition to simplifying assumptions, such as ignoring functional M-capacity, ignoring uncontrolled Contextual Overdetermination effects or ignoring the Partial-Intersections strategy that subjects can use, we had to make statistical (model-dependent) simplifying assumptions in order to ignore that TSP5 and TSP5* are necessarily violated by the first and last items in the subsets.

Table 5 gives the theoretical expected proportions of examinees (i.e. conditional probabilities Pr $[Md_j(1)|Mp_t]$) estimated by the Latent Class Analysis program using Lazarsfeld's model. These are the best fitting theoretical probabilities that jointly satisfy both the constraints of Lazarsfeld's model and these data. We have marked, with a "staircase" line along the main diagonal, the Mp/Md Trade-off boundary that separates areas where M-power $\geq$ M-demand from where M-power $<$ M-demand. Readers may wish to compare this empirical data matrix with the theoretical matrix of Fig. 3 (and with Predictions of Table 2) searching for quantitative-structural patterns. The many structural correspondences are very gratifying.

We make a few comments using the first item subset as example. First, we notice in the first row, which gives proportion of subjects in the population falling under each Mp-type t (or cumulative M-class), that only 3% of subjects (0.0320) fall under type $t = 1$ (expected response pattern 0, 0, 0, 0, 0, 0). This indicates that most examinees fall within Mp-types that the task can assess. Secondly, probability (Pr$[Md_6(1)|Mp_6]$), or main probability of passing item 6 given $Mp = 6$, has a relatively low value (0.6568) and thus a *large error rate* $(1 - 0.6568 = 0.3432)$—the largest of all items. In contrast, Pr$[Md_6(1)|Mp_5]$ is *small* (0.0634). This contrast suggests that the class 6 item discriminates better for relatively less able examinees (those who should fail this item) than for more able examinees. The converse occurs with the class 3 and class 4 items, which have a smaller error rate for the passing response (respectively, $1 - 0.9966 = 0.0034$; and

TABLE 5
Parameter Estimates for the 4 Subsets of 6 Test Items under Lazarsfeld's
Latent-distance Model

	Latent Class (Mp = t)						
	$t = 1$	$t = 2$	$t = 3$	$t = 4$	$t = 5$	$t = 6$	$t = 7$
1st subset of 6 test items							
π_t^x	0.0320	0.1712	0.2042	0.1310	0.0349	0.1872	0.2396
$\pi_{2(1)|t}$	0.0028	0.9972	0.9972	0.9972	0.9972	0.9972	0.9972
$\pi_{3(1)|t}$	0.1448	0.1448	0.9966	0.9966	0.9966	0.9966	0.9966
$\pi_{4(1)|t}$	0.1628	0.1628	0.1628	0.9975	0.9975	0.9975	0.9975
$\pi_{5(1)|t}$	0.1424	0.1424	0.1424	0.1424	0.8683	0.8683	0.8683
$\pi_{6(1)|t}$	0.0634	0.0634	0.0634	0.0634	0.0634	0.6568	0.6568
$\pi_{7(1)|t}$	0.0583	0.0583	0.0583	0.0583	0.0583	0.0583	0.9417
2nd subset of 6 test items							
π_t^x	0.0537	0.1840	0.1382	0.0631	0.0600	0.2293	0.2718
$\pi_{2(1)|t}$	0.0000	1.0000	1.0000	1.0000	1.0000	1.0000	1.0000
$\pi_{3(1)|t}$	0.3225	0.3225	0.9953	0.9953	0.9953	0.9953	0.9953
$\pi_{4(1)|t}$	0.1297	0.1297	0.1297	0.8716	0.8716	0.8716	0.8716
$\pi_{5(1)|t}$	0.0585	0.0585	0.0585	0.0585	0.7574	0.7574	0.7574
$\pi_{6(1)|t}$	0.0000	0.1064	0.1064	0.1064	0.1064	0.6931	0.6931
$\pi_{7(1)|t}$	0.0000	0.1375	0.1375	0.1375	0.1375	0.1375	0.8625
3rd subset of 6 test items							
π_t^x	0.0493	0.1246	0.0669	0.1435	0.1072	0.2128	0.2958
$\pi_{2(1)|t}$	0.0030	0.9970	0.9970	0.9970	0.9970	0.9970	0.9970
$\pi_{3(1)|t}$	0.3688	0.3688	0.9923	0.9923	0.9923	0.9923	0.9923
$\pi_{4(1)|t}$	0.0768	0.0768	0.0768	0.8933	0.8933	0.8933	0.8933
$\pi_{5(1)|t}$	0.0211	0.0211	0.0211	0.0211	0.6708	0.6708	0.6708
$\pi_{6(1)|t}$	0.0000	0.0000	0.0000	0.0000	0.0000	0.6407	0.6407
$\pi_{7(1)|t}$	0.1076	0.1076	0.1076	0.1076	0.1076	0.1076	0.8924
4th subset of 6 test items							
π_t^x	0.0640	0.1482	0.1126	0.1505	0.1425	0.1682	0.2141
$\pi_{2(1)|t}$	0.0000	1.0000	1.0000	1.0000	1.0000	1.0000	1.0000
$\pi_{3(1)|t}$	0.3512	0.3512	0.9947	0.9947	0.9947	0.9947	0.9947
$\pi_{4(1)|t}$	0.1827	0.1827	0.1827	0.8781	0.8781	0.8781	0.8781
$\pi_{5(1)|t}$	0.0261	0.0261	0.0261	0.0261	0.6786	0.6786	0.6786
$\pi_{6(1)|t}$	0.0000	0.0944	0.0944	0.0944	0.0944	0.6848	0.6848
$\pi_{7(1)|t}$	0.0000	0.0553	0.0553	0.0553	0.0553	0.0553	0.9447

Note: The MLLSA program was unable to estimate some of the conditional probabilities and fixed them to values of either 1 or 0.

$1 - 0.9975 = 0.0025$) than they do for failing responses (respectively, 0.1448, and 0.1628). Thus, the FIT can still be improved.

Finally, Table 6 presents the actual empirical percentage of subjects assigned by the program to each adopted latent class t, separately for each age group. We highlight only two important points. First, the reader will notice that latent class $t = 5$ is empty: Subjects either remain in class $t = 4$ or jump to class $t = 6$. This can be accounted for in terms of the *Partial Intersections Procedure* explained in the section on the Figural Intersections Task and its Process/Task Analysis; perhaps the pretraining practice received by our children with the FIT-relevant task had an unexpected effect: To induce subjects to create automatised (LC) attentional L-structures which disregard the irrelevant figure but hold a relevant figure f_1 as background. Alternatively, readers might infer that item $j = 5$ is not a good one. But then they should check, in Table 5, the error rates for passing and failing responses in item $j = 5$; they are both adequate, 13% and 14%, suggesting that item $j = 5$ is acceptable.

Secondly, we might ask how these data relate to data on percentage of passing in dichotomous, qualitative, more or less misleading developmental tasks like those of Piaget and neo-Piagetians. In our theory, these tasks should be passed, when properly designed and administered, only when subjects' M-power is equal to or greater than the task's M-demand; and M-demand can be interpreted as minimum M-power needed by a subject to solve the task. Thus, we can convert percentages in Table 6 into estimates of qualitative neo-Piagetian or Piagetian percentages by cumulating these percentages *from $t = 7$ down to $t = 1$*. With this procedure, the t-value where the percentage reaches a developmentalist's stage-characteristic passing level s, i.e. larger than 65% and smaller than 75%, will be the value (*estimated in terms of expectable M-power*) of our children's attained developmental stage for each age group.[6] When these calculations are made, using Table 6, it appears that 5-year-olds have a stage-characteristic M-value of 2 ($t = 2$ cumulative percentage is 61; but $t = 1$ is 100); the stage-characteristic M for 6-year-olds is also 2 ($t = 2$, 90%; $t = 3$, 56%). In contrast, the stage-characteristic value for 7- and 8-year-olds is 3 (respectively, $t = 3$, 68%; and $t = 3$, 78%). Then the stage-characteristic value for 9 and 10yearolds is 4 (respectively, $t = 4$, 79%; and $t = 4$, 75%); and that for 11- and 12-year-olds is 6 (respectively, $t = 6$, 66%; and $t = 6$, 81%). Finally, the stage-characteristic M-value for 13-year-olds is 7 ($t = 7$, 71%). Our task analysis of the Partial Intersections strategies in the FIT easily predicts that 11- to 12-year-olds and 13-year-olds could overperform relative to their ideal theoretical M-level values,

---

[6]Notice that this procedure of cumulating percentages from high t-values to low t-values, until the stage-characteristic passing level s, where 65% < s < 75%, has the merit of minimising the effect of overperformance due to prior learning (superior repertoire or intratask learning). It does because a child who has an M-power of $k + u$ (e.g. 6) has also an M-power of k (e.g. 2), and so these percentages can be meaningfully cumulated; but this cumulation has the effect of minimising the impact of extreme performances in favour of modal performances.

TABLE 6
Percentage of Subjects assigned to Each Latent Class within Each Age Group for the
First Subset of 6 Test Items

Latent	Age (Years)									Total
Class (t)	5	6	7	8	9	10	11	12	13	
1	38.46	9.80	2.86	0.00	0.00	0.97	0.00	0.00	0.00	18
2	30.77	33.33	28.57	22.22	7.87	10.68	6.74	0.00	0.00	85
3	26.92	31.37	25.71	29.17	13.48	13.59	20.22	5.66	7.14	110
4	3.85	9.80	21.43	18.06	16.85	12.62	6.74	13.21	7.14	76
5	0.00	0.00	0.00	0.00	0.00	0.00	0.00	0.00	0.00	0
6	0.00	7.84	11.43	23.61	33.71	32.04	30.34	32.08	14.29	138
7	0.00	7.84	10.00	6.94	28.09	30.10	35.96	49.06	71.43	140
Total	26	51	70	72	89	103	89	53	14	567

given in Table 1. These are structural results predicted by the theory—as a comparison with Table 1 (Pascual-Leone, 1970), and our task analysis of Partial-intersection strategies, show. *Thus, these data both fit Lazarsfeld's latent-distance model, which assumes a discrete (noncontinuous) latent metric (Lazarsfeld & Henry, 1968), and fit the stage-characteristic M-power developmental predictions of neo-Piagetians.* Since both metrics, Latent Class Analysis and quantitative-structural developmental analysis, are discrete, and since the developmental pattern of structural M-growth grows only every other year (see Table 1), we must rule out the existence of a continuous latent metric; and thus conclude that M-power (*the hidden measure of M*) grows in a discontinuous manner, discretely. This result is perhaps the most controversial one. Many distinguished researchers are intent on showing that measures of M-capacity grow continuously and not discretely (e.g. Lindenberger, 1992). These researchers often mistake the theoretical *measure* of M with *M-capacity itself* (which grows con-tinuously), and they use unreliable ways of assigning discrete M-values. But Lazarsfeld and Henry have already emphasised that latent, continuous distributions cannot fit a latent-distance model, because for continuous distributions "it is very hard to find good approximations to local inde-pendence" (Lazarsfeld & Henry, 1968, p. 149). Local independence is our postulate P4. Furthermore, elsewhere (Goodman, 1979; Johnson, et al., 1989; Pascual-Leone, 1987; Todor, 1977, 1979) we have demonstrated, using visuo-spatial, motor, and language tasks, the existence of *discrete developmental traces* faithful to the growth pattern of Table 1 and to the main-diagonal staircase pattern of pass/fail probabilities that Lazarsfeld's model has computed for our FIT data matrix.

CONCLUSIONS

The first conclusion is that Lazarsfeld's model is, as predicted, a good representation of FIT data. The second conclusion, which confirms claims of Pascual-Leone and associates (Johnson, et al., 1989; Pascual-Leone, 1970; Pascual-Leone & Ijaz, 1989), is that the hidden variable M measured with FIT has the measurement power of an interval scale. There are two sources of evidence for this conclusion. (1) Lazarsfeld's latent-distance model is known to imply the power of an interval scale (Clogg & Sawyer, 1981; Lazarsfeld & Henry, 1968). (2) Our theoretical structural predictions (TSP1–TSP6*) involve multiple predicted asymmetrical relations defined between ratios of t-values (M-power) and j-values (M-demand)—see Fig. 3; these theoretical ratios could not possibly be retrieved in the data unless the empirical metric were that of an interval scale.

The third conclusion is that our latent variable, mental attentional capacity, exhibits the psychometric and developmental characteristics of a discrete variable. This is not to say that the hidden developmental growth of M-capacity is discrete: We expect it to be continuous because most other "quantitative" biological variables develop in a continuous fashion. Results imply, however, that the behavioural measure (i.e. the latent information-processing variable), obtained by counting—directly or indirectly—the number of schemes that a subject can muster, is a discrete variable: It grows discontinuously, and after three years of age grows every other year until adolescence (Table 1).

The fourth conclusion, is that our detailed discussion and investigation of the relational structure (conditions for measurement) in the FIT data support our model of mental attention. This is the new concept that mental attention is a complex organismic function that can be decomposed into different operators (E, M, I, F). Using these concepts we constructed a new task and have demonstrated a level of quantitative-structural prediction in developmental processes never attained by competing theories, whether theories of attention, or of mental effort, cognitive resources, or working memory.

The final conclusion is that our original methods of process/task analysis (metasubjective analysis) deserve more careful attention from researchers. We have attempted to give a demonstration of their usefulness in investigating structural foundations for applied measurement. From this broad perspective of measurement our semantic-pragmatic methods of analysis have yielded new insights. These insights can be illustrated with reference to what psychometricians call "error of measurement" or "noise". This is a semantically ill-defined concept that, in practice, includes all variables that psychometricians cannot control. For instance, the psychometric literature (e.g. Clogg & Sawyer, 1981; McCutcheon, 1987) regards the Latent Class models we have used, as probabilistic versions of Guttman's scale—

probabilistic because they take into consideration, in distinct ways, "error of measurement". But our results indicate otherwise: Both our Mp/Md Trade-off processes (which explain the latent Guttman scale) and our Contextual Overdetermination Trade-off processes (which give it probabilistic character and pattern the latent variable's manifestation) are *organismic processes*; they are both signal, not noise produced by an act of empirical measurement.

REFERENCES

Allport, G. (1980). Cognitive mechanisms are content-specific. In G. Claxton (Ed.), *Cognitive psychology: New directions* (pp. 26–64). London: Routledge & Kegan Paul.

Baddeley, A.D. (1992a). Working memory. *Science, 255*, 556–559.

Baddeley, A.D. (1992b). Is working memory working? *Quarterly Journal of Experimental Psychology, 44A*, 1–31.

Baillargeon, R.H. (1993). *A quantitative study of mental development*. Unpublished doctoral dissertation. Toronto: York University.

Binet, A. (1911). Qu'est-ce qu'une émotion? Qu'est-ce qu'un acte intellectuel? *L'Année Psychologique, 17*, 1–47.

Bjorklund, D.F., & Harnishfeger, K.K. (1990). The resources construct in cognitive development: Diverse sources of evidence and a theory of inefficient inhibition. *Developmental Review, 10*, 48–71.

Case, R. (1992). The role of the frontal lobes in the regulation of cognitive development. *Brain and Cognition, 20*, 51–73.

Clogg, C.C. (1988). Latent class models for measuring. In R. Langeheine and J. Rost (Eds.), *Latent trait and latent class models* (pp. 173–205). New York: Plenum.

Clogg, C.C., & Sawyer, D.O. (1981). A comparison of alternative models for analyzing the scalability of response patterns. In S. Leinhardt (Ed.), *Sociological methodology* (pp. 240–280). San Francisco: Jossey-Bass.

Dempster, F.N. (1992). The rise and fall of the inhibitory mechanism: Toward a unified theory of cognitive development and aging. *Developmental Review, 12*, 45–75.

Eliason, S.R. (1990). *The categorical data analysis system version 3.50 user's manual* [computer program]. University of Iowa.

Fuster, J.M. (1989). *The prefrontal cortex* (2nd ed.). New York: Raven.

Goldman-Rakic, P.S. (1987). Development of cortical circuitry and cognitive function. *Child Development, 58*, 601–622.

Goodman, D.R. (1979). *Stage transitions and the developmental traces of constructive operators: An investigation of a neo-Piagetian theory of cognitive growth*. Unpublished doctoral dissertation. Toronto: York University.

Goodman, L.A., & Kruskal, W.H. (1979). *Measures of association for cross classifications*. New York: Springer. [Contains articles appearing in the *Journal of the American Statistical Association* in 1954, 1959, 1963, 1972]

Hasher, L., & Zacks, R.T. (1979). Automatic and effortful processes in memory. *Journal of Experimental Psychology: General, 108*, 356–388.

Holland, J., Holyoak, K., Nisbett, R., & Thagard, P. (1986). *Induction: Process of inference, learning, and discovery*. Cambridge, MA: MIT Press.

Horn, J.L., & Hofer, S.M. (1992). Major abilities and development in the adult period. In R.S. Sternberg & C.A. Berg (Eds.), *Intellectual development* (pp. 44–99). Cambridge University Press.

James, W. (1955). *Pragmatism and four essays from the meaning of truth*. New York: New American Library. (Originally published as *Pragmatism*. New York: Longmans, Green and Co, 1907)

James, W. (1966). G. Allport (Ed.), In *Psychology: The briefer course*. New York: Harper & Row.

Johnson, J. (1991). Constructive processes in bilingualism and their cognitive growth effects. In E. Bialystok (Ed.), *Language processing and language awareness by bilingual children* (pp. 194–222). Cambridge University Press.

Johnson, J., Fabian, V., & Pascual-Leone, J. (1989). Quantitative hardware-stages that constrain language development. *Human Development, 32*, 245–271.

Johnson, J., & Pascual-Leone, J. (1989). Developmental levels of processing in metaphor interpretation. *Journal of Experimental Child Psychology, 48*(1), 1–31.

Kahneman, D. (1973). *Attention and effort*. Englewood Cliffs, NJ: Prentice-Hall.

Lazarsfeld, P.F., & Henry, N.W. (1968). *Latent structure analysis*. Boston: Houghton Mifflin.

Lindenberger, U. (1992). *Working memory and intellectual development*. Poster Workshop: Developmental aspects of working memory. Fifth European Conference of Developmental Psychology, Seville, September 1992.

McCutcheon, A.L. (1987). *Latent class analysis*. Sage University Paper on Quantitative Applications in the Social Sciences. Beverly Hills: Sage.

Moscovitch, M. (1992). Memory and working-with-memory: A component process model based on modules and central systems. *Journal of Cognitive Neuroscience, 4*, 257–267.

Norman, D.A., & Shallice, T. (1980). *Attention to action: Willed and automatic control of behaviour*. CHIP Report 99. San Diego: University of California.

Pascual-Leone, J. (1970). A mathematical model for the transition rule in Piaget's developmental stages. *Acta Psychologica, 32*, 301–345.

Pascual-Leone, J. (1974). *A neo-Piagetian process-structural model of Witkin's psychological differentiation*. Paper presented at the 2nd conference of the International Association for Cross-Cultural Psychology, Kingston.

Pascual-Leone, J. (1978). Compounds, Confounds, and models in developmental information processing: A reply to Trabasso and Foellinger. *Journal of Experimental Child Psychology, 26*, 18–40. [see p. 29]

Pascual-Leone, J. (1980). Constructive problems for constructive theories: The current relevance of Piaget's work and a critique of information-processing simulation psychology. In R. Kluwe & H. Spada (Eds.), *Developmental models of thinking* (pp. 263–296). New York: Academic Press.

Pascual-Leone, J. (1984). Attention, dialectic and mental effort: Towards an organismic theory of life stages. In M.L. Commons, F.A. Richards, & G. Armon (Eds.), *Beyond formal operations: Late adolescence and adult cognitive development* (pp. 182–215). New York: Praeger.

Pascual-Leone, J. (1987). Organismic processes for neo-Piagetian theories: A dialectical causal account of cognitive development. *International Journal of Psychology, 22*, 531–570.

Pascual-Leone, J. (1989). An organismic process model of Witkin's field-dependence-independence. In T. Globerson & T. Zelniker (Eds.), *Cognitive style and cognitive development* (pp. 36–70). Norwood, NJ: Ablex.

Pascual-Leone, J. (1990). An essay on wisdom: Toward organismic processes that make it possible. In R.J. Sternberg (Ed.), *Wisdom: Its nature, origins and development* (pp. 244–278). Cambridge University Press.

Pascual-Leone, J., Baillargeon, R.H., Lee, C., & Ho, G.W. (1991). *Towards standardization of mental capacity testing*. Research Report No. 199. Toronto: York University.

Pascual-Leone, J., & Goodman, D. (1979). Intelligence and experience: A neo-Piagetian approach. *Instructional Science*, *8*, 301-367.

Pascual-Leone, J., Goodman, D.R., Ammon, P., & Subelman, I. (1978). Piagetian theory and neo-Piagetian analysis as psychological guides in education. In J.M. Gallagher & J. Easley (Eds.), *Knowledge and development: Piaget and education* (Vol. 2, pp. 243-289). New York: Plenum.

Pascual-Leone, J., & Ijaz, H. (1989). Mental capacity testing as a form of intellectual-developmental assessment. In R.J. Samuda, S.L. Kong, J. Pascual-Leone, J. Cummings, & J. Lewis (Eds), *Assessment and placement of minority students. A review for educators* (pp. 143-171). Toronto: Hogrefe.

Pascual-Leone, J., & Irwin, R.R. (1992). *Non-cognitive factors in adult learning*. Research Report No. 208. Toronto: York University.

Pascual-Leone, J., & Johnson, J. (1991). The psychological unit and its role in task analysis. A reinterpretation of object performance. In M. Chandler & M. Chapman (Eds.), *Criteria for competence: Controversies in the conceptualization and assessment of children's abilities* (pp. 153-187). Hillsdale, NJ: Lawrence Erlbaum Associates Inc.

Pascual-Leone, J., Johnson, J., Goodman, D., Hameluck, D., & Theodor, L. (1981). I-interruption effects in backward pattern masking: The neglected role of fixation stimuli. In *Proceedings of the 3rd Annual Conference of the Cognitive Science Society*. Berkeley, California.

Pascual-Leone, J., & Morra, S. (1991). Horizontality of water level: A neo-Piagetian developmental review. *Advances in Child Development and Behaviour*, *23*, 231-276.

Pascual-Leone, J., & Smith, J. (1969). The encoding and decoding of symbols by children: A new experimental paradigm and neo-Piagetian model. *Journal of Experimental Child Psychology*, *8*, 328-355.

Pascual-Leone, J., & Sparkman, E. (1980). The dialectics of empiricism and rationalism: A last methodological reply to Tabrasso. *Journal of Experimental Child Psychology*, *29*, 88-101.

de Ribaupierre, A., & Pascual-Leone, J. (1984). Pour une intégration des méthodes en psychologie: Approches expérimentale, psychogénétique et différentielle. *L'Année Psychologique*, *84*, 227-250.

Salomon, G., & Perkins, D.N. (1989). Rocky roads to transfer: Rethinking mechanisms of a neglected phenomenon. *Educational Psychologist*, *24*, 113-142.

Schacter, D.L., & Tulving, E.(Eds.) (1992). [Special issue] *Journal of Cognitive Neuroscience*, *4*(3).

Smolensky, P. (1988). On the proper treatment of connectionism. *Behavioral and Brain Sciences*, *11*, 1-74.

Spearman, C.E. (1927). *The abilities of man, their nature and measurement*. New York: MacMillan.

Stuss, D.T. (1992). Biological and psychological development of executive functions. *Brain and Cognition*, *20*, 8-23.

Todor, J.I. (1977, October). Cognitive development, cognitive style and motor ability. In B. Kerr (Ed.), *Human performance and behavior: Proceedings of the 9th Canadian Psycho-Motor Learning and Sport Psychology Symposium* (pp. 26-28). Banff, Alberta, Canada.

Todor, J.I. (1979). Developmental differences in motor task integration: A test of Pascual-Leone's theory of constructive operators. *Journal of Experimental Child Psychology*, *28*, 314-322.

Wickens, C.D. (1984). Processing resources in attention. In R. Parasuraman and D.R. Davies (Eds.), *Varieties of attention*. New York: Academic Press.

APPENDIX

Normalisation of the strength of X- and Y-strategies used in theoretically calculating TSP5, TSP5*, TSP6, TSP6*

For any item j, the strength of the X- and Y-strategies can be evaluated by obtaining respectively the Mp/Md and Md/Mp ratios. These ratios are normalised dividing each of them by the total of all Mp/Md (or Md/Mp) ratios for that item.

We add over cells above and, separately, below the main diagonal and normalise by dividing by the sum of the cell ratios within item j, because *Lazarsfeld's model constrains probabilities to be equal across cells within each item*. Because the cell probabilities above (or below) the main diagonal within an item are computed in Lazarsfeld's model relative to the item vector above (or below) the main diagonal as a whole, we must do similarly when estimating the strength of the X- and Y-strategies. For example, in the case of TSP5 and TSP5*, for a given item j, the *strength of the X-strategies* above (or below) the Mp/Md trade-off boundary can be calculated as the normalised sum of the Mp/Md ratios equal to or greater than 1 (or less than 1). For $j = 5$, for instance, the sum of the Mp/Md ratios (see Fig. 3) in the seven cells is 5.6, so that the strength of the X-strategies above and below the Md/Mp trade-off boundary is calculated, respectively, as follows: $(5/5 + 6/5 + 7/5)/5.6 = 0.64$; and $(1/5 + 2/5 + 3/5 + 4/5)/5.6 = 0.36$. Similarly, the *strength of the Y-strategies* below (above) the Mp/Md trade-off boundary can be evaluated as the sum of the Md/Mp ratios equal to or greater than 1 (or less than 1. For $j = 5$, for instance, the sum of the Md/Mp ratios (see Fig. 3) in the seven cells is 12.96. The strength of the Y-strategies below and above the Md/Mp trade-off boundary can be estimated as follows: $(5/1 + 5/2 + 5/3 + 5/4)/12.96 = 0.80$; and $(5/5 + 5/6 + 5/7)/12.96 = 0.20$.

TSP6 and TSP6* are calculated similarly with the following exception: The strength of X- (and of Y-) strategies is defined in terms of the ratio Mp/Md (or Md/Mp) *for each given cell* divided by the corresponding total sum of ratios for the Mp-class (column) in question. We now compute separately for each cell the strength of X- or Y-strategies (and normalise dividing by the sum of the column's ratios) because, unlike with cells of each item j (each row), cells of each type t (column) are unconstrained in Lazarsfeld's model in terms of their respective probabilities.

Observed Frequencies of Response Patterns for the 4 Subsets of 6 Test Items in the
Relevant Version of the Figural Intersection Task

Index	Response Pattern *M-demand* 2 3 4 5 6 7	1st Subset[a]	2nd Subset[b]	3rd Subset[c]	4th Subset[d]
1	0 0 0 0 0 0	16	20	17	23
2	1 0 0 0 0 0	56	44	39	37
3	0 1 0 0 0 0	03	10	10	09
4	1 1 0 0 0 0	74	69	58	73
5	0 0 1 0 0 0	00	00	00	00
6	1 0 1 0 0 0	14	10	06	12
7	0 1 1 0 0 0	00	00	01	04
8	1 1 1 0 0 0	78	46	96	101
9	0 0 0 1 0 0	00	00	00	01
10	1 0 0 1 0 0	08	01	00	00
11	0 1 0 1 0 0	00	00	00	00
12	1 1 0 1 0 0	17	17	13	14
13	0 0 1 1 0 0	00	01	00	00
14	1 0 1 1 0 0	03	01	01	02
15	0 1 1 1 0 0	00	00	00	00
16	1 1 1 1 0 0	60	44	58	60
17	0 0 0 0 1 0	00	00	00	00
18	1 0 0 0 1 0	00	06	00	02
19	0 1 0 0 1 0	00	00	00	00
20	1 1 0 0 1 0	11	16	04	14
21	0 0 1 0 1 0	00	00	00	00
22	1 0 1 0 1 0	00	00	00	00
23	0 1 1 0 1 0	00	00	00	00
24	1 1 1 0 1 0	15	29	30	45
25	0 0 0 1 1 0	00	00	00	00
26	1 0 0 1 1 0	00	00	00	00
27	0 1 0 1 1 0	00	00	00	00
28	1 1 0 1 1 0	03	10	02	07
29	0 0 1 1 1 0	00	00	00	00
30	1 0 1 1 1 0	00	01	00	00
31	0 1 1 1 1 0	00	00	01	00
32	1 1 1 1 1 0	64	59	45	32
33	0 0 0 0 0 1	00	00	01	00
34	1 0 0 0 0 1	04	07	01	04
35	0 1 0 0 0 1	00	00	00	00
36	1 1 0 0 0 1	06	16	15	07
37	0 0 1 0 0 1	00	00	00	00
38	1 0 1 0 0 1	00	02	00	01
39	0 1 1 0 0 1	00	00	00	00
40	1 1 1 0 0 1	16	19	31	15
41	0 0 0 1 0 1	00	00	00	00
42	1 0 0 1 0 1	00	01	01	00

| | M-demand | | | | |
| | 2 3 4 5 6 7 | | | | |

Index	Response Pattern	1st Subset[a]	2nd Subset[b]	3rd Subset[c]	4th Subset[d]
43	0 1 0 1 0 1	00	00	00	00
44	1 1 0 1 0 1	00	07	08	04
45	0 0 1 1 0 1	00	00	00	00
46	1 0 1 1 0 1	01	00	01	00
47	0 1 1 1 0 1	01	00	00	00
48	1 1 1 1 0 1	38	31	32	26
49	0 0 0 0 1 1	00	00	00	00
50	1 0 0 0 1 1	00	01	00	00
51	0 1 0 0 1 1	00	00	00	00
52	1 1 0 0 1 1	00	06	01	05
53	0 0 1 0 1 1	00	00	00	00
54	1 0 1 0 1 1	00	00	00	00
55	0 1 1 0 1 1	00	00	00	00
56	1 1 1 0 1 1	09	16	24	13
57	0 0 0 1 1 1	00	00	00	00
58	1 0 0 1 1 1	00	00	00	00
59	0 1 0 1 1 1	00	00	00	00
60	1 1 0 1 1 1	00	04	05	01
61	0 0 1 1 1 1	00	00	00	00
62	1 0 1 1 1 1	00	00	00	00
63	0 1 1 1 1 1	00	00	00	00
64	1 1 1 1 1 1	81	83	76	66
Sample size		578	577	577	578

[a]Items 1, 2, 3, 4, 5, and 6 refer to items 26, 16, 14, 4, 6, and 33, respectively.
[b]Items 1, 2, 3, 4, 5, and 6 refer to items 13, 05, 03, 11, 17, and 25, respectively.
[c]Items 1, 2, 3, 4, 5, and 6 refer to items 21, 10, 23, 15, 18, and 36, repectively.
[d]Items 1, 2, 3, 4, 5, and 6 refer to items 28, 19, 30, 29, 27, and 20, respectively.

Subject Index

international journal of behavioral development

Edited by LINDA SIEGEL

(Ontario Institute for Studies in Education, Canada)

The International Journal of Behavioral Development exists to promote the discovery, dissemination and application of knowledge about developmental processes at all stages of the lifespan - infancy, childhood, adolescence, adulthood and old age. Established in 1978, the journal is a foremost international publication devoted to reporting interdisciplinary research, theoretical reviews, book reviews and other items of scientific communication. The journal is the official journal of the International Society for the Study of Behavioral Development.

RECENT AND FORTHCOMING PAPERS

Only Children and Sibling Children in Urban China: A Re-examination, X. Chen, K.H. Rubin

Fostering Independence in Mother-Child Interactions: Longitudinal Changes in Contingency Patterns as Children Grow Competent in Developmental Tasks, T.A. Kindermann

An Observational Study of Five-Year-Old South African Children in the Year Before School, C. Liddell, J. Kvalsvig, N. Strydom, P. Qotyana, A. Shabalala

Tanzanian and United States Mother's Beliefs About Parents' and Teachers' Roles in Children's Knowledge Acquisition, A.V. McGillicuddy-De-Lisi, S. Subramanian

Work and Love: Their Relationship in Adulthood, S.B. Merriam, M.C. Clark

Comparison of Children's Cognitive Representation of Number: China, France, Japan, Korea, Sweden, and the United States, I.T. Miura, Y. Okamoo, C.C. Kim, C.M. Chang, M. Steere, M. Fayol

Biomedical and Social-Environmental Influences on Cognitive and Verbal Abilities in Children One to Three Years of Age, V.J. Molfese, L. Holcomb, S. Helwig

ABSTRACTS

Abstracts for *International Journal of Behavioural Development* are published by the following: Assia, Biosis, Current Contents, PsychINFO, Research Alert, Social Sciences Citation Index, Sociological Abstracts, University Microfilms.

SUBSCRIPTION INFORMATION

Volume 17 (4 issues), 1994, ISSN 0165 0254
(50% increase in number of pages for 1994)
Individuals: EC £56.00 / USA $106.00 / Rest of World £63.00
Institutions: EC £140.00 / USA $266.00 / Rest of World £147.00
Members of the ISSBD receive the journal as part of their membership

ORDERS AND ENQUIRIES TO: Lawrence Erlbaum Associates Ltd, 27 Church Road, Hove, E. Sussex, BN3 2FA, England.

For Product Safety Concerns and Information please contact our EU
representative GPSR@taylorandfrancis.com
Taylor & Francis Verlag GmbH, Kaufingerstraße 24, 80331 München, Germany

www.ingramcontent.com/pod-product-compliance
Lightning Source LLC
Chambersburg PA
CBHW062026270326
41929CB00014B/2337

9 7 8 1 1 3 8 8 7 7 3 1 3